CHOOSING TO LEAD

CHOOSING TO LEAD

WOMEN
AND
THE CRISIS OF
AMERICAN
VALUES

*

Constance H. Buchanan

Beacon Press
BOSTON

Beacon Press
25 Beacon Street
Boston, Massachusetts 02108-2892

Beacon Press books
are published under the auspices of
the Unitarian Universalist Association of Congregations.

00 99 98 97   8 7 6 5 4 3 2

Text design by Wesley B. Tanner/Passim Editions
Composition by Wilsted & Taylor
Printed on acid-free, recycled paper that contains
at least 20 percent postconsumer fibers.

Library of Congress Cataloging-in-Publication Data
can be found on page 278.

Contents

Acknowledgments

I never expected a divinity school to be the place in which my work would take shape. Starting out in the early 1970s to be an historian, however, I discovered that the academic world of history did not take seriously women, questions of meaning and value, or social responsibility. At Harvard, among theologians, I found an academic setting which had been brought face to face with the need to address these things by a growing influx of women students. At the Divinity School, I discovered with faculty colleagues and students the multifaceted conversation for which I had been looking.

This book is a product of that conversation. In writing it, I have understood more clearly why, as for so many women in past and present, the language of religion has been crucial to discovering my own voice. Critical appropriation of this language gives women what they have been denied by society, history, culture, and paradoxically, religious traditions themselves. It gives women the tools to claim full moral agency in interpreting and shaping their own lives, the life of society, and human perceptions of ultimate truth.

Choosing to Lead reflects my own views. Because it is my part of a broader conversation, however, writing it has been a far from solitary process. In addition to the voices cited in the notes and bibliography, I have been constantly aware of other voices that have influenced me—voices the reader will not be able to hear. These are voices of faculty colleagues whose thinking and priorities have helped shape my own. They are voices too of the almost one hundred scholars who have been appointed over the years to Harvard's Women's Studies in Religion Program and of members of the program's scholarly Advisory Committee. And they are voices of many friends and family who have lived with this book and cared about it, perhaps with little idea how they contributed to it by a simple question or encouraging comment about its progress.

It is a pleasure to acknowledge, in particular, several who have had considerable impact on my work and to express my deep appreciation for the special role they played in the life of this book. With characteristic generosity, Derek Bok shared with me material on the decline of civic engagement from his own work in progress and commented on the first two versions of what was to become the proposal for *Choosing to Lead*. George Rupp supported the project at important points. When his own work was especially pressing, he read the initial draft of each chapter, making several suggestions that were critical to the book's conception and strengthened it significantly. Another of the chief influences on the book has been the long-standing conversation Clarissa Atkinson and I carry on about issues it addresses and many others. She too read the whole manuscript, more than once, and more than once enriched it by pushing for more precise analysis and nuanced judgment. At a crucial stage, Deborah Valenze also brought her expertise on historical and contemporary women to the manuscript. She helped me to hear my own voice, to understand more clearly what I was trying to say, and to say it better. Finally, Theda Skocpol brought her concern for just solutions and her deep knowledge of American social policy to bear in commenting on the penultimate draft.

This book had important support from others as well. I am very grateful for the encouragement Ronald Thiemann, Dean of Harvard Divinity School, offered. He not only made time and computer equipment available to help me get it done, but urged me to say what was on my mind. The Rockefeller Foundation made it possible for me to spend a month at its Study Center in Bellagio,

Italy, where the beautiful natural setting and the company of artists, as well as other scholars, gave me new perspective on the project. Among the many friends this book has had along the way, I owe special thanks to the following for their interest and their often provocative questions and comments: Alberta Arthurs, Alison Bernstein, Ann Braude, Barbara Garrey, Nadja Gould, Anne Klein, Helen Hunt, John E. Masten, John H. Masten, Caryl Phillips, Wayne Proudfoot, Elisabeth Schüssler Fiorenza, Lynn Szwaja, and Pamela Walker. Carolyn De Swarte Gifford was a valued resource for my thinking about Frances Willard and kindly provided me with edited selections from Willard's journal before it went to press. Americanists Ellen Fitzpatrick and Maureen Fitzgerald each took time from their own writing to make helpful comments on the manuscript. And as the book was in its last stages, Margaret Miles's skilled support reminded me of the years of our shared learning about women and institutional change that mark every page.

Each day, I felt deeper gratitude for Lucia Rahilly's ability and dedication as a research assistant. She fearlessly traversed Harvard's library system to meet the book's interdisciplinary demands, entered countless textual changes and notes with speed and accuracy, and handled the computer with aplomb when it came time to devise programs to produce the chapter notes, bibliography, and complete manuscript. Ann Romberger, Mary Shotwell, and Suzanne Seger also contributed their intelligence and enthusiasm at different stages. I was fortunate to have an editor, Susan Worst, who cared about the book and set about skillfully sharpening its focus, pushing me to say no more and no less than I had in mind.

Finally, my family played a crucial role in shaping this book. My father, Albert B. Buchanan, and my older sister, Ann Buchanan Tytus, both of whom died well before this book was even imagined, were never far from my mind as I wrote it. Without them, it would not look the way it does. My father trained my basic instincts about religion. He taught me to be deeply critical of the self-justifying and destructive uses human beings find for it. But he also taught me to respect and understand religion as a central force in human life, and to recognize that it can serve as a resource for principles of justice and compassion on which the creative renewal of society depends. My sister, by her command of New York City when we were growing up there, and later by her example in local politics and in educational innovation here and in South America, ingrained in me the certainty that women are as responsible as men for shaping the world. My mother, Barbara M. Buchanan, continues to give me firsthand knowledge of the courage and ability women can bring to the task of improving social institutions. Because of her, it was not difficult to recognize the dedication to this same task that nineteenth- and early-twentieth-century "organized women" demonstrated. Finally, the book owes much to my brother, Mark L. Buchanan. It would have been enough to be able to count on his experienced analysis of national policy and politics, and on his quick grasp of what the book was about, but he also was its loyal champion from start to finish.

C.H.B.
Cambridge, July 1995

CHOOSING TO LEAD

CHAPTER ONE

Addressing the Crisis of American Values

Many Americans attribute the increasing disorder of individual, family, and community life to "the breakdown of moral values and social structure."[1] The disorder that concerns them is exemplified by family disruption, poverty, violence, and drugs. Public debate places women, particularly mothers, at the very heart of this national values crisis, but it seriously misreads how and why they are so central. A new analysis of the link between motherhood and the welfare of American society is crucial to understanding why fundamental social values are threatened. *Choosing to Lead* offers this analysis. Moreover, it argues that women have the potential to play an important role in leading the nation out of its values crisis and explores the barriers—practical, historical, and especially moral—that they must overcome to do so.

THE PUBLIC DEBATE

Many who fear that our primary social institutions—including marriage, "the" family, neighborhoods, and public school systems—are disintegrating perceive decay of the moral fabric of American life as both the cause and consequence. These institutions, with religious ones, have traditionally been the central social sites for values formation, but they are said to be no longer transmitting basic values effectively. As a result, according to the consensus that has emerged, *individual* values, such as sexual responsibility, the work ethic, and respect for authority, are eroding, especially among the urban poor. This diagnosis of the American values crisis depicts the nation as confronted by a choice between restoring individual values and unstoppable social deterioration.

Since the Reagan era, both the values crisis and this diagnosis have become increasingly familiar features of the national debate. The President, members of Congress, policymakers, social critics, television commentators and radio talk show hosts, newspaper columnists, and many other opinion shapers refer to them daily. One of the striking aspects of public debate about this crisis is the degree to which it is dominated and its terms are defined by men. Women play a comparatively small role in the debate. This is due in part, of course, to the fact that few women have risen to positions of prominence that make them public analysts. Yet the small number of women in top leadership positions itself reflects the fact that American women still are not expected to have a public voice and to speak about the state of society as a whole. This lack of expectation is evident in private life as well. There, a silent consensus often confers on men the authority to frame the national situation, despite the deep concern about society that many women express in national polls and elsewhere.

It seems particularly ironic that women are playing such a small role in public debate about the values crisis given the fact that motherhood is a central focus of this debate. A powerful bi-partisan consensus identifies "illegitimacy," especially among unwed mothers receiving public assistance, as a major cause of the country's moral and social deterioration. This view seems persuasive to many Americans, although it is championed especially by the political and religious right. Former Vice-President Quayle promoted it in his famous speech to the 1992 Republican Convention when he argued, in reference to the Los Angeles riots, that a "poverty of values," beginning with sexual promiscuity, is causing the breakdown of "the" family as a moral unit that leads to violence.[2]

The logic of this consensus about "illegitimacy" depicts single mothers as violating basic values of personal responsibility with regard to marriage, parenthood, schooling, and work.[3] These mothers, especially among the "underclass," are said to feed the erosion of American values by transmitting their own poverty of values, along with their poverty, to new generations who engage in socially destructive behavior and are not self-sufficient.

Yet it is in part precisely *because* motherhood is a central focus of this debate that women play a small part in it. The public consensus about single mothers gets its persuasive power from implicit appeal to a belief central to the dominant American culture that fundamentally influences women's lives. This belief links "good" women, as wives and mothers, with the moral order of society. The dominant culture gives families, in particular mothers, responsibility for the daily moral lessons that turn children into self-sufficient citizens who contribute to the good order of democratic society. The public consensus about poor unwed mothers gains its power by using this standard of the "good" mother to evaluate them: if these were "good" mothers, its logic goes, they would be building the social order, not undermining it. The language about motherhood central to the public debate is being used to portray women as deviant.

But it is not just the performance of poor unwed mothers that is under scrutiny. American women are at once judged by and part of national concern about how well *all* mothers are doing their job. Most are torn between the daily reality of juggling work in and outside of the home and the ideal of the "good" mother, searching for a sound way to reconcile the two. They belong to a culture that believes that when society is working well it is because women are being "good" mothers, rearing children to civic virtue, and that when society is not working well it is because mothers are failing at their chief task. This traditional Western cultural belief was first expressed in its American form after the Revolution in the notion of "Republican motherhood."[4]

During the 1992 presidential campaign, it was national concern about *mothers'* domestic labor that conservative politicians played on, lamenting the increasing numbers of single mothers and the entrance of a majority of mothers into the paid labor force. At the Re-

publican Convention, speakers presented both single motherhood
and women's paid work as undermining the quality of mothering
received by American children. In contrast, concern in the family
values debate about fathers' absence from families focuses chiefly
on their economic role. When it comes to fathers' moral contribution, most emphasize the importance of their *presence* as head of
family, not their active daily responsibility for children's development.

Since the 1992 election, national concern about women's work
outside the home has continued, generating both debate about the
impact of childcare on children's development and guilt in many
employed mothers. But the economic necessity that sends most
mothers into paid work has muted criticism of their labor force participation. Now, the larger issue of how all American mothers are
doing has come to be addressed instead through the focus on how
well *certain* mothers, notably single mothers, are doing. And the
liberal view that families should be valued however they are structured, which candidate Bill Clinton represented during the 1992
campaign, has given way in national politics to the consensus that
single-parent families are inadequate. This consensus focuses on
restoring the two-parent family by discouraging out-of-wedlock
births and divorce.[5] President Clinton put it bluntly during the
1994 elections: "I know not everybody is going to be in a stable traditional family like you see on one of those 1950 sitcoms, but we'd
be better off if more people were."[6]

Because it is hard for anyone, let alone mothers, to be disloyal
to the traditional cultural ideal of the "good" mother, appeal to this
ideal by critics of single mothers leaves many women who do not
wholly agree with the criticism ambivalent. While women on the
political and religious right often join in this criticism, many others
find themselves silenced by the implications of simple agreement
or disagreement. These women wish to challenge whether the consensus about female-headed families represents an adequate grasp
either of the values crisis that is tearing the social fabric or of the
situation of single mothers, especially those on public assistance.

Women who might offer such a challenge are stymied, however, because they do not have available to them a critical assessment of the *moral* terms of the public debate, one that clarifies how it is being driven by a fundamental cultural belief about the way women and the moral order of society are connected. Yet women who seek a better analysis of the nation's values crisis have a crucial contribution to make to this debate. As citizens, individuals, and mothers, these women have both a compelling interest in its outcome and expertise about the social realities it ought to address.

What these women need in order to participate fully in the values debate is the moral insight to articulate confidently a new analysis of the situation of American families and its implications for work, communities, and society as a whole. Developing this moral insight and confidence depends on gaining a critical, historical understanding of the traditional dominant cultural beliefs that are shaping the debate—beliefs about society's organization into public and private spheres. Women who want to put forward a new analysis need to understand, in particular, traditional beliefs about the "good" mother, the role of women in the welfare of society, and the relationship between the two. These beliefs are integral to the larger set of cultural beliefs about the "natural" sexual division of labor. This division of labor makes the private sphere the main arena of women's activity and the public sphere that of men's, giving authority in both spheres to men.

These traditional cultural beliefs continue to drive public debate about the way society is and ought to be organized, overwhelming both our knowledge of well-documented major changes in social reality and our ability to respond to these changes. Women, especially married or single mothers, because they still bear primary responsibility for the unpaid daily work of sustaining family and community bonds of mutuality and obligation, are acutely aware of this gap between society's ideals and social reality. They see the lack of structural support for this unpaid work and the increasing erosion of these bonds not just in families, but in society more broadly. Women, in short, see the cost to American so-

ciety of continuing to treat this crucial work as women's work
rather than as a priority that also should be integral to the lives of
men and of social institutions beyond "the" family. As a consequence, women are especially aware of a deep collective, as well as
personal, need to find realistic and sound ways to translate traditional values to fit new social arrangements.

To accomplish this work of translation, in alliance with men
who also recognize its urgency, women must begin by exploring
how traditional cultural beliefs are driving the public debate about
values off the mark and limiting their own participation in it.

BLAMING THE "BAD" MOTHER

One of the chief ways traditional beliefs about public and private
are distorting debate about the values crisis is by making it easy to
blame mothers and motherhood for the nation's severe problems.
Because they make the "good" mother responsible for the basic
moral health of the social fabric, traditional cultural beliefs about
public and private provide an authoritative rationale for its moral
decay: "bad" mothers. The power of the "good" mother as a cultural symbol makes the liberal and conservative focus on "bad"
mothers who violate the basic moral order of society seem reasonable. Evidence to support the social "truth" that unmarried or
never married mothers are "bad" is drawn from a complex orches-
tration of public concern about their values in general, the impact
of father absence and poverty on the development of children, and
social attitudes (especially those of whites) about sexuality and the
"underclass."

In short, public consensus identifies these single mothers as a
major cause of a range of grave social problems on the grounds that
they fail to transmit to their children basic values essential to reproducing the patterns of personal and civic relationship a healthy
society depends on. Conservative analyst Charles Murray made
this point in his influential editorial in the *Wall Street Journal* in October 1993. Noting that 30 percent of all live U.S. births in 1991

were to unmarried women, he argued that "illegitimacy" is "the single most important social problem of our time—more important than crime, drugs, poverty, illiteracy, welfare, or homelessness because *it drives everything else*. Doing something about it is not just one more item on the American policy agenda, but should be at the top."[7] Murray declared that the need to address "illegitimacy" was made all the more urgent by the fact that, in a year in which 22 percent of white births were to single women, the "black story" of "illegitimacy" had become "old news." He warned that because "illegitimacy" is most common among low-income white women it signals the emergence of a new white underclass: "[T]he brutal truth is that American society as a whole could survive when illegitimacy became epidemic within a comparatively small ethnic minority. It cannot survive the same epidemic among whites."[8]

Others hold "bad" mothers responsible for many of society's gravest problems because they see them as lacking not only individual values, but also what traditional beliefs identify as women's "natural" maternal capacity for childrearing. George Will, a widely read conservative political columnist, argued in his *Newsweek* column that "Mothers Who Don't Know How" are causing the intergenerational transmission of poverty and America's "urban regression": "A mother reared in poverty is apt to have a barren 'inner world' of imagination and emotional energy, a consequence of impoverished early experiences. . . . Very early intervention can 'jumpstart' their mothering skills. But there are too many single mothers who need this . . . expensive attention."[9]

Conservatives and, to a lesser degree, liberals strengthen their diagnosis that "illegitimacy" is central to the nation's moral decay by shifting their focus on single mothers (never-married and divorced) to a focus on *teenage pregnancy*. As sociologist Kristin Luker points out, worry about welfare and poverty in the public debate typically involves rhetorical and analytical slippage in which single motherhood becomes the cause of poverty and teenage pregnancy takes the place of single motherhood, unwed motherhood, and teenage motherhood.[10] Thus, both debate and policy proposals focus on teenage pregnancy, despite the fact that only 3.8 percent of welfare recipients are teenagers and these teenagers make up only 4.9 percent of recipients who are not married.[11] This focus overlooks, typically, the fact that most unwed mothers in the American population are not teenagers. The number of births to unwed mothers is rising much more rapidly among older women than among teenagers, with teenagers actually constituting a decreasing proportion of unwed mothers in the United States.[12]

Yet the emphasis on teenage pregnancy allows public debate to focus on a vulnerable population easily labeled as lacking in character and personal responsibility by both conservatives and liberals.[13] Given familiar stereotypes of promiscuous teenage girls, black teenage girls especially, it is not difficult to persuade American society to think of them as sexually irresponsible and unwilling to be self-sufficient.[14] And while identifying the problem as the sexuality of young women seems to many Americans not only plausible but also innocuous, it taps into a real concern of many: teenagers disadvantaged by class, race, and gender.[15] A conservative like Murray is not loath to make graphically clear the gender and racial bias behind moral assessment of unwed mothers' "undisciplined" sexual appetites. Reducing their pregnancies to physical gratification, he employs a familiar, if shocking, sexual double standard to deny the father's responsibility: "As far as I can tell, he has approximately the same causal responsibility as a slice of chocolate cake has in determining whether a woman gains weight."[16] Thus, according to the logic of the public debate, the moral weakness of "children who have children" lies at the heart of society's moral deterioration.

This focus, by making black teenage women the moral lightning rod for the nation, draws on sex and race stereotypes to send strong moral signals to single mothers up and down the social scale about what is and is not socially approved maternal behavior. In American society, the bad teenage girl who gets "in trouble" has always served as a cautionary tale to others about womanhood. Now unwed black teenage mothers are being used to convey a general moral warning about single motherhood: no family structure can be legitimate or healthy in the absence of a father at its head.[17] Thus, many conservatives and liberals draw from these teenagers the broader lesson that "Dan Quayle Was Right": *any* family not headed by a father seriously disadvantages children developmentally and economically, causing the range of social ills confronting the country.[18]

This broader lesson about father absence appears to confirm that single mothers de facto cannot be "good" mothers. Yet this view of single mothers is not supported by the research literature. There is evidence that children living with one parent are likely to be somewhat disadvantaged compared with children whose families conform to the two-parent social ideal.[19] However, the literature is not conclusive on the subject of whether it is the loss of income or of the father, two factors that are difficult to separate, which disadvantages children in female-headed single-parent families. Contrary to what many believe, while divorce and single motherhood may be associated with low income and poverty, family disruption is not the primary cause of poverty, low achievement, and delinquency.[20] Furthermore, the negative impact of marital disruption has been exaggerated by studies, most of which, until recently, have failed to distinguish between the harm caused children by divorce and by long-term family conflict leading up to it.[21] Too often, blaming single mothers takes the place of efforts to arrive at a more precise understanding of both the shifting social conditions that have made the two-parent family so vulnerable and what harms children's well-being. This approach of interpreting female-headed families and absent fathers as the cause of social problems, rather than a symptom of them, was established in the public debate by Senator Daniel Patrick Moynihan in his 1965 report on "the" black family.[22]

In sum, the public consensus about single mothers proposes addressing the country's perceived moral decline among the poor, where it is argued by many to be worst, by restoring motherhood to an economically self-sufficient, two-parent family it can then make the proper nursery of civic virtue. This strategy and the diagnosis of the values crisis it grows out of fail to recognize that most teenage mothers are caught up in persistent poverty and are not its begetters. They begin as disadvantaged young women for whom the central social institutions of the country—families, schools, job markets, the medical system—are not working. Teen pregnancy may be, in this context, the sole meaningful option for many young women who as a result of gender, poverty, race, and failure in school have few others.[23] Furthermore, assuming that a poverty of values is characteristic chiefly of the poor hardly reflects an adequate grasp of the moral malaise Americans perceive. Social disintegration is not limited to urban or disadvantaged ethnic populations, where lack of resources to buffer or hide it make it particularly evident. Instead, it is being experienced up and down the social and economic scale in such things as family "breakdown," domestic violence, youth violence and crime, drugs, corruption among those in positions of authority, deep racial and ethnic divisions, and declining civic responsibility and initiative.

The perception that moral decline is pervasive suggests that much more is at stake, in short, than strengthening personal values and behavior, particularly among the disadvantaged, within a basic social structure that is otherwise sound. It suggests that aspects of the way American society is *structured* are part of the problem and that the association of moral values chiefly with individual behavior needs further examination. This association is a familiar way of thinking about moral values in America, but it is not sufficient for understanding the moral basis of the country's social ills.

BEYOND PRIVATE SOLUTIONS
TO THE VALUES CRISIS

In addition to making it easy to blame mothers, dominant cultural beliefs are driving public debate about the nation's values crisis off track by defining as natural and immutable society's traditional or-

ganization into public and private spheres. These beliefs provide a
map of society so familiar that it is employed uncritically and unconsciously by many political leaders, policy experts, social commentators, ordinary citizens, and even scholars. Precisely because
they *are* beliefs, these traditional beliefs do not have to correspond
with social reality in past and present to retain their power.[24] More
than simply describing the structure of society, "public" and "private" are categories that prescribe a certain set of social arrangements. They represent basic notions in the dominant American
culture about the way society is and ought to be ordered. This
means that public debate about the values crisis is being shaped by
an embedded *moral* discourse that governs the organization and
analysis of society. Because this discourse goes largely unexamined, a whole level of values analysis is missing from the debate.

Because we do not yet have a thorough grasp of how this cultural
discourse about public and private governs our worldview, the
nation is stalled in understanding and addressing its grave social
problems. We lack, in particular, understanding of how these inherited beliefs encode our modern secular value system, the moral
knowledge of the dominant culture that shapes Americans' lives.
Important scholarly debate about the origins and function of these
beliefs notwithstanding, the way in which they currently are shaping and reinforcing dominant American social values has not been
explored sufficiently. To a significant degree, this is because debate
about these beliefs has been carried on in academia among theo-
reticians and historians, cut off from policy studies within univer-
sities and from public debate outside. As a result, too little attention has been paid to the impact of these beliefs on the way the
nation's values crisis is understood.

To illustrate, we need only look carefully at a belief like that
in the "good" mother to see that it carries with it basic values
assumptions not only about women, but also about how society
should be organized. These structural assumptions are shaping
public debate without being properly examined. They have to do

not only with the family and responsibility for childrearing and caregiving, but also with the relationship of the family and these tasks to public institutions and their responsibilities, and with the social role of men. Because belief in the "good" mother orients public debate to an understanding of values as individual and of childrearing as the private responsibility primarily of individual mothers, few ask how motherhood and childrearing as social values are supported by the larger social structure that undergirds and depends on families.

Addressing the nation's values crisis requires more, in short, than moving backward to recapture traditional values conceived of chiefly as individual traits or possessions. It requires moving forward to a more complex understanding of the relationship of these values to institutional structures of all kinds and to the way society is organized into public and private spheres. Without this understanding we cannot do justice to the values many Americans want to reinterpret and sustain for the future.

CHANGING STRUCTURES, REINTERPRETING VALUES

This brings us to the third way in which the public debate about values is being driven astray by traditional cultural beliefs about public and private. The structural assumptions built into the debate by these beliefs no longer fit the structure of American life. For example, the idea that the work of motherhood should be the private responsibility of women still governs a society in which neither "the" family nor other institutions are organized to support this work the way they once did for the majority. By the early 1990s, less than 10 percent of American families conformed to the two-parent nuclear model with "breadwinner" father and full-time mother at home.[25] Yet public debate continues to tie families' valued nurturing and character-forming role to the traditional sexual division of labor in this nuclear model. It does so despite evidence we will discuss shortly that this model's full-time mother has disappeared, its sole- and even primary-breadwinner father is becoming a thing of the past, and its relationships have been revealed as, more frequently than not, idealized.

To gain a more accurate sense of the country's problems, in short, we must assess not only how our social vision is patterned by traditional beliefs about public and private, but also what changes in the structure of American life these beliefs are obscuring. Several of the well-documented, interrelated structural shifts that affect the institutions of motherhood and "the" family, but are overlooked by a focus on individual values, will help illustrate this point. When these shifts are taken into account, the experience of poor single mothers can no longer be read as a story simply of their personal "poverty of values."

First, both women and men have shown a rapidly increasing preference in recent decades for postponing marriage until their mid-twenties. This preference has changed sexual activity for *all* teenagers, not just poor ones. Such activity used to take place for a brief, largely premarital period. Together with biological changes causing earlier onset of puberty, however, the rise of age at first marriage has created more than a decade of sexually mature activity that begins for teenage women and men while many are living at home. The American population as a whole is witnessing a redefinition of the sexual agency of all teens, something which has special ramifications for women.[26]

Second, motherhood and marriage are increasingly separated. This is true not just for teenagers, but for even more rapidly growing numbers of older mothers. By 1988, 26 percent of all live births in the country were to single women.[27] Single-parent families have grown among the disadvantaged and the privileged, and across lines of age and race. Their increase has been caused by yet a third major shift in the structure of society. Over much of the twentieth century, women's increasing economic independence has made it more possible than in the past for women from all social strata to live without a husband. While conservatives in particular argue that welfare is the cause of the growth in single-parent families, it is not. Single motherhood is growing among the better off as well as the poor and has kept growing despite the decline in the real value of welfare benefits after 1974.[28]

A fourth structural shift that has caused a decrease in the economic incentives marriage holds for women stems from the steady narrowing of the gender wage-gap since 1970. Experienced by adults up and down the social ladder, this narrowing has been mainly the result not of women's gaining equal pay, but of the decline in men's earning power relative to women's. The decline has been most dramatic for low-skilled men at the bottom of the ladder. Their absolute loss in earnings means that for some marriage has become less attractive because they no longer can fulfill a primary "breadwinning" role in the family.[29]

A fifth major structural change in American life reflects the increasing economic independence and responsibilities of women. Work outside the home was once common predominantly among minority and white lower-class women, with only 26 percent of women with children aged six to seventeen and 10.8 percent of those with children under age six in the paid labor force in 1948. Now mothers from most social groups are employed. By 1993, 70.6 percent of women with children aged six to seventeen were in the paid labor force and 56.8 percent of those with children under six; 59.8 percent of those with children under eighteen were in it full-time and full-year.[30] This development is in part a consequence of economic insecurity and a declining standard of living for the majority of Americans, not just the "underclass." Together these factors have resulted in overwork and a shrinkage of leisure hours for family, marriage or relationships, and other personal priorities.[31]

Along with additional changes in the structure of women's and men's lives that will be discussed in upcoming chapters, these structural shifts have crucial implications for marriage, motherhood, and families. They are evidence that the economic contract between women and men, which once was a key element of the institutional structure of marriage, is eroding. They are also evidence that the meaning and value of women's work, both reproductive and productive, is in the process of being fundamentally reorganized socially, as is the traditional sexual division of labor between women and men. The social and cultural change these shifts represent is deeply rooted, taking place across the whole of society and shaped by trends reaching back into the early decades of this century.

It is unrealistic to think that American society could, if it wanted to, simply roll back these complex changes. Instead, we must recognize that basic patterns of adult life and work are not determined by nature, contrary to traditional cultural belief, but are given much of their shape by history. The responsibility of American women and men today is to face the historical challenge, brought to a head by various long-term forces, of helping to fashion meaningful new patterns of adult life for their children to inherit.

LIMITING WOMEN'S PUBLIC PARTICIPATION

Finally, in addition to exploring how dominant cultural beliefs about public and private are undermining public debate about the nation's values crisis, women and men who wish to find realistic and sound ways to translate traditional values to fit new social arrangements must explore how these beliefs also limit women's participation in this debate.

With its emphasis on women's public role in their private capacity as mothers, consensus in the debate asserts a particular view of women's citizenship. In doing so, it reveals the unfinished revolution regarding women in American society. Despite the fact that many politicians, journalists, institutional leaders, and scholars write and speak as if women were already full public participants, or as if their becoming so were simply a matter of time, the nature of women's citizenship is actually hotly contested.

The view that women are central to the solution to the nation's moral decline in their private capacity as mothers draws its persuasive power from traditional cultural beliefs. By appealing to these, in particular to the belief that mothers secure the nation's moral and social order, this view indirectly and implicitly reinforces the idea that being a "good" mother is women's fundamental public contribution and the essence of their citizenship. Traditional beliefs define mothers' "natural" capacity for childrearing, as well as childbearing, as their chief political responsibility and role. The notion that the most important dimension of women's citizenship is fulfilled by "natural" instincts, rather than by women's *conscious* public commitment as individuals, is a key element of traditional cultural beliefs about public and private.[32]

These beliefs ensure that a double standard still lurks beneath the widely held assumption that women today are already full participants in American public life. By making this double standard seem part of the natural and proper structure of society, these beliefs continue to function as a barrier to women's realizing the full potential of their public participation and leadership. Whether or not those in the current debate who emphasize motherhood intend to reinforce women's traditional association with the domestic world, and thus to subvert their progress toward full participation in public life, their conception of women's citizenship defines women's political role chiefly as serving the nation by serving the family.[33] As we shall see, the problem with this view is not the value it places on motherhood, but the way its conception of motherhood limits women's public role and denies them a direct relationship with government.

The fact that motherhood remains for many Americans the central focus of women's public contribution, while independent individualism (not fatherhood) is the focus of men's, demonstrates that there is more to the definition of public participation than voting rights. In fact, although many Americans espouse equality between the sexes, women are not yet seen and for the most part do not yet see themselves as full public participants. Most are not expected, and do not yet expect, to formulate public priorities for the whole of society and assert them with authority.

The chief evidence of this is that the overwhelming majority of local, state, and federal elected officials still are male, like the top officials in most fields, but there is further evidence as well. A recent study of citizen participation found that women are significantly less likely than men to be active in politics by "making a campaign contribution, working informally in the community, contacting an official, and affiliation with a political organization" nationally or locally.[34] Women also are less likely than men to follow politics in the mass media or to believe that they can understand and influence politics and policy.[35] And in recent years the drop in women's newspaper readership rates has been substantially larger than men's, a differential that also reflects the fact, according to experts, that the news nationally continues to be overwhelmingly (white) male in content and editorial perspective.[36] In sum, as political philosopher Seyla Benhabib notes, our very definition of the public sphere still is based in theory and practice on the norm of male participation: "Two centuries after the American and French revolutions, the entry of women into the public sphere is far from complete, the gender division of labor in the family is still not the object of moral and political reflection, and women and their concerns are still invisible in contemporary theories of justice and community."[37]

In short, in the face of the staying power of traditional cultural beliefs, the women's movement has had limited success in leading women to full public participation. This may be in part because its emphasis on women's rights and access as the main agenda for women's political activity is not persuasive enough to move most liberal women, let alone conservative ones, to seek effectiveness and claim authority in public matters. Thus, estimates indicate that only about one-third of voting American women identify themselves as feminists.[38] This statistic, along with the gender gap in voting that has been evident since the 1980s and demonstrates women's "distinctive and liberal political views on foreign policy matters and social spending issues," suggests that many women are interested in a broader public agenda.[39] In other words, the most effective way to improve women's status in society may be to recognize their interest in more than a "social feminist" agenda (reproductive freedom, childcare, parental leave, and comparable worth).[40] It may mean linking women's concern for their rights with their larger sense of social responsibility.

A CHOICE BETWEEN BEING MATERNAL OR BEING LIKE MEN

Making this link between women's rights and their concern for society as a whole requires attending to something that has received far too little attention from most feminist leaders and scholars: the question of women's *moral agency*. This question is central to defining a new kind of political presence for women in American society that goes beyond one based on being either maternal or like men.

Traditional cultural beliefs about public and private control the terms that shape and limit alternatives for women's public participation by conflating women and motherhood, a Western pattern that has analogues in other cultures. Scholars already have given significant attention to the denial of women's individuality inherent in defining their essential identity in terms of such maternal traits as nurturing, relationality, and emotional expressiveness. This conflation eliminates "contexts within which motherhood is irrelevant to women's behavior."[41] Equally important, however, is that even when motherhood *is* relevant to women's behavior, conflating women and motherhood denies that mothers are at the same time women and individuals as well.

By teaching us to place greatest social value on women's biological capacities, dominant cultural beliefs about public and private separate women's moral agency from their conscious moral and intellectual capacities. So while traditional beliefs present women's maternal nature as endowing them with special virtue, these beliefs actually enshrine a moral double standard by defining women's moral capacity, in contrast to men's, as based on "natural" moral traits that are a matter neither of reason, consciousness, nor will. There is, in short, a moral paradox at the heart of dominant cultural beliefs about public and private: they present women as at once morally superior and morally inferior. Overcoming this paradox is central to American women's assertion of public leadership in the present, as it was in the past.

Thus, dominant beliefs about public and private have ensured that there are only three main options for conceptualizing women's public participation. All three represent a choice between being maternal (responsibility) or being like men (rights): women can be citizens in their capacity as mothers; they can be maternalists, citizens who bring a maternal perspective to society; or they can become citizens according to the male norms of the rights-bearing individual. The first of these three options, like "Republican motherhood," emphasizes women's actual motherhood. The second, maternalism, espoused today by both nonfeminists and some feminists, is characterized not only by concern for public programs to benefit mothers and children, but even more fundamentally by criticism of the public world's orientation to rights-bearing individualism and by assertion of the higher value of what are seen as women's distinctive maternal values and thinking.[42] The third position, one that has been identified as the classic feminist position, emphasizes women's equal rights based on a male model of individualism.

In the case of all three options for women's public agency, furthermore, these beliefs about public and private also have ensured the cultural expectation that women *as women* will make a difference by improving society morally—that they will make it better. Mothers will do so by producing through their citizen-children civic virtue. Maternalists will do so by mothering the public world as they do their private families, bringing to it humane care for the vulnerable and the obligation to put others ahead of self-interest. And even as citizens on the male model of the rights-bearing individual, women commonly are expected to bring greater integrity and social improvement to their public engagement and leadership. This expectation was expressed early in this century, in words we might easily hear today, by a young woman anticipating women's formal entrance into public life after winning the vote:

[T]he advent of women into political life would mean the loosening of a great moral force which will modify and soften the relentlessly selfish economic forces of trade and industry. . . . [T]he ideals of democracy and of social and human welfare will undoubtedly receive a great impetus.[43]

CONCLUSION

In the following chapters, I will argue that the consensus on single mothers prevailing in today's public debate, especially the restigmatizing of "illegitimacy" among disadvantaged teenagers, offers a solution to our national values crisis that is seriously flawed. It is wrong because the set of dominant cultural beliefs about public and private, which operates largely undetected in analyses of American life, both restricts women from full participation in public life and prevents clear definition of the nation's grave problems and formulation of sound new public vision. Although these traditional beliefs lead the public debate to perceive correctly how central women and motherhood are to the health of the nation's social fabric and to its current problems, they mislead in the way they define this centrality.

Choosing to Lead joins analysis of religion with that of gender (in relation to race, ethnicity, and class) and history to redefine the national crisis of values. Religion is an important tool for analyzing and criticizing the traditional cultural beliefs that are a principal variable in this crisis and in analyses of it. These beliefs, like most values of the dominant American culture, have been powerfully shaped by Western Christianity and Judaism.

This interdisciplinary approach will help us get beyond today's use of a naturalistic model of motherhood that blames women and limits their public participation. It will offer an historical view of motherhood as a social institution from which we can learn much about both the country's values crisis and the values that encourage the social responsibility and connectedness required to address this crisis. This interdisciplinary approach also will help us see that while women have always shaped American values, for the most part in private, they are faced now with an unprecedented opportunity to do so publicly, which is crucial to the life of the nation. Moreover, this approach will reveal that in facing this opportunity American women are part of historical traditions of women's public leadership and distinctive vision for society. When viewed critically, these traditions are an important source of insight and encouragement in breaking new ground for the present. Whether and how women choose to guide their destiny at this critical point in American society is central to their own fate and to the country's ability, through commitment to the value of human welfare, to turn around its moral decline.

I will begin by investigating how American life has been organized into private and public worlds, each a social ethos that orients women and men to different moral roles and traditions in society. I turn first to the continuing association of women with the domestic world and men with the public.

CHAPTER TWO

A Woman's Place Was *in the Home:*
The Domestic Sphere

Paradoxically, the family responsibilities of the majority of American women have increased even though their place is no longer physically in the home. Married or not, most mothers today must support or help support their families financially. By 1994, 55 percent of all employed women and 48 percent of employed married women were providing half or more of their households' income.[1] At the same time, as wives and homemakers, women continue to bear disproportionate responsibility for the daily affective, physical, and moral work of family life. Despite having moved into the workplace, in short, women still are associated in a fundamental way with the domestic sphere. As a result, in a society that continues to regard responsibility for the unpaid daily labor of family and community commitment as incompatible with full public participation, they also still face constraints outside the home.

Women's persisting association with the domestic sphere is the main reason their voices are not more prominent in the debate about the nation's values crisis. Besides limiting the time in a day available for politics, this association keeps women from full public participation in two major ways. On a cultural level, it defines their legitimate purview even in public matters as children, the home, caregiving, and women themselves, limiting their authority to speak about society as a whole. Thus, the cultural conception of women's natural place in society identifies them still as suited to shaping American values on a limited and personal, rather than a collective and institutional, basis. The staying power of this norm was graphically illustrated when it was invoked to help put political pressure on First Lady Hillary Rodham Clinton to replace her leadership of health-care planning, a policy initiative with wide economic and social consequences, with a focus mainly on women and children. The second major way the association of women with the domestic sphere regulates women's public voices is by limiting their access to top positions of institutional leadership.

Women's association with the domestic sphere persists despite the fact that most are leading workforce lives increasingly like those of men. Women have always worked and many have always worked outside the home for pay, although the economic value to families of these contributions has been obscured by the notions of the male "breadwinner" and "family wage." What is new for most women, however, is major or sole responsibility for family income. By the turn of the century, women, the majority of them mothers, will constitute almost half of the national workforce.[2] American mothers, having entered the paid labor force in growing numbers over the last century and in recent years as a result especially of declining national and state economies, are winning a new right to work in society's eyes. Economic necessity, the new family-related financial responsibility of the majority, not the meaning of paid labor to women as individuals, is making the most widely accepted case for this new right. That this right is also a duty is evident too in changing welfare prescriptions for poor, single mothers. Whereas once welfare policy was based on the social assumption that poor mothers, like others, should stay home with their children, now there is widespread social agreement that these mothers too should work outside the home.

As this dramatic change in the social norm regarding women and paid work is taking place, however, the traditional cultural ideal for women is simply adapting to keep pace. The social reality of families in which most women's labor went predominantly into the home, a reality which rested on heterosexual marriage and the possibility for the majority of men of being the sole or primary wage earner, has disappeared. Yet the dominant cultural belief that women are responsible in society for family well-being, especially for children, but also for the ill, elderly, and those with disabilities, is *not* disappearing. Also resisting change is the belief that women's individual talents and interests are secondary to this "true" work for which they are suited by nature. As a result, the expansion of women's family responsibilities to include "breadwinning" represents a one-sided shift in the gender division of labor in American society. Men as a group are experiencing nothing like a corresponding redefinition and growth of their family duties, although some men are working toward new models of partnership and fatherhood.

Women's situation calls attention to the growing gap between the value society claims to place on the unpaid daily work of family and community welfare and the structural support it actually gives this work. The gap involves tremendous cost to women, who are making valiant efforts to fill it, as well as to the status of this unpaid work as a social value and to the American social fabric. Now, as in the past in American society, the fate of human welfare is inextricably linked through motherhood with women's fate. Because women's traditional role is simply being stretched to incorporate the new norm of their paid employment, their unpaid family and community labor, along with their potential as full participants in the public world, is being jeopardized.

Understanding the social implications of the persisting association of women with the domestic sphere requires deeper analysis of the social values in which this association is anchored. Failure to understand the moral roots of modern women's situation is limiting our comprehension of it and the central role it plays in the nation's values crisis. This failure is limiting too our ability to address the crisis effectively.

THE PERSISTENCE OF THE PUBLIC
AND PRIVATE DISTINCTION

There are and always have been in American society multiple "publics"—groups of people having common interests or characteristics. The public represented by white, privileged men, however, has successfully advanced historically the claim to represent the American public sphere, defining and directing national political and social life. One of the chief sources of its defining and directing power is the set of governing cultural beliefs about public and private. Far from being simply descriptive terms, "public" and "private" sustain the power of the dominant public by presenting society's governing gender ideals and the values associated with them as the basis for society's organization into two spheres. Thus, these terms also organize both the fundamental moral resources of American society and the way we perceive these resources. Dominant beliefs about public and private persist because they present a credible *moral* map of social reality, a view of the way men and women are "by nature" and the way society consequently is supposed to work.

This moral view of society, which most social analysts overlook, has enormous staying power because of what it accomplishes for society. By providing an implicit moral explanation for the social reality they describe, dominant beliefs about public and private make their description of this reality appear at once reasonable and authoritative. This description gains persuasive power through its claim to be an apprehension of the moral order of nature itself. The *moral* authority of these cultural beliefs has been integral to their power to dominate.

To critically assess these beliefs about public and private, therefore, we must go beyond the idea that morality is a matter of individual behavior, especially sexual behavior, and recognize it as also a social and structural phenomenon. Morality has to do with the social order. It is a matter of the social identity and status cultures assign social groups and their members, of the social roles appropriate to these assignments, and of ideas about the proper relationship of individuals, genders, races, classes, and groups of all kinds. These assignments and ideas are based on classifications of human difference that represent cultural *judgments* about the moral nature and comparative status of different kinds of human beings. For example, traditional beliefs about public and private define women in terms of distinctive maternal moral traits that are said to be natural. In this way, these beliefs make motherhood the source of women's virtue, setting the social standard and role for a "good" woman. Yet they present women's assigned moral identity and status not as a value judgment, but as an objective, "scientific" discovery about the nature of this kind of human being. They also do not acknowledge that the moral perspective from which this and other assignments have been made is that of privileged men of the dominant Anglo-Saxon culture that historically has shaped American social reality.

We must recognize, in short, that the structure of society and social relations defined by beliefs about public and private represents the dominant culture's social organization of human morality. Based on their claims about morality, these beliefs identify social players, define their roles, and set the parameters of their arena of action on the social stage.[3] They accomplish "the hierarchical ordering of differences, by which morality is the province of some and not others" and also designate moral space—what kind of morality is appropriate to which sphere and its institutions (e.g., an ethic of altruism to the home and one of self-interest to the marketplace).[4] The way these dominant beliefs define the moral order of society goes largely unrecognized, however, because they themselves teach us to think of morality as primarily individual and private, not structural and social. This is nowhere as evident as in the way these beliefs define sexuality as personal and private rather than public. Until very recently, for example, the sexual behavior of public figures in the context of their public roles was believed to be a private issue unrelated to the fulfillment of their public responsibilities. Yet as a result of growing revelations not only of extra-marital affairs, but also of institutional patterns of sexual harassment and sexual exploitation of children and others, Americans are increasingly aware that institutional power has brought with it protected sexual entitlements and expression that the very notion of "public" has obscured.

GENDER AND THE MORAL STRUCTURE
OF SOCIETY

Beliefs about public and private root the moral order of American society in biology. Specifically, they present the social order as rooted in gender, leaving unacknowledged the dominant culture's privileging of the white race. Gaining authority from the claim to represent natural meaning, gender actually represents the cultural process of *assigning* meaning to human biology and clusters of social values to the male and female. As a cultural product, gender norms make systematic links, defined as biological and universal, between particular values and the sexes. In doing so, these norms also obscure the actual diversity of the way gender is expressed in American life in relation to race, ethnicity, socioeconomic status, and sexuality. Finally, the values these norms link with each sex reflect a basic underlying cultural value: the superior value accorded the male—the hierarchy of masculinity over femininity. This hierarchy, along with the unacknowledged hierarchy of race, determines the values, tasks, and opportunities socially prescribed for women and men and legitimates the larger pattern of social and political arrangements.

Through these gender-linked value clusters and this gender hierarchy, dominant cultural beliefs provide the logic for organizing the sexes and the values they represent into public and private spheres, and for giving priority culturally to values symbolized by the masculine. Gender, then, in addition to explaining and in turn being explained by the categories of "public" and "private," also comes to symbolize them. So, for example, femininity, which the dominant culture associates with such "natural" traits as the capacity to nurture, emotional expressiveness, and dependence, also is associated with the private sphere. Thus, women come to represent the private world of the home and all the social values associated with it.

Some American women symbolize the private more than others, however, because physically and socially they represent most closely the dominant culture's feminine ideal. Within the dominant belief system, gender interacts with the other "natural" categories of race and ethnicity, as well as class, to create a moral hierarchy among women. Thus, minority and poor women are seen as capable only of *approximating* the feminine ideal set by the dominant white culture. Their status as women is qualified by their standing outside the dominant racial group; for example, the status of black women is defined by their being "non-white" as well as female. Yet as we shall see, women from varied racial, ethnic, and class groups, although in very different social circumstances than privileged white women and with very different social outcomes, nevertheless are seen, in comparison with men of their group, as representative of the feminine. It is not the case, as often is argued, that only privileged women are viewed as the "'natural' bearers of morality" and of other feminine traits.[5]

What follows, therefore, is an exploration of the persisting dominant moral definition and destiny of *all* women. We must examine the moral basis of the cultural sex-gender system—the dominant, socially constructed values that anchor it—to gain insight into traditional cultural beliefs about public and private. Understanding the moral economy these beliefs continue to hold in place in society—the social distribution and interaction of values they legitimate—is crucial to understanding what it will take for American women to change this economy and become full participants in public life. Understanding this traditional moral economy is crucial too to understanding how women can play a central role in addressing the nation's moral and social crisis more effectively.

In particular, we must explore the traditional gender system's moral paradox regarding women. The governing cultural judgment that women's moral weakness necessitates their dependence on men has been obscured by the cultural attribution, given this dependence, of superior moral qualities to women's nature. The dominant culture historically has defined American women's morality as instinctual and limited. This definition, by identifying women's morality with dependence and their biological capacity to nurture, actually negates the culture's attribution of moral superiority to women and reinforces its evaluation of them as morally deficient. The full moral agency of women is denied with their moral consciousness when they are defined as "naturally" good at relations that are socially important.[6]

Because maternal traits have defined women's morality, critical assessment of the gender-linked moral economy embedded in traditional beliefs about public and private must begin with examination of the association of these traits with "goodness" for women. In fact, this association is neither natural nor unchanging, but has a history. As we shall see, this history has been misunderstood, even by historians of American women, in ways that narrow our understanding of modern women's situation and leave barriers in the way of their public leadership. Contrary to the prevailing historical view that the experience of nineteenth-century middle-class women gave rise to American women's association with the domestic sphere, this association goes much deeper culturally and much further back in time.

RELIGION AND THE MORAL PATTERNS OF WESTERN CHRISTIAN CULTURE

As we have seen, the fact that we are likely, when we think about what a woman is and what her social role is meant to be, to assume that both have been defined basically by nature is itself a hallmark of dominant cultural beliefs about public and private. These beliefs obscure the extent to which the social conception of womanhood, like all social conceptions, is not determined by natural "facts," but is a product of the history of human *interpretation* of nature. Indeed, the "good" woman is a creation of the history of Western culture, and this history has a great deal of light to shed on her. We can turn to it to ask: How did the identity of American women come to be associated so profoundly with the home, motherhood, and morality? Where did the idea of the private sphere come from and how have women come to symbolize it? What has American women's association with domesticity and their exclusion from the public sphere meant historically for their lives? How has this association helped to shape broader American social, political, and cultural patterns?

As we turn to history to explore these questions, we need also to turn to the study of religion. We tend to think of religion as private—as personal and set apart from the public world. Yet historically it has played a major role in fashioning and articulating the central moral patterns of every culture, including the social organization of gendered values and tasks. Recognizing religion as a public force requires attending both to explicitly religious values per se and to religion's powerful influence in defining what society has come to view as its secular values. Religion has influenced the pervasive dimension of meaning and evaluation inherent in all human thought and action, social relations and institutions.

The intellectually naive modern idea that religion is a narrow and marginal category of human life is sharply called into question by the history of womanhood in the West. The dominant conception of womanhood in American culture that links the female, morality, and the domestic comes from an old and broad tradition. Christianity and Judaism, Western society's primary belief systems, helped fashion and articulate this conception as it evolved from the interpretation of historical developments in light of biblical text.

Specifically, in the sixteenth century in Europe, a religious and social revolution, stimulated by profound economic and political changes, created the newly central family and household and redrew the lines between the public and private worlds.[7] This revolution produced a new set of cultural beliefs about public and private that regulated and justified a new sexual division of labor familiar to our modern eye. It developed these separate spheres and beliefs about them through a set of Christian teachings about womanhood, motherhood, the proper social organization of male and female activity, and the relationship of the home to church and state. These teachings set forth fundamental conceptions about the organization of individual and social life that have been dominant in the West for more than four hundred years.[8] In doing so, Western religion has not been unique. One of the chief features of religious traditions in cultures around the globe has been their historical role in defining and articulating gender systems, many of which have striking continuities with the Western system.

The Western tradition of womanhood, governed by male authorities—who were mainly ecclesiastical, celibate until the reformations, and elite by virtue of education and privileged status—did not influence the lives and institutions of Christian believers only, although for centuries that would have meant the majority of the population in Europe. Rather, it shaped the foundations of all the institutions of the dominant European culture—intellectual, ethical, medical, legal, political, economic, artistic, educational, as well as religious. It also shaped the American culture that arose out of the European and was forged from its institutions. In defining women's identity and purpose in moral terms, the dominant pattern in Christianity has been to define the *moral status* of women, within every category of human difference, as inferior to that of men. Religion has presented the position of men and women as asymmetrical; women have been viewed as created second, of lesser value and subordinate to men.

The significance of this biblically rooted anthropology in which men have been seen as primary, created in the image of God, is that they have been defined as representing the human and its capacity for moral agency. Incorporating ancient myths of female evil common in the Mediterranean world, the Christian church in the West, beginning with Paul and the Church Fathers, while it honored women, also built this historical and theological tradition of their inferiority. Eve's responsibility for the fall of Adam in the Garden of Eden was made into a cultural principle of women's moral weakness, representing emotion over reason, body over soul, and carnality over spirit. The curse interpreted as brought down on Eve's head in Eden for causing the fall of man was a punishment to be borne by generations of women living in "sorrow and travail."[9]

It is this basic moral dualism, a cultural "glass ceiling" defining women's secondary status, that anchors and undergirds the privileged status of men over women in American culture. By defining women's moral status in society as inferior to that of men and their social destiny as restricted by their reproductive capacity, this Christian tradition of womanhood has influenced powerfully the fundamental terms of the cultural problem still faced by American women, as well as the cultural resources for change available to them.

THE "GOOD" MOTHER

One of the primary ways in which Christianity has helped define womanhood and the notion of the private sphere in American society is through its presentation of motherhood as a universal "natural" reality, rather than as a social institution that has a history. Christianity has anchored motherhood in the eternal, obscuring the way women's experience varies "not only among families and individuals but according to time, place, race, class, and culture" by describing its biological aspects as "changeless": "Women's lives were organized and their capacities defined by their status as mothers, potential mothers, and non-mothers, but motherhood itself was not perceived as an institution shaped by culture and subject to history."[10]

In fact, in the history of Christianity, the relationship of womanhood and motherhood has varied in important ways over time. This relationship changed significantly in sixteenth-century Europe when a new Christian conception of domesticity arose, setting new cultural and social terms for domestic life that have dominated in the West, albeit with significant modifications, down to the present. This conception is embedded in the contemporary

Western political, social, and economic institutions it helped to fashion.[11]

From the fifteenth to the seventeenth centuries, the institutions of family and state emerged to form the basis of European society, taking the place of the kinship alliances which once had done so.[12] Together with geographical expansion, religious reform

> stimulated and accompanied transformations in politics and society, economic and intellectual life. The world within the household was altered as profoundly as the world outside, with long-lasting repercussions for marriage and parenthood, for the experience of family life, and the place of the household in church and society.[13]

Along with Christian humanists, Protestant and Catholic reformers were caught up in these transformations. They brought the theological and institutional power of Christianity to bear in helping to shape and explain the conjugal family. As the foundation of morality and social order, this family unit was new at the time, although it is familiar to modern eyes. In fashioning new understandings of the work of parents, reformers reworked theological doctrines, giving revised meanings to religious symbols in light of their own family experience.[14]

Drawing on ancient sources, especially Hebrew Scriptures, reformers like Martin Luther articulated a new ideal of Christian motherhood, one that defined a new relationship for women between virtue and domesticity.[15] Whereas holiness in earliest Christianity was not especially relevant to motherhood and in the Middle Ages could best be achieved by virgins or women who *overcame* the obstacles of marriage and children, in the early modern period holiness and motherhood came to be deeply joined. As historian Clarissa Atkinson has demonstrated, in the sixteenth century motherhood as a symbol, cultural belief, and institution in the West was transformed into the natural and true vocation of *every* woman. Through motherhood alone women might find virtue and even sainthood. Now, in a new way, women had no alternative to becoming wives. To be a "good" woman was to be a "good" mother:

In an ideal society, adult women were wives and mothers—protected, productive, fulfilled. Their sexual, spiritual, and intellectual energies were absorbed in the production and training of Christians for the churches, workers for the marketplace, and citizens for the state. A woman's duty was to give birth to children (as many as possible), to nourish them physically and morally, and to prepare them for the work of church and society, if they were boys, for motherhood if they were girls. She was inclined toward this work by her physical and psychological being; grace, now identified with nature, need no longer triumph over nature to produce a good woman.[16]

TRUE WOMANHOOD

While motherhood, like the dominant cultural beliefs about public and private of which it was part, continued to evolve over time in the West, the early modern period established the continuing framework within which this evolution was to take place—the redefined relationship between women, virtue, and domesticity. By the nineteenth century in America, this early modern doctrine of the "good" woman had survived and evolved into the notion of True Womanhood.[17] However, when most historians of American women look for the appearance of cultural belief associating women with the private sphere, they point to a set of social attitudes that "first became conspicuous in the early nineteenth century."[18] Probably the most influential early study of True Womanhood, that by historian Nancy Cott, implies that the nineteenth century was the first to witness the emergence of a cultural doctrine defining "women's domestic influence and maternal duties" as a positive social role:

> Its configuration took shape as early as 1780 and was well established by 1820. . . . The doctrine of woman's sphere opened to women (reserved for them) the avenues of domestic influence, religious morality, and child nurture. It articulated a social power based on their special female qualities rather than on general human rights.[19]

Cott's study has persuaded many not simply that this doctrine was more explicit in the nineteenth century, but that much about it was entirely new:

Within this "cult" (it might almost be called a social ethic), mother, father, and children grouped together in the private household ruled the transmission of culture, the maintenance of social stability, and the pursuit of happiness; the family's influence reached outward, underlying success or failure in church and state, and inward, creating individual character. Not the understanding of families as cells making up the body of society but the emphasis placed on and agencies attributed to the family unit were new, and the importance given to women's roles as wives, mothers, and mistresses of households was unprecedented. . . . this ethic made women's presence the essence of successful homes and families.[20]

While the popular press that emerged and flourished in the early nineteenth century might make the doctrine of separate spheres *seem* new to modern scholars, however, it was not new in American culture and probably not even newly conspicuous to most Americans. The doctrine expressed in True Womanhood was already very prominent as an ideal imparted daily in myriad ways throughout society. In the institutions of home, school, and church alone, it would have been familiar to women and men through imagery, conversation, prayer, reading the Bible and other devotional literature, sermons, and classroom lessons.

What *was* new in the first decades of the nineteenth century is that the notion of the "good" woman was exposed to rapid social change. This exposure necessitated that it be updated and also defended, as its status shifted in some respects from that of an unquestioned, received truth to one newly subjected to negotiation.[21] In fact, the social ethic restricting women to the private household was promoted in popular literature at just the time a constellation of social and economic forces were both reinforcing and challenging the relegation of middle-class women to the domestic world.[22] The challenge came in particular from nineteenth-century feminism, which sought to redefine women's social status and options.[23]

True Womanhood was first and foremost a *moral* definition of women. It defined morality as women's nature—piety and purity —and by describing what women were like prescribed what they

should be like. This nineteenth-century ideal for women, like earlier ones, expressed the close cultural association of women and religion, an association stronger for women than for men, especially
but not only within Protestantism, the dominant American religious tradition. Women made up the numerical majority of wor-
shipers, while men, who were a minority in Protestantism, were
its leaders and official representatives. Women were seen by men,
whose institutional authority defined womanhood, as "naturally"
religious because they were "naturally" more dependent on both
God and men. The two forms of dependence were understood as
working together; religion, it was thought, would promote a
woman's proper orientation to home and to male dominance.[24] As
one influential writer of the period summarized, the True Woman
was to reflect in her way of being—passive, responsive, obedient,
and humble—her awareness that man was created by God as her
superior: "A really sensible woman feels her dependence. She does
what she can, but she is conscious of inferiority, and therefore
grateful for support."[25] Finally, purity—specifically, sexual virtue
and its maintenance against the force of male passion—was another
key attribute that constituted the moral superiority of True Womanhood.[26] In short, as historian Barbara Welter emphasizes, agency
—will, initiative, work, sexual passion, intellect, recognition—belonged to men, equipping them to move out into the world to take
on the hard realities of life.

The American home was a major focus of cultural belief in True
Womanhood and preoccupied middle-class women's magazines
and related literature in antebellum America. Woman was depicted
as unable to act in the world without being undone by the forces
of evil, but able to find safety and her natural place in the home.
Furthermore, she had an important role to play there as moral
guardian of the home's occupants and the symbol of its moral difference from the world. The ideal of the True Woman included her
social function of creating a home. Made by God to put duty to
husband and children—to family—at the center of her life, the True
Woman achieved her proper moral status and authority in her roles

as wife and mother. As she did so, she created a moral counterforce to the world's materialism and other evils: "the domestic fireside is the great guardian of society against the excesses of human passions."[27] What made woman a moral force was her maternity—her maternal intuition, suffering love, and dedication—which was anchored in and anchored her piety. As in the early modern doctrine of domesticity, motherhood was the center of women's being:

> To identify women with the heart was to imply that they conducted themselves through life by engaging the affections of others. The cultural metonymy by which the nurturant maternal role stood for the whole of women's experience further confirmed that "heartfelt" caring was women's characteristic virtue.[28]

In short, maternity gave women what real power, position, and independence they were allowed in nineteenth-century America. While a modern feminist scholar might find it hard to believe, a single woman who was a noted novelist was not "sentimentalizing domesticity" or "inflating" the power women might find in the home in the nineteenth century when she wrote in her diary of her desire for a household over which to preside; she was reflecting the social fact that marriage and motherhood, not a successful career, represented what real influence and status women might attain.[29]

WOMEN AND MORALITY IN AMERICAN SOCIETY

The fact that many historians of American women have not recognized that True Womanhood was a nineteenth-century version of the early modern doctrine of the "good" woman and domesticity is significant. It has seriously skewed our understanding of nineteenth-century American women and, because the history of these women has deeply affected our thinking about women's potential for public leadership, it also has skewed our view of the situation of modern women.

However, historical research that recognizes religion as a principal influence in the cultural patterns of meaning expressed in social arrangements helps correct our understanding of women in both past and present. This research reveals the complex moral roots of the association of American women with virtue and domesticity that are overlooked by many modern feminists. Deeper analysis of these complex roots is crucial if we are to understand better not only women's past and present status in society, but also its relationship to what the dominant culture perceives as the moral order of society as a whole.

While the importance of morality as a social category has been overlooked by many scholars, it was grasped to a significant degree by the first to explore True Womanhood. Barbara Welter not only recognized that the doctrine set forth a "complex of virtues" thought to constitute womanhood (piety, purity, submissiveness, etc.), but she also related True Womanhood to the broader problem that worried nineteenth-century American society: the profound moral threat represented by the social changes it was undergoing.[30] The True Woman's task was to be virtuous and obedient, assigned as she was by male authority to maintain the moral order inherent in the social order. This assignment was explicitly to *preserve* the division between private and public spheres by remaining in the private sphere. In the mid nineteenth century, as they had since the sixteenth-century reformations, Christian clergy communicated this religious and cultural message to women starkly, often in sermons: "Yours is to determine whether the beautiful order of society shall continue as it has been [or whether] society shall break up and become a chaos of disjointed and unsightly elements."[31]

In a situation strikingly parallel to today's, emphasis on this message in various contexts was necessitated by male authorities' fear that society was disintegrating morally. They called on women to resist change for themselves in order to anchor traditional values. Male fear grew out of the instability of a mobile and rapidly growing materialistic society, the impact of an expanding market economy on the lives of nineteenth-century men, and the threat social change posed to the distinction between male and female roles.[32] In short, what was particularly new about True Womanhood in the nineteenth century was society's heightened sense, as a result of industrialization and urbanization, of the contrast between the immorality of the marketplace and the morality of the home.

Instead of continuing to analyze True Womanhood in the context of these broader social patterns of values and meaning, however, many pioneers in women's history laid the foundation for a more limited analysis of it. They were more concerned with the history of *feminism* than of women or American society in general. Theirs was an historical decision to study women in a particular way, bringing to center stage certain women's struggle for individual rights, along with signs of their identification as women and their emerging solidarity. This approach cast domesticity in a fundamentally negative light, accepting traditional historians' devaluation of it in comparison with the public sphere, despite the fact that "women of the past centuries rarely perceived, as modern feminists do, an antithesis between women's obligations in the domestic realm and their general progress."[33] Even feminist historians who consciously strove to "judge domesticity on its own terms, as of its own time," including those who recognized that many women used it as a rationale for public activity, did not fully escape this modern feminist view that the association of women and domesticity is problematic. Furthermore, this focus on emerging nineteenth-century feminism attributed the "appearance" of the domestic doctrine by the 1830s to the rapid social and economic modernization then transforming America, especially the increasing separation between the spheres of home and the emerging market economy, as the focus of production and exchange shifted from the one to the other.[34]

Moreover, many historians of feminism, analyzing this cult of domesticity as a product of the early nineteenth century having primarily economic and class-linked roots, tied it to the identity of middle-class, Protestant women of the urban Northeast. These scholars presented True Womanhood as "rooted in the experience of Yankee middle-class mothers but applied to the female sex as a whole."[35] Thus, many came to see domesticity narrowly as a bourgeois idea, a class identity of privileged women, one that was developed for and by them into the ideology of "the lady." For these historians, white urban ladies were the agents and symbols of new class distinctions as they epitomized this new domestic norm, incorporating it into their religious vision for urban reform and gaining from it a sense of moral superiority to working-class women.

To be sure, an important part of the nineteenth-century evolution of the doctrine of domesticity *was* its role in the development of middle-class American femininity and even of the feminism that at once built on and reacted against the social power middle-class women derived from domesticity.[36] Nevertheless, tying it so narrowly to one group and reducing it chiefly to the class-based value of respectability as an instrument of social control distorts the past.

Treating domesticity this way underestimates its social pervasiveness, deep cultural roots, and moral significance. Unmoored from its broader historical and cultural contexts, the cult of True Womanhood has been seriously misread. It has been understood from the perspective of scholars interested especially in the history of modern feminism as the creation of a new social ideal for women. And this feminist perspective too often has marginalized the moral and explicitly religious in social analysis, reducing morality to a class-based issue. Many historians who have brought women to prominence as historical actors, that is, ironically have adopted established analytic approaches developed by mainstream historians of nineteenth- and early-twentieth-century America who focus on men, on the evolution of American social policy, and on the origins of the American welfare state. The new focus on women often is worked out, in other words, in the context of a class-centered history based on the Marxist premise that religion is little more than a bourgeois mechanism of social control.[37]

The insufficiently critical acceptance by historians of women of this approach seriously limits our understanding of the association of women and morality in American society. The nineteenth-century cult of domesticity has come to be understood as the *source* of the nineteenth-century's identification of womanhood with morality and the home.[38] Middle-class women, representing their class standard of respectability, have come to be seen chiefly as agents of social control efforts aimed at the poor and native-born and immigrant ethnic and minority populations. Thus, morality, control, motherhood, and its social extensions ("social housekeeping" and later social work) have been linked together in service of this class- and race-driven analysis.

What is problematic about this feminist interpretation of society and economy is not its claim that morality might serve the class, race, and gender interests of the privileged. Certainly, it did so in the nineteenth century and it does today. But this is never all that morality is or accomplishes, and the claim that it is reduces the complexity of the moral and religious dimensions of historical social change. Both these dimensions come to be treated as mere symbols of nineteenth-century women's relegation to the private sphere or as artifacts of middle-class identity. Behind this treatment lies a narrow and marginal view of religion as private only, a matter of personal belief and piety, or institutional, a matter of ministerial authority.

Most scholars of American women, that is, interpret religion as a variable *inside* the established framework of public and private spheres that reinforces women's assignment to the private and their exclusion from the public. Religion often is depicted, as if in a drama, in the role of gatekeeper—even of prison guard—in the lives of historical women. Recognizing religion as shaping only the values or beliefs people hold, however, and not also the *structural* values their social institutions and arrangements embody and promote, misses the major aspect of its historical significance. To extend the dramatic metaphor, what is at stake is the difference between seeing religion in a play as a character (a Protestant minister), a building that is part of the scenery, or a prop, and seeing it as a key element in the design of the roles of all the characters, of the dramatic action among them, and of all the institutions represented by the building scenery.

By not understanding that religion is integral to the design of the whole, many historians have failed to see religion's role in shaping the larger cultural history of the West of which nineteenth-century American society was a part. They have failed too to recognize the extent to which a moral framework that religion has helped fashion and has expressed shapes the American social order, its dynamics, and the way both are perceived. These failures have led to treatment of religion as simply a part of American society, rather than as a powerful force in constructing and legitimating fundamental American social structures and patterns we are still dealing with today.

It is particularly interesting that modern feminists treat religion in this reductive fashion, given women's rights activist Elizabeth Cady Stanton's efforts a century ago to underscore its importance. In launching a project to reinterpret the Bible, Stanton recognized belief in women's moral inferiority as the chief barrier to their equality in all areas of society. She also recognized the central role played by biblical text in authorizing this inferiority:

> The Bible teaches that woman brought sin and death into the world, that she precipitated the fall of the race, that she was arraigned before the judgment seat of Heaven, tried, condemned, and sentenced. Marriage for her was to be a condition of bondage, maternity a period of suffering and anguish, and in silence and subjection, she was to play the role of a dependent on man's bounty for all her material wants, and for all the information she might desire on the vital questions of the hour, she was commanded to ask her husband at home. Here is the Bible position of woman briefly summed up.[39]

Stanton, unlike many modern feminist historians, recognized the powerful role Christianity played in American culture, as in European culture more broadly, in shaping the notion of the private sphere. To be sure, her words interpret that notion through the lens of a particular experience of womanhood and motherhood, that of a white, middle-class, nineteenth-century American woman who might depend on a husband for all her "material wants." Most poor and slave women lived in quite different conditions. Nevertheless, their lives too were shaped by the inseparability in Christian teachings of women's inferior moral status, motherhood, and domesticity. Precisely because Stanton saw how deeply rooted belief in women's moral inferiority was in the American cultural value system, including the values of American women, she warned that it was naive to think this belief would simply give way with time.[40]

By insisting that we take seriously religion and its role in helping to forge and articulate the moral judgments represented by cultural beliefs about public and private, Stanton helps us understand better contemporary women's situation and its broader implications for society.

MORAL STATUS AS WOMEN'S MODERN PROBLEM

Now we can see that the mother who is so American that she sets the standard for national identity—"as American as motherhood and apple pie"—is neither timeless, as many assume, nor quite recent, as some historians would have it, nor a product simply of the emerging nineteenth-century bourgeois woman's claim to respectability, as still others have argued. The Republican mother of the post-revolutionary period (whose role was to produce virtuous male citizens), the True Woman of the mid nineteenth century, and television's Harriet (ideal wife to Ozzie) are all updated versions of the "good" mother on whom much has depended in the West for the last four centuries.

Today she still helps anchor the nation's complex social world. Holding maternal traits in place as the natural essence and virtue of women, the "good" mother continues to hold in place the American ideal of womanhood. She sustains a conception of womanhood that, as the history of motherhood demonstrates, emphasizes a particular solution to the problem of the relationship between virtue and femininity. This problem stems from the ancient Western cultural judgment of women's moral deficiency, which continues to make the achievement of virtue a defining task of womanhood in America. This task is neither for white, middle-, and upper-class women simply, nor for the religiously observant alone. Rather, the dominant culture has made the achievement of virtue a universal task for women across economic and racial boundaries.

Assigned secondary moral status within their racial, ethnic, and class groups, all women in American society share the task of becoming a "good" woman. To be sure, the precise nature of this moral predicament and specific norms for its resolution—what a "good" woman is—have varied in important ways for women through American history and according to norms of race, ethnicity, class, religious tradition, and region of the country. And women have played a significant role in resisting and changing, as well as accepting, cultural definitions of the "good" woman. Yet, all women have encountered the basic conception that a "good" woman is a "good" mother setting the terms and the agenda of their cultural and social situation. The persistence of American culture's identification of women with the home and the family demonstrates that this conception continues to set those terms today. It is so deeply rooted that anyone seeking to improve the situation of contemporary women cannot avoid the problem of virtue and femininity at its heart, but must acknowledge and address it.

In addition to reconstructing the moral status of women, however, we must attend to a related problem: the secondary status in the hierarchy of American social values assigned to the "good" mother's unpaid labor of family and community commitment. The Christian domestic ideal that emerged with and helped shape the new institutions of family and state in early modern Europe helped create the new distinction between private and public *values* these institutions embodied. By relegating motherhood to the institutional base of the private home, this ideal helped organize motherhood's social function and meaning in a particular way. Assigning women the work of maintaining the value and the values of "the" family, an assignment especially evident now, as in the mid nineteenth century, in the midst of rapid social change, was essential to this organization. Relegating the labor of family caregiving as a social value and function, along with women and mothers, to the private world of the home, this sixteenth-century domestic ideology separated all three from the public sphere. As a result, neither women, motherhood, nor caregiving have been socially structured as public values, responsibilities, or priorities of the world outside the home. Indeed, as Seyla Benhabib notes, one of the chief distinguishing marks of contemporary American moral and political discourse is privatization of the values women's work represents.[41] "The" family and children all exist, with women, in the sphere of processes characterized as natural rather than social, and hence are excluded from the public agenda.

Recognizing the *moral* as historical, as socially constructed and changing, has important implications for the private sphere and the values it represents. Both are removed from the realm of the "natural." Once we understand how virtue was joined with motherhood, maternal qualities, and womanhood in Western society by developments of the sixteenth century, we can see this particular association as historical. We can see that in the West, women have not always been viewed as having these moral qualities; in particular, motherhood has not always been women's avenue to virtue. There was an historical moment in which, for complex reasons, a new cultural norm emerged associating these maternal traits with "goodness" for women. Its authority based in the authority of God and nature, this norm established a new understanding of "the way things were and the way they were meant to be." It established the new belief that woman was called to marriage and motherhood as her true vocation, the work for which her very being was shaped and her only path to virtue.

Recognizing that motherhood has a history and a changing moral meaning, and that women too have been defined in other ways at other times by Western culture, undercuts claims that these particular socially defined and selected maternal traits constitute the unchanging essence of women's identity. Recognizing that motherhood's meaning is not eternal allows us, as Atkinson points

out, to assume responsibility for the social reconstruction and reinterpretation of motherhood. Equally important, it allows us to recognize and address the complex moral dimension of this task.

Before we can reconstruct the moral status of motherhood, however, we must acknowledge the surprising staying power of cultural beliefs associating women with the private sphere. Belief in
women's distinctive moral traits runs so deep in American culture
that many today resist any argument that they are not natural. Others claim that women are *socialized* to distinctive moral qualities and
behavior. Champions of both positions want to sustain the traditional idea of women's virtue and often assume that this virtue will
translate predictably into distinctive moral action. They overlook
the fact that moral agency is not automatic but a complex mix of
conscious choice with situation and instinct, whether native or ac-
quired. It is not the religious and political right alone that perpet-
uates belief in women's "difference."

A TRADITION OF PRIVATE VALUES

The deep association of domestic values with women persists not
simply because it remains the teaching of biblical traditions, but
even more because the religious values that helped fashion and articulate it have passed, largely unrecognized, into the dominant
American *secular* value system. Their roots unseen, these values
have become an inseparable part of dominant moral beliefs in modern American culture about how society is and ought to be structured. Their very familiarity gives them validity. Americans literally recognize these values as truth. Indeed, the power of their
validity is such that when they appear embedded in sophisticated
modern theory in a range of fields they lend authority to other
claims and in turn are reinforced by them. The presence of these
secular values, however, and the fact that they began as religious
ones, goes undetected largely because of the lack of sophistication
about religion, history, and gender displayed frequently by social
scientists and analysts of many kinds. Two prominent examples of
powerful and widely read modern theory illustrate this.

A particularly striking case, one that demonstrates the contemporary role of the "good" mother in holding the economy in place, is the theory of Gary S. Becker, who in 1992 won the Nobel Prize. Basic to his market-focused economic theory, the notion of the "good" mother is a centerpiece of Becker's *A Treatise on the Family*. Rooting the division of labor between household and market mainly in "intrinsic differences between the sexes," Becker argues that women have a "comparative advantage" in domestic labor—in his terms, that it's the right place for them to work.[42] Claiming that women are more suited "by nature" to the task of producing and caring for children and perhaps even to taking care of the household than to any other task, he unwittingly offers an updated, secular version of the argument of sixteenth-century humanists and religious reformers:

> Women not only have a heavy biological commitment to the production and feeding of children, but they also are biologically committed to the care of children in other, more subtle ways. Moreover, women have been willing to spend much time and energy caring for their children because they want their heavy biological investment in production to be worthwhile. In addition, a mother can more readily feed and watch her older children while she produces additional children than while she engages in most other activities. . . . Men have been less biologically committed to the care of children, and have spent their time and energy on food, clothing, protection, and other market activities.[43]

In what he presents as a simple rendering of "basic" facts about the biological difference between the sexes, Becker provides the "natural" underpinnings for the particular social organization that has divided the private world of the household from the market in American society. Like all "facts," however, biological data are not objective, but culturally influenced human interpretations of physical reality.[44] These interpretations, like Becker's, superimpose on such data a map of social roles and organization the data seem to justify.

In the name of *economic* theory, Becker actually is offering a moral-structural logic for a particular American social and economic organization that has been historically constructed. He presents that organization, however, as natural and universal. It is an organization that presupposes, in agreement with Martin Luther, the conflation of womanhood with motherhood and the establishment of heterosexual marriage as the basis of the public and private social order.[45] Becker's explicit claim that this social organization is a given carries the implicit claim that it is morally right. This moral claim is strengthened by the authority of his further claim that the sexual division of labor is a universal fact both in human history and in nature:

> Consequently, biological differences in comparative advantage between the sexes explain why households typically have both sexes, but also why women have usually spent their time rearing children and engaging in other household activities, whereas men have spent their time in market activities. This sexual division of labor has been found in virtually all human societies, and in most other biological species that fertilize eggs within the body of the female.[46]

In fact, anthropologists do not understand the social meanings of the categories "male" and "female" to be universal and unchanging, but rather to vary significantly across cultures and time. They reject the claim that there are "biological facts" of difference between the sexes that are the same in every society and that these "facts" determine the social relations of the sexes.[47] They reject, that is, the idea that biological difference in reproductive roles contains inherent cultural meanings and consequences for the way gender is organized socially, or even that "natural" difference exists between the sexes to which every culture gives its own specific meanings and consequences. Rather, they argue that Western ways of understanding the "biological" difference between "male" and "female" are simply one cultural definition of difference and hence of relations between human beings:

> Having rejected the notion that there are presocial, universal domains of social relations, such as a domestic domain and a public domain, a kinship

domain and a political domain, we must ask what symbolic and social processes make these domains appear self-evident, and perhaps even "natural"
fields of activity in any society.[48]

A second instance of sophisticated modern theory influenced
significantly by traditional, religiously shaped, cultural gender beliefs, although again unrecognized as such, is psychologist Carol
Gilligan's *In a Different Voice: Psychological Theory and Women's Development* (Harvard, 1982). This widely read work on women's distinctive style of moral reasoning must be called a classic among
studies of gender. Yet despite its author's expertise and insistence
on her narrow purpose of questioning the way in which male development has been made the psychological standard for human
development, the book's extraordinary persuasive power stems especially from what readers *see* in it.

What they see is confirmation in modern *psychological* language
of the traditional conception of womanhood. Gilligan's theory
about women's distinctive moral voice strikes a deeply resonant
cultural chord because it appears, quite contrary to her intent, to
document scientifically the familiar beliefs about women's morality
that the privileged women in her study articulate. Thus, analyzing
and contrasting an ethic of care and an ethic of justice, norms of
"embeddedness in lives of relationship" versus autonomy, Gilligan
maps as psychology the moral profile to which the dominant culture socializes women:

> [T]he conventional feminine voice emerges with great clarity, defining the
> self and proclaiming its worth on the basis of the ability to care for and
> protect others. The woman [in the study] now constructs a world perfused
> with the assumptions about feminine goodness that are reflected in the ste-
> reotypes of . . . Broverman et al. [49]

These "assumptions about goodness" in the modern feminine sex-
role stereotype are, in psychological language, warmth, expressiveness, subjectivity, dependency, and passivity, attributes and
values associated with women that have evolved only slightly from

those of the mid nineteenth century. They are a modern version of early modern Christian teachings on motherhood.

The continuing power of dominant cultural beliefs about womanhood explains why enthusiasts and critics alike have largely ignored Gilligan's insistence, in sharp contrast to Becker, that women's association with the distinctive traits or moral reasoning she analyzes is neither natural nor absolute.[50]

CONCLUSION

Religiously shaped social belief about women has become so powerful a part of the modern American system of values that it operates undetected, in and outside of academia, as an authoritative analysis of reality. It does so, among other reasons, because it continues to be a common language that captures what have become important values for many women. Calling for reconstructing the traditional association of women with the private sphere, which persists at high cost to both women and society, recognizes this. It will allow American women's commitment to many domestic values to play a crucial public role in addressing the nation's values crisis.

The best proof of this commitment is in women's actions. Many are sustaining their unpaid family and community labor in the face of new economic demands at great personal cost. For the most part, these women are far from naive; they are aware of the self-sacrifice entailed. Neither are they lacking in intelligence; women who juggle family and work commitments display both impressive ingenuity in creating the arrangements that make doing so possible and the kind of ability on the job that often stands out despite these additional burdens. These women, in short, are consciously choosing to sustain, against significant odds, values they see as giving human life meaning and importance that are not the values to which the public world outside the home is oriented. Whether and how they will keep sustaining these values is a question of major significance not only to these women and their families, but also to American society as a whole.

Many women hesitate, poised on the brink of the public world. It has been argued that for them the prospect of becoming full participants in the world outside the home is a "fearful freedom" that threatens them with having not only to support themselves, but to break free of feminine dependence and define themselves fully as individuals as well.[51] There is an important element of truth in this argument; self-definition is a daunting project few humans face, let alone with equanimity. It is understandable that in a culture in which this project has not been expected of women, which provides them with neither the historical traditions nor other social resources that support it, many might hesitate. There is, however, another reason women hesitate that is overlooked when their predicament is constructed as a choice between special protections (difference) and equal rights (sameness).

Poised between the public and private worlds, searching for sure footing into the future, many women are eager to find a moral option other than the apparently untenable ones of turning back or pressing ahead full steam. Increasingly, they are aware that the public world into which they are moving, while it depends on the private world of the home, operates on the basis of a different values agenda. In growing frustration, they question much of what they encounter in it. And seeing that the question of what they value is intimately bound up with the question of who they are becoming and where society is headed, they are concerned about more than maintaining many of the values of the home. What concerns many women is the gap between the public world they are encountering and the one they want to see, and the challenge of formulating the personal and public vision that will make them effective agents in remaking this world.

CHAPTER THREE

The Erosion of Authority

Many women do not claim the ability to speak about society as a whole because of their habit of deferring to the authority of voices other than their own. The chief challenge that women face in becoming full public participants is not "simply" gaining access to opportunity, but also learning to claim public authority. The reasons for this are cultural as well as personal and social. The "good" mother has helped hold in place the cultural ideal of masculinity and the public sphere by representing a different set of values and bearing daily responsibility for the domestic world that supports the public one. But she also has helped hold the larger social and moral order in place by being excluded from equal rights, opportunities, and authority in the public world.

In recent decades, exclusion has appeared on the verge of becoming a thing of the past. Women as a group have made significant progress toward achieving equality and access, a situation of which privileged women have been positioned to take best advantage. Nevertheless, this progress has been halting, throwing into doubt widespread expectation that it is merely a matter of time until women reach parity with men in the public world. Women's continuing association with the private sphere and the public sphere's resistance to incorporating them at all levels on an equal basis, especially in top leadership positions, suggest the power of traditional public values to adapt and persist in reinforcing women's exclusion from authority. It is important to understand why and how public values do this.

Cultural association of masculinity with the public sphere—the world outside the home—is at the center of traditional values. On one level, the link is obvious. Most people readily acknowledge that men dominate institutions both numerically and in terms of their overwhelming presence in leadership positions. On another level, however, there is far less agreement that this matters—that masculinity significantly affects the nature of institutional life and public affairs. Many scholars, journalists, and other experts remain content to analyze American public life as if the dominance of men has been an incidental feature of it.

The notion that even though the public world is dominated by men its structures, roles, and concerns are not gendered (and race-inflected) in substance sheds important light on traditional cultural beliefs. These beliefs present the public world as the domain of values that are universal, inclusive of all perspectives and experience. In doing so, they build on and reinforce traditional assumptions identifying femininity with the particular and masculinity with the human. It is this assumption about masculinity that allows traditional beliefs to obscure the gendered character of the public world. While these beliefs present the female voice as limited to its own self-interested and narrow view, they present the male voice as capable of speaking socially for more than itself. Nothing reveals this distinction as clearly as the norm in modern American politics of referring to the priorities and perspectives of women (or indeed of any group other than the privileged males who constitute the public power elite) as those of a "special interest." The implicit comparison is with the perspective of privileged men, which has been seen as inclusive, above special interest and particularity.

The cultural ideal that men represent the human has held in place the association of masculinity with authority. One of the chief values of American society that the power of the public sphere upholds is the masculinity of authority and the authority of masculinity. We must examine this social value in order to understand the staying power of traditional beliefs about public and private and their ability to keep women from full public participation. Examining the link between masculinity and authority is crucial, too, to understanding how these cultural beliefs are obscuring the erosion of authority currently taking place in American society. This erosion and the need for new models of leadership it is creating are part of the nation's values crisis. They make it all the more vital that women claim the authority to speak about society as a whole.

THE CRISIS OF MALE AUTHORITY

Many who applaud the persistence of the traditional division of labor between men and women, public and private, assume that it is primarily women's increasing numbers and progress in the public world that threaten traditional patterns of authority in American life. Yet a second development under way in American society has even greater immediate implications for men, authority, and social institutions of all kinds. It receives comparatively little attention in debate about the national values crisis, even though its social effects are becoming evident. This development is the erosion of the governing cultural conception of masculinity in American society, of belief in masculinity's "natural" association with authority, and consequently, of the traditionally dominant meaning of authority itself. This erosion is a critical factor in the current state of all American social institutions, from "the" family to democracy itself.

A central reason why the erosion of masculine authority is not recognized as a major dimension of the nation's values crisis is that most experts, journalists, and politicians, the majority of whom are white males, do not analyze gender as a crucial variable in public life. They believe that both the public realm and their own perspectives are gender-neutral. As a result, they do not recognize the cultural link between masculinity, fatherhood, and authority in the public world. So, with the exception of a small number of recent historical studies that recognize fatherhood's public and cultural dimension, fatherhood is perceived overwhelmingly as a private role. Men on the political and religious right especially are concerned with the erosion of fathers' authority in "the" family. Yet even here the focus of concern is narrow. Conservatives and liberals assert the importance of fathers' role in regard to rebuilding the families of the "underclass" by reforming welfare, reducing "illegitimacy," and enforcing child support. Their tendency to tie fathers' weakened role in the family chiefly to poverty and to the black community in particular, however, obscures the extent to which the weakening of fatherhood is a pattern emerging across class, race, and ethnic lines—apparent even among the more privileged. Also going largely undetected is the relationship between the erosion of fatherhood and the erosion of male authority not only in families, but in government, the law, the economy, the professions, sports, religion, and other areas of society.

Since the sixteenth century, the promise to uphold truth and fairness and to protect the vulnerable has been central to the essential meaning of masculinity in the West and to masculinity's governing definition as the trustworthy representative of the universal and the human. The moral core of male authority and the status of masculinity as the primary value of American public life has rested on this promise. Now the promise is crumbling in the face of three growing and growingly visible national patterns that involve the physical, emotional, and economic vulnerability of women and children to men in public and private. These patterns are workplace sexual harassment, the weakening public status of fatherhood, and domestic violence, marital and date rape.

To be sure, however common the aggression and abandonment represented by these three patterns are, they do not characterize the relationship of most American men with women and children. Yet aggression and abandonment do not have to be the statistical norm to have a powerful cultural impact. Public discovery in recent years of their prevalence has shaken cultural faith in male protection, once so unquestioned. Because institutional power, fatherhood, and intimate relations are key moments in the assertion of masculine authority, these three patterns strike at the heart of the dominant cultural meaning and power traditionally assigned masculinity. The erosion of trust that results is especially evident in the increasingly common presentation in the media of white males as "bad guys."[1] Criticism of men given access by privilege to the highest ranks of public institutional authority represents more than a challenge to the special entitlements they have enjoyed. It represents a crisis of male authority that has profound implications for American society.

Understanding what the model of authority in American society has been is, therefore, crucial to addressing our national values crisis effectively. We must examine the social values that historically have linked masculinity, fatherhood, and authority. Because these values also have defined *women's* relationship to authority, they have important light to shed on the special challenge and opportunity the crisis of authority represents for contemporary women. Women must not only reconstruct their own relationship to authority, especially as they seek full participation in the public world outside the home, but they also must help to define anew the nature and meaning of authority in American society.

THE MASCULINITY OF AUTHORITY

Traditional dominant cultural beliefs promote a coherent social order that establishes the defining authority of men in American society. As we have seen, this social order is also a moral framework. At its center is a governing conception of authority which reflects the cultural belief that men are suited and entitled by nature to power, a cultural belief shaped historically by the social power of white, privileged men. The distinction this moral framework makes between private and public masks the fact that they are firmly linked by the traditional authority of men in *both* the domestic and larger worlds.

This conception of authority attests to the powerful social and cultural role of religion in the West. Judaism and Christianity helped fashion and express the Western notion of authority as masculine and of masculinity as authoritative by likening men to God on a symbolic level, by describing them as made in God's image, and by putting in their hands the institutional power to interpret divine and human reality. Religion's articulation of men's capacity to represent the universal, the truth and the power of the divine, has had an effect on more than religious institutions. As a public force, religion has helped shape and sustain the model of authority for Western systems of governance and for social institutions of all kinds.

Teachings about men's likeness to God have given masculinity its special character in the dominant culture: its perceived ability to represent the human. This ability makes masculinity fit to represent the public dimension of human life, and makes "publicness" itself central to the definition of what it means to be male. Given the racial and class hierarchy among men, all men have not had equal access to the ability to represent the human. Representing the whole has been the province especially of privileged men, who have the social and material resources to fulfill the masculine ideal. At the same time, all men have had greater access to the ability to speak for the whole than women of their own racial, ethnic, and class group have had. A good illustration of this is the Million Man March in Washington, D.C., in October 1995, which claimed to represent the black community to itself and to the nation yet barred black women from participating.

The ancient link between masculinity, authority, and fatherhood is another fundamental theme in the history of the cultural association of masculinity and authority. Radical egalitarian reformulations of family and family commitments evident in Christianity's origins gave way to the identification of men's patriarchal authority with the authority of God, both ideologically and institutionally. Christianity adapted Greco-Roman and Jewish-Hellenistic patriarchal domestic codes that made the natural primacy of the father in the household the model for the state.[2] Thus, in the West, patriarchal values prescribed by sacred text and institutionalized in the Christian church by Church Fathers at once reflected and helped define the broader social conception of authority.

In the sixteenth century, as we saw earlier, Catholic humanists and Protestant religious reformers reworked Christian domestic ideology. What they did had important *new* implications for fatherhood. Marriage and parenthood became "essential vocations" for both men and women.[3] By reason of God's subjection of Eve to her husband Adam in the Garden of Eden, all women became newly subject to the authority of men, not only in the home but in the wider world. In Martin Luther's words: "He rules the home and the state, wages wars, defends his possessions, tills the soil, builds, plants, etc. The woman, on the other hand, is like a nail driven into the wall. She sits at home."[4] And just as new meaning was given to the link between femininity, obedience, and motherhood, it also was given to the link between masculinity, authority, and fatherhood. Reformers attributed a new *moral* character to fathers and fatherhood, which both confirmed and added to the natural association of authority with men. Seeing fatherhood as the highest calling for men, they identified justice and righteousness with masculine authority, "an assumption of benevolence and correctness that made disobedience a sin as well as a crime."[5] In this way, humanists and religious leaders all but merged fatherhood with divinity. While they did so within Roman Catholicism too, the logic seemed especially natural within Protestantism now that ministers were expected to marry, and it was prompted in part by this development.[6]

At the same time, reformers strengthened the exclusion of women from authority in private or public. Women might attain virtue through motherhood, but in the home they were subordinate to their husbands, and they were denied public authority altogether. Martin Luther gave wide exposure in his lifetime and beyond to the idea that it was unnatural for women to lead. A powerful example, given the social importance both of biblical text and apostolic leadership, was his promotion of biblical interpretation that erased evidence of women's leadership in early Christianity. Junia, the woman who helped Paul establish the early Christian church and whom Paul called "outstanding among the apostles" (Romans 16:7), was transformed into a man, Junias.[7]

The eclipsing of Junia shows that the Western cultural association of masculinity with authority does more than exclude women from leadership. It makes femininity and authority fundamentally incompatible. This negative association accomplishes several things. By denying women the capacity to represent either ultimate truth and authority or the human, it denies them the capacity to function in the public world. Unable to represent more than female particularity, women are defined culturally as lacking the ability to speak to issues of human meaning and value, of collective purpose and direction—the ability to *envision*. In every social group, thus, women must struggle against traditional beliefs that present the authority and scope of their vision as properly bounded by the home and family, even in cases where their actual activity is not. In contrast, the vision of privileged men is understood as essential to the interpretation and direction of the world. Even men without privilege are ascribed, in comparison with women of their social group, some degree of authority about affairs in the world outside the home. As a result, women themselves, through both prescribed subordination and self-denial, become oriented to the maleness of authority. In this way, women's proper relationship with authority has been defined culturally not simply as serving male authority, but even more basically as helping to construct it.

The sixteenth-century addition of a moral dimension to fatherhood and authority completed, as Clarissa Atkinson concludes, the particular constellation of moral, psychological, and emotional dynamics which gave rise to patriarchy's modern form. The public power of patriarchal authority had come to include the benevolent moral power of husband and father. This was reflected in the way early modern kingship modeled its authority on the now central conjugal family:

> More loudly and explicitly than ever before, rulers and political theorists presented royal authority in terms of patriarchy: identifying themselves with the fathers of families, kings claimed the loyalty and obedience owed to domestic rulers. . . . James I of England made this plain when he declared: "I am the Husband, and all the whole Isle is my lawfull Wife."[8]

Humanist and religious reformers had helped construct and articulate a cultural conception of authority as identified not with fatherhood alone, but with its justice and benevolence. This conception was to govern Western society and culture for centuries, crossing the Atlantic into the institutions fashioned by the Founding Fathers and personified in George Washington, the "Father of Our Country." The reformers together had revised the conception of authority for family and society that, along with motherhood, guaranteed the moral and social order.[9] Fatherhood had come to represent the male capacity and promise to use authority in the service of truth, fairness, and protection of the vulnerable. This promise governed the state, market, church, and household.

Evolving and changing, but remaining intact in its essential outlines, this model of authority has continued to shape American society until very recently. Over the course of the nineteenth century, even as fathers increasingly ceded to mothers responsibility for the actual work of the moral and spiritual development of the family, they retained their moral authority as head of the family. Likewise, the moral dimension of fatherhood was not dissociated from public authority even when leaders began to take less direct responsibility for the moral health of institutions and the people in them. (A telling symbol of this was the fact that, by the end of the nineteenth century, the President of Harvard College, which educated many of the society's leaders and served as a model for other educational establishments, had given up his traditional responsibility for teaching ethics to seniors.) As we near the close of the twentieth century, however, the long association of masculine leadership with the benevolence and justice of fatherhood has itself begun to erode, and with it the cultural conception of authority this association has defined.

THE EMBLEMATIC EVENT

For several reasons, the 1991 televised hearings of Anita Hill's testimony to the Senate Judiciary Committee charged with investigating the character and competence of Clarence Thomas for appointment to the Supreme Court have been called a defining moment in American public life. They exhibited the exclusive privilege of white men in such a way as to lead numbers of white and minority women to become more engaged in politics and to run for public office. Even more significant, however, although it has received little explicit attention, was the way the Committee's handling of allegations of sexual harassment against Thomas symbolized and hastened erosion of the cultural identification of authority and white men already under way.

The Senate, in particular members of the Senate Judiciary Committee, wanted to be perceived as neither sexist nor racist, and to show that they understood the importance of taking sexual harassment seriously. Yet when it came to untangling the multiple interacting layers of gender, race, and justice in the allegations Hill brought against Thomas, they seemed incapable of offering the leadership required. It was their inability to do this serious work, the *way* they handled the allegations, that in the long run made their authority appear so unreliable. In the hearings' aftermath, strong skepticism about the Senators' authority, due to their treatment of Hill, eventually shifted public opinion away from support of Thomas. It was this public skepticism, not simply criticism of the Senators' failure to recognize the seriousness of sexual harassment, that was conveyed by the phrase "they just don't get it"— skepticism born of the Committee's inability to bring justice and fairness to the matter before them.

Defining what precisely "it" was that members of the Judiciary Committee did not "get," analysts have argued that Committee members failed both to comprehend important realities in American life crucial to any just handling of the matter and to address these realities with principled courage. The Senators could not grasp the reality of sexual harassment, the "volatile politics of gender and race" Thomas manipulated to depict himself as the victim of a "high-tech lynching," or the distinctive social reality of black women erased by the white male perspective that dichotomizes "minorities and women."[10] Involving as they did sexual harassment, race, and gender, that is, the hearings combined precisely those elements that could deliver a significant blow to the authority of the white, male public sphere. They at once exhibited and tested the full cultural promise of masculine authority to put truth above self-interest and to protect the interests of the vulnerable. The powerful all-white Committee represented this cultural promise especially, but the aspirant to the Supreme Court represented it too. The promise was heightened by the institutional responsibility of Senators to represent all citizens and the particular responsibility for American justice of Committee members and the nominee to the Court.

The Judiciary Committee's failure to deliver on this promise presented a potent visual tableau of the inadequacy of white, male leadership—inadequacy, as we shall see, also visible to many Americans in their daily lives. The Committee failed chiefly through its members' inability to do several things: to recognize the particularity of their own perspectives, to get beyond that particularity, and to entertain seriously experience and interests other than their own. As a result, the Hill-Thomas hearings depicted more than the exclusion of women of all races (and of black and minority men in significant numbers) from the highest ranks of public power. It depicted and, at the same time, deepened erosion of the dominant cultural conception of masculinity as a symbol of justice and protection in American life.

In this way, at the highest and most visible levels of American government, the hearings were a kind of modern morality play enacting the crisis of masculine authority. The members of the Judiciary Committee failed to deliver on their constitutional and political responsibility, as well as their cultural responsibility as men, not because they failed to accept Hill's charges as accurate, but because they failed to represent fairly the interests of women and specifically of the black woman before them. This failure was caused by their inability to *see* experience that differed from their own. Doing so would have meant recognizing her charges as morally, legally, and socially integral to judgment about whether Thomas was suited by competence and character to the post for which he was being reviewed. It would have meant investigating these charges seriously.

The Senators' failure to represent fairly Hill's interests as a black woman undercut traditional cultural belief in the universality of the male perspective—in its capacity to represent the human. Members of the Committee revealed their blindness to how their white, male way of looking at things limited their understanding. What they did not "get," as leading analysts of race and gender in America have pointed out, was Anita Hill. An educated black woman, she had no reality or credibility for white men with little firsthand experience of working with black professional women. A year after the hearings, in a speech at Georgetown University, Anita Hill pointed to the Senate's failure to understand her: "they failed to relate to my race, my gender, my race and gender combined, and in combination with my education, my career choice and my demeanor."[11] Hill represented none of the dominant culture's stereotypes of black women as Mammy, oversexed-black-Jezebel, traitor-to-the-race, welfare queen (or, I might add, teenage, black single mother).[12]

The Senators' behavior in the hearings contradicted in several other ways the deep cultural belief that men are naturally equipped to give full and fair attention to the range of human realities. It demonstrated that the Senators gave priority to representing their own reality. Reluctant initially even to delay the vote on Thomas's nomination in order to hear the sexual harassment charge, the dismissive attitude of the Judiciary Committee's Democratic and Republican leadership reflected the view that sexual harassment was not significant enough to claim their attention in a Supreme Court confirmation process or to become a political factor between them.[13] This revealed the predisposition of members, in particular the Committee chair, to use their power to advance their own interests, to the exclusion of interests other than their own. While their predisposition reflected in part, quite rightly, caution in making a judgment about the likely truth of the charge, it also reflected a

striking disregard for justice, truth, and their constitutional duty
to investigate the character and competence of the nominee. As the
subject of a growing body of law and legal debate that had reached
all the way to the Supreme Court by 1986, sexual harassment was,
after all, something of which we might expect Judiciary Committee
members to have been aware. It was also a regulatory responsibility
of Thomas's both as Chairman of the Equal Employment Opportunity Commission and Assistant Secretary of Education for Civil
Rights in the Department of Education.

The deeper corrosive effect of the hearings notwithstanding,
their short-term effect was to confirm traditional social values, including the authority of the Senators and of Thomas, and hence to
contribute to his confirmation. The traditional distinction between
public and private played a crucial role in this confirmation. This
distinction, which the Senators demonstrated their inclination to
preserve by their reluctance to hear the charges, was reinforced
by Thomas. His defensive strategy, laid out in his angry opening
statement, cleverly set traditional beliefs about public and private
firmly in place as a framework for the hearings. Manipulating these
beliefs, along with the politics of race, Thomas depicted the Senators as a white lynch mob. Thus, he redefined the hearings as a
public contest taking place between men, specifically between a
group of white men and a black man. Defining the hearings in this
way excluded Anita Hill, as a woman, from the important struggle
taking place, marginalizing her claims as a subject in her own right,
and leaving her only the role of traitor to a black man.

Thomas further manipulated the terms of the hearings' inquiry
by adamantly refusing to answer questions about "what goes on in
the most intimate parts of [his] private life, or the sanctity of [his]
bedroom."[14] Thus, as his sexual conduct in the office was being in-
vestigated, he successfully associated himself with the cultural belief that sex is personal and *private*, properly located in the bedroom
and there inviolate. He also implied that his behavior conformed
to this belief, clothing himself in the standards of propriety it has
represented. In this way, Thomas invoked a set of traditional as-

sumptions about the way things are and ought to be that prevented questioning about his sexual activity outside the workplace. Doing so helped to supply credibility to his later flat denials of Hill's allegations about his sexual activity in the office.[15] Relegating sex to the private sphere, and thus giving it status in the hearing secondary to the public contest of men over race, also allowed Thomas to emphasize the public importance of his work, especially his struggle against racism to ascend to the Supreme Court. Here, he engaged too the power of traditional cultural beliefs that assign public significance, and hence greater value, to the work of men over the work (and even the rights) of women.

Thomas reinforced a powerful dynamic in his favor by appealing to these cultural beliefs about work. They strengthened not only the rationale for the Committee's failure to inquire fully into facts related to the charge of misconduct,[16] but also its members' blindness to the distinctive *context* of the charge: the reality of women and work, specifically of black women and work. Instead of trying to understand the situation of a black professional woman in the workplace and seemingly unaware of the social revolution under way in the definition of women's work, the Judiciary Committee operated within the confines of its own assumptions in its inquiry.

As a result, the Committee arrived at an unbridgeable gap between its assumptions and Hill's behavior. This gap produced the litany of puzzling questions that would not go away, questions that seemed to many in the hearing room and watching their televisions to go unanswered: Why didn't Hill leave her job? Why didn't she come forward with charges at the time? How could a man so many respected do what was alleged? Why did Hill follow Thomas to the EEOC? Why did she telephone him in later years? These questions begged for the kind of informed evaluation of the allegations in the context of black women's work that never took place. The Committee never sought to educate itself or the American public about the reality of sexual harassment as a variable in a black professional woman's career.

Had they given serious attention to understanding this reality, the Senators would have learned things that had significant implications for their interpretation of the charges and the facts. They would have learned that sexual harassment, the use of sex to dominate in the workplace, not only subordinates a woman but also has a powerful message to send about her work. Redefining her in the workplace as a sexual object, it communicates that she does not belong and sets aside the meaning and value of her work to herself and to the workplace. By denying a woman's commitment and right to her work, harassment strips away the dignity and sense of self-possession she finds in both. In a culture that has traditionally identified women, especially black women, and the "true" work for which nature has suited them with their sexuality, harassment is an attempt to halt the reconception of women's work. It usurps a woman's hard-won freedom to define herself to herself, let alone to others, in terms of her individual talents, interests, and commitments and their economic worth.

Recognizing the meaning and value a woman's work has for her self-definition and livelihood makes it easier to see why Hill responded to harassment by fighting to *regain* her work identity and equilibrium, hoping the harassment could be forgotten. When she thought the harassment had stopped, to do otherwise than follow Thomas from the Department of Education to the EEOC for the opportunity to continue her civil rights work would have jeopardized further the kind of work and the hard-won professional identity Hill prized early.[17] A double standard was evident in the Senators' denying Hill the work commitment and ambition valued in men. To have left the Department of Education would have made sense only from the perspective of those who viewed Hill primarily as a woman mistreated in a personal way, not as a woman professional. This perspective reveals that Hill's questioners shared with harassers the assumption that a woman's *presence* in the workplace creates the problem, one solved by removing her from it. As a professional woman, in short, Hill's options were defined by the realities of male power in the workplace. As anyone knows who has watched men assess a female candidate for a position, they are likely to ask first about any deviation in her career from the male norm of professional development in the field. A man would have left Thomas's employ only for a demonstrably better opportunity elsewhere; a woman doing otherwise would damage her career.

Likewise, the question of why Hill did not press charges makes sense only to those who do not take seriously the importance of Hill's work to her. Far from saving or helping a career, sexual harassment charges are likely to undermine a woman's advancement permanently. At any point along the way, because male employers view women who file harassment complaints as "troublemakers," Hill would have risked professional stigma. Only when she reached the relative security of tenure did she come forward, and then reluctantly. Her behavior is all the more understandable, moreover, in the context of a national and workplace culture which in 1981 did not yet recognize sexual harassment as illegal. Five years later, the Supreme Court took the step of declaring it so, but not until a decade later did the Court declare harassment a civil rights violation and hold the employer automatically liable for damages. Yet even in 1991, as the Senate and the hearings demonstrated, the national climate still tended to give credence to the male harasser.

In short, the Senators' failure to try to understand the meaning of sexual harassment in the context of women's work left the logic of Hill's professional situation obscured. It also left intact an unseen moral framework for the hearings. When Senators building a case for Thomas asked their questions, they invoked three persisting beliefs about the division of labor between men and women in American society that functioned decisively beneath the hearings' surface. These beliefs are that a man's right to paid work is greater than a woman's; that work outside the home does not play as central a role in a woman's life as it does in a man's; and that a woman's career is of lesser value than a man's.

The strategy was successful. By the hearings' end, these traditional beliefs about gender and work had led the majority of Senators and the public to see Hill's story as unpersuasive. Furthermore, these beliefs, interacting with white racial guilt and with varied liberal and conservative political agendas regarding race, reinforced the reluctance of the majority of Americans polled to harm the career of an African-American man headed for the Supreme Court. As a cultural equation skillfully manipulated in favor of Thomas, these beliefs helped deliver him the benefit of the doubt.

SEXUAL HARASSMENT

The Hill-Thomas hearings are not only emblematic of the broader pattern of erosion of masculine authority, they also shed light on the role workplace sexual harassment is playing in this process. The hearings and their aftermath dramatically deepened the challenge sexual harassment represents to the traditional cultural association of masculinity with authority. They created a place for harassment at the center of public attention, causing the American public to recognize it as a legitimate and serious problem.

One of the first signs of this recognition was that the hearings even changed the public's mind about the allegations against Thomas. Whereas at the time of the hearings more Americans believed Thomas's denial of the charges against him, in the long term more came to believe Hill.[18] By publicly depicting both the power imbalance commonly faced by women lodging harassment complaints and the gender and race bias in justice that can result, the hearings helped crack the legitimacy long automatically granted male authority. They conveyed the message that the decision makers were neither neutral nor unbiased, a message frequently conveyed by sexual harassment cases. Precisely because such cases often reveal male self-interest so graphically, they have a profound effect on attitudes toward male authority. Judgments about the neutrality of authority are crucial to judgments about its fairness, when the public assesses authority's legitimacy.[19]

Since the hearings, growing evidence of the prevalence of sexual harassment in institutions of all kinds has become the object of sustained public concern, as other dramatic public cases—Tailhook (the U.S. Navy), Packwood (the U.S. Senate), and Harris v. Fork-lift Systems, Inc. (the basis for the November 9, 1993, Supreme Court ruling on sexual harassment)—have driven home. These highly visible cases, along with others in federal law enforcement agencies (the FBI, the Bureau of Alcohol, Tobacco, and Firearms, and the Immigration and Naturalization Service), the United Nations, and the U.S. Air Force, Army, and Navy Reserves, have been especially significant. Involving prominent male leaders as they do, such cases confirm the growing awareness many ordinary Americans have of sexual harassment in their own workplaces, accentuating their questioning of male authority.

When men involved in harassment are public officials, the impact on masculinity as a symbol is especially great. Their behavior is perceived as also betraying the public trust and the higher standards expected of such figures. The impact is even greater still when public figures perceived as special champions of fairness for the vulnerable are found to have engaged in harassing behavior. This is true, for example, of former Senator Robert Packwood (Republican of Oregon), known for his public record of advocacy for women's rights; of Navy officers, known not only as defenders of the public but also as "gentlemen"; and of David E. Johnson, the Episcopal Bishop of Massachusetts known for aggressive enforcement of antiharassment policies pertaining to clergy in his diocese, whose own apparent sexual exploitation of women was made public by church officials following his suicide.

While women's workplace experience with male authority has been highly varied and in many respects positive, increasing public attention to patterns of sexual harassment of white and minority women, especially by male supervisors and peers, cuts to the heart of confidence in male institutional leadership. It erodes the trust placed in male authority by women and society in general, revealing the predatory dimension of male power that subjects women, even in the workplace, to physical vulnerability or the threat of it. This is shocking enough. However, sexual harassment sends the further message that authority figures, who are expected to be fair and to safeguard multiple interests, do not respect the dignity of women's work. Most damaging of all, awareness that harassment is an aspect of labor-force discrimination against women brings significant disillusionment with belief that men's exercise of authority is disinterested. Sexual harassment is an act of subordination aimed at women's status in institutions. It represents men's use of power to resist and derail women's progress toward institutional authority; whatever their outcome, cases typically damage a woman's career.

What is especially corrosive about this form of sexual misconduct is evidence that it is not new, but has for years been shielded from view, its perpetrators (when known) often protected by their institutions and colleagues. The American public has learned in recent years that the authority of men, traditionally unquestioned, often has been used to allow individuals and institutions to put their own self-interest before justice, even in legal, government, and ecclesiastical institutions devoted to serving justice. In such cases, maintaining a man's position, in particular by maintaining his job or professional status, has been seen as more important than a woman's dignity, well-being, rights, or job. Evidence that such protection continues today is profoundly damaging to male authority. Hence the particular potency of cases, like the Hill-Thomas hearings, that reveal male leaders' unwillingness to go beyond rhetoric in recognizing the seriousness of the issue and handling it fairly.

Even putting in place institutional policies and procedures designed to address sexual harassment is no guarantee of progress. Male entitlement is so strong that institutional cultures protect it even in the face of new regulations. In the words of a New York labor and employment lawyer describing how law firms protect the powerful: "These firms think that by having a policy, that will insulate them from liability. The reality is that you're generally dead in the water if you make a claim against a powerful partner at these places."[20] This protection of male interests was evident in some companies' response even to the 1991 Civil Rights Act designed to strengthen the rights of those suffering discrimination, including sexual harassment. Hoping to avoid high damage awards, these companies required employee claims to be settled by binding arbitration (often by a panel of white, male managers) instead of the federally mandated jury trials that would have ensured more diverse panels.[21]

One of the most damaging instances of the slowness of male authorities to respond to harassment has been played out in recent years in the American military and Congress in the sexual harassment investigation arising from the Tailhook Convention of September 1991. In April 1993, the official report on sexual misconduct at the Convention identified 140 Navy and Marine pilots charged with involvement in "indecent assaults, indecent exposure, conduct unbecoming an officer, dereliction in duty, and making false statements" in the harassment of 83 women, who were fellow officers, subordinates, and guests. Commenting when the report was released, Admiral Frank B. Kelso, chief of naval operations, characterized the Convention as a "watershed event that has brought about cultural change."[22]

Although a full investigation and accountability were promised, as well as sweeping change to address the Navy's and Marine Corps' problems with the treatment of women, less than a year later the last three cases against the pilots were dismissed. Not one of the officers originally charged was convicted in a court martial. Furthermore, in 1994 Kelso was eased into an honorable retirement and lauded by Secretary of Defense Perry as "a man of highest integrity and honor," despite the Navy judge's conclusion that Admiral Kelso failed to tell the truth about his own activities at Tailhook and used his authority to hinder the investigation. This early retirement and tribute effectively foreclosed any further Navy inquiry into its judge's allegations and Kelso's conduct. Disgust at these outcomes caused the *New York Times* to editorialize that "a fiasco has ended with a charade."[23]

Weeks later, the impression that the nation's military leaders—

the Secretary of the Navy, the Secretary of Defense, and the Chairman of the Joint Chiefs of Staff—were protecting Kelso and the male power structure he represented was reinforced yet again. With the active support of these officials, the Senate Armed Services Committee voted overwhelmingly to confer on Kelso the four stars and pension of full retirement honors, despite his accountability as chief admiral for Tailhook and the judicial allegation that he had manipulated the investigation to protect himself and others. Just two of the twenty-two Senators on the Committee, one of whom was its only woman member (Kay Bailey Hutchison, Republican of Texas), voted against the decision. The impression the Senate Committee communicated was that it was *acting* to protect male Navy officers' interests, but merely giving lip service to the protection of women's.

A few days later, in the debate prior to the vote in the full Senate, Senator Hutchison tried to persuade her colleagues against voting for Kelso's full pension. She implied that they, like Kelso and the Navy, might be widely perceived as having shielded those responsible instead of providing vigorous leadership on Tailhook: "It's no secret to anyone that few officers believed that the Navy was serious about getting to the bottom of Tailhook '91. Officer after officer stymied the investigation."[24] Despite this warning, the full Senate, following the Committee, proceeded to vote to reward Kelso, its implicit connection of justice with male entitlement eerily reminiscent of the Hill-Thomas hearings. This decision came on the heels of new testimony heard by the Armed Services Committee of the House of Representatives. The testimony concerned complaints about harassment by women officers from the Navy Reserves, the Air Force, the Marine Corps, and the Army (lodged at the time of Tailhook or after) that were ignored by the new systems put in place to protect complainants, investigate problems, and punish offenders. Not only were these complaints ignored, but the women who made them suffered physical, psychological, and professional reprisals and one left her branch of the service.[25]

In both the Thomas and Kelso cases, despite the warnings of

women Senators and Representatives, the Senate resolutely protected men's public status over claims on behalf of women's personal and professional rights. It did so in the Kelso case even in the face of growing public doubts about such use of male authority. Not only did the heated Senate debate produce a larger negative vote than originally estimated, but two leading Republican Senators, Arlen Specter (Pennsylvania) and Alfonse M. D'Amato (New York), chastened by public reaction to their handling of Hill's allegations, voted against the four-star rank. What was most indicative of new levels of public questioning, however, were the actions of the seven women Senators and nine Congresswomen. Confident of the power their actions would have with the public, they demonstrated even more dramatically the female solidarity they first had shown at the time of the Hill-Thomas hearings. Strategically grouping themselves to get in the range of TV cameras, the women appeared together on the floor of the Senate behind Senator Barbara Boxer (Democrat of California) as she admonished supporters of Kelso from the podium.[26]

It might be argued that in its idealization of traditional masculinity the military is prone to more extreme patterns of sexual harassment and discrimination than other American institutions.[27] Yet the maleness of other institutional cultures, many of which have organizational models originally heavily influenced by the military, echoes in substance these patterns in the treatment of women. And while sexual harassment may be something power structures defined and dominated by men have been slow to acknowledge as requiring serious attention, working Americans are very familiar with it. In a 1987 United States Merit Systems Protection Board survey, 42 percent of women federal employees reported being sexually harassed, compared to 14 percent of male employees.[28] At the time of the Hill-Thomas hearings in October 1991, a national *New York Times*/CBS News poll found that about four out of ten women in the country had been the "object of sexual advances, propositions, or unwanted sexual discussions" from male supervisors in the workplace; to protect her career, only one out of

eight made a formal complaint. One-half of the men polled said
there had been occasions when their words or actions might have
been interpreted by a female colleague as harassment.[29] And studies show that sexual harassment of women takes place in workplace
relationships other than peer relationships or those of superior to
subordinate. For example, a 1992 study reported in the *New England Journal of Medicine* urged attention to sexual harassment in
medical schools and professional development on the basis of the
finding that 77 percent of female physicians surveyed had been
sexually harassed at least once during their career by a patient.[30]
Recent separate surveys of women rabbis and women ministers in
the United Methodist Church found that similar percentages of
women, 70 percent and 77 percent respectively, experienced work-
related harassment, more than half saying it came from laypeople,
as well as other rabbis or ministers.[31]

Finally, with a logic as stunning as it was unfortunate, by 1994
the challenge workplace sexual harassment represents to the traditional cultural association of masculinity with authority had trav-
eled beyond the Supreme Court and the highest ranks of civilian
and military leadership to the American presidency. Only weeks
after the Kelso decision, charges of sexual harassment were lodged
against President Clinton by a former state employee for an inci-
dent alleged to have taken place when he was Governor of Arkan-
sas. Whatever future legal action determines their merit to be,
these charges were responded to nationally by a chorus of analysts.
Many of these renewed a prominent refrain in national debate
about sexual harassment: that emphasis on the significance of sexual harassment is driven by the naiveté and puritanism of women's
rights advocates.[32] The refrain asserts the traditional view that sexual harassment, like sexual conduct in general, is a private matter
and ought not to be seen as connected to public responsibilities or
as having public significance.

What was notable, however, in the exchange between traditional voices and those insisting on the serious nature of the charges
was an analysis by a leading liberal political commentator that

broke through the existing terms of the harassment debate.[33] Without reaching a conclusion about these new charges, the commentator set forth the argument that President Clinton's character was marked by a lack of moral compass consistently expressed in his public policies as well as his personal sexual behavior. What was especially striking about this argument, which established an assessment of the President that was to be repeated often, was what it indicated about the impact of sexual harassment. Only three years after the Hill-Thomas hearings, the case could now be made in a widely read national news magazine that the private morality of the most powerful public figure in the country (and perhaps the world) was related to his public morality. The impact sexual harassment had come to have on male authority was indicated by the commentator's claim that the President's lack of principled action in public and private was eroding the authority of the American presidency at home and abroad. More than thirty years earlier, while a different yet direct connection also could have been drawn between the sexual behavior and public policies of President John F. Kennedy, Clinton's role model, it never was.

THE EROSION OF FATHERHOOD

As we saw earlier, since the early modern period in the West, fatherhood has constituted an important element of the basis of male authority in family and society. Now the traditional meaning of fatherhood is eroding, the best efforts of many devoted and successful American fathers notwithstanding. Erosion of fathers' commitment to use authority in the service of truth, fairness, and protection of the vulnerable is a further sign of the crisis in the governing cultural meanings of masculinity and authority in American society.

Three chief causes are behind the weakening public status of fatherhood. The first of these is the eroding "breadwinning" role of fathers. According to dominant cultural belief, a good father is first and foremost a good provider. As Western capitalist society industrialized, while a mother was responsible for childrearing and homemaking, a father's chief role became providing cash income for the family economy. By the early twentieth century, in a marketplace oriented to wage labor, this cultural belief had become institutionalized in the male "family wage." The idea that it was in the natural order of things for women and children to be economically dependent on men was reflected in the structure of the workplace and the national economy. This structure gave many men access to jobs that paid a wage sufficient to make women's and children's paid labor unnecessary, and it excluded women who worked outside the home from such positions and pay. Even in the lower classes, where men were least likely to have jobs that made them sole providers, the visibility of their cash contribution to the family economy and the differential between male and female wages normally obscured work women did for which they received no wage or a significantly lower one. Today, however, the father as "breadwinner" is rapidly disappearing. Whereas in 1950 almost 60 percent of American households were made up of a married couple in which the male was the sole or primary wage earner, by 1990 that number had decreased to less than 14 percent.[34]

Various factors have contributed to undermining the once dominant pattern of male "breadwinning." Changes in the national economy over the course of the twentieth century have meant the stagnation of the male wage, the loss for many men of the "family wage," and the rise of the two-paycheck family. The impact of these changes is increasingly apparent in the middle class, although at the bottom of the economic ladder family structures differing from the norm (i.e., employed wife and female-headed, single-parent families) have been prevalent since before 1960.[35] The majority of men in two-paycheck families today just barely remain the primary wage earner. Still, largely because pay discrimination means women earn lower wages than men and their continuing responsibility for children means they often work part-time, it is the male wage that continues to keep many families from poverty. The financial impact of divorce on women and children and the poverty of female-headed families illustrate this fact dramatically.[36]

Women's growing presence in the labor market has long been viewed by conservative commentators as subverting the male provider norm on which that market has been based. Overlooking the disappearance of the male "family wage" and the fact that in many families women have always combined paid and unpaid labor, these commentators often suggest that the male "breadwinning" role has been weakened chiefly by the modern women's movement, with its challenge to both the traditional sexual division of labor and discrimination against women in the paid labor force. Some, in fact, view men's "provider" role as having been lost to women who have been encouraged to find liberation in paid employment. This view is illustrated even in the more balanced account of Robert Griswold, one of the few male scholars who study fatherhood. Griswold concludes that it is *women's* demands that have politicized fatherhood and *women's* participation in the paid labor force that has "rendered the traditional attitudes and behaviors of fathers dysfunctional and obsolete."[37]

Others, however, see men as having abandoned the provider role rather than having lost it. Social critic Barbara Ehrenreich, for example, argues that a largely unnoticed male revolt against the "breadwinner ethic" was under way in the 1950s, well before the modern feminist movement arose.[38] By the end of the 1970s and the beginning of the 1980s, she writes, "healthy" manhood, which since the sixteenth century in the West has been understood as finding its highest fulfillment in fatherhood, was possible without fatherhood and conformity to the old expectations of marriage and "breadwinning":

> We began in a moral climate that honored, in men, responsibility, self-discipline and a protective commitment to women and children. We moved . . . toward a moral climate that endorsed irresponsibility, self-indulgence and an isolationist detachment from the claims of others.[39]

Furthermore, as the economic commitment of many privileged and poor fathers weakens, what was once seen as a symbol of a father's *multiple* levels of attachment to his family now appears increasingly to have been many men's *chief* family attachment. The rise of the phenomenon of "deadbeat dads," divorced fathers who default on their child support payments, and never-married fathers who take no financial responsibility for their children, is the most unsettling evidence of some fathers' lack of substantial ties of any kind to their families.

In a culture based for centuries on belief that the father-headed family is the primary social institution, the second major cause of the weakening public status of fatherhood is awareness of fathers' growing absence from families and of mothers' growing responsibility for them. It is more and more evident in a society that used to believe "father knows best" that many families depend physically, emotionally, and now economically as well on mothers. This social reality, the product of various factors, including poverty, the fact that 50 percent of marriages end in divorce, and increasing numbers of female-headed, single-parent families, is becoming the reality of numerous families up and down the economic ladder. Of children born in 1994, more than half will live with only one parent, usually their mother, for part or all of their childhood.[40] A growing number of families in all sectors of society are being formed and sustained apart from the traditional marital relationship between men and women. This has important implications for mothers and children, as well as fathers.

Finally, the third main cause contributing to erosion of fatherhood is abuse of children by men, especially biological fathers and stepfathers. Although its emerging complexity has so far eluded neat definition, measurement, or analysis, child abuse is a growing national problem across social groups. Contrary to a common stereotype that links it to blacks, a recent study indicates that child maltreatment occurs at a higher rate in white communities than in black ones.[41] Its incidence and significance are connected with masculinity in important respects. Fathers and males in general have been little studied as factors in child maltreatment other than sexual abuse; most research has focused on mothers because of their primary role in childrearing.[42] In reported cases of child sexual abuse, however, the violence of fathers, stepfathers, and nonrelated males stands out.[43] Furthermore, child abuse is related to marital abuse; men who victimize their wives are more likely than nonabusive men to victimize their children, and mothers who are the victims of abuse are more likely to abuse their children.[44]

Even if fathers were no more abusive than mothers, however, because of the way fatherhood differs from motherhood in cultural significance, child maltreatment still would have a particularly powerful effect on fatherhood as a social institution and symbol. The distinctive meaning of fatherhood, part of the dominant belief system of society, is commonly referred to as a moral "fact." For example, a nationally prominent conservative journalist, bemoaning the erosion of respect for fathers, wrote on the occasion of Father's Day in 1994 that motherhood is rooted in love, while fatherhood is rooted in authority.[45] Likewise, the director of the National Fatherhood Initiative, a conservative group dedicated to restoring paternal authority, identified the inherent and irreplaceable qualities that only men bring to a family as "discipline, risk-taking, and decisiveness."[46]

Such defenses of traditional cultural beliefs indicate why it is that, when men and fathers abuse, part of the parenting role they betray is the special trust society has invested in them as protectors. When women abuse, however, they are seen as violating their maternal "nature," which is not identified with authority socially and culturally. Highly visible public cases of men's abuse confirm and feed the weakening of masculinity's cultural identification with authority. Such a case was that of Woody Allen, the film director, actor, and comedian widely loved for his mix of wisdom and harmlessness. From intense media coverage, the public learned that Allen was having an affair with the twenty-one-year-old daughter of his partner, Mia Farrow, and that Farrow had accused him of sexually abusing their own seven-year-old adopted daughter, a charge of which he was later cleared. That even Allen, a nationally respected interpreter of modern life and values, especially those of elite New Yorkers, might be a sexual opportunist (or worse) in his domestic life seemed to suggest that no father any longer could be an object of automatic trust. The national pattern of abusive step-fathers and stepfather figures had gained visibility from this case among the ranks of the most privileged.

Finally, the sexual abuse of children (and adults) by male reli-gious leaders has been especially damaging to the public status of fatherhood, corroding the positive association of masculinity and fatherhood with authority not only for the faithful, but for Amer-ican society as a whole. For believers, religious leaders are religious symbols of fatherhood, but in a society whose institutions have been profoundly shaped by biblical religion, they are also cultural symbols of fatherhood.

Beginning in the mid-1980s, a national pattern of child sexual abuse, notably by Christian leaders, began to be revealed. Most visible, along with cases in mainstream Protestant traditions, have been the cases of abuse within the Roman Catholic Church. By the decade ending in 1994, 400 cases of sexual abuse by priests had been reported nationally, causing most dioceses to review their pro-cedures for handling such cases.[47] Yet it was not until 1993 that the Pope publicly addressed the problem. At that time also, the Na-tional Conference of Catholic Bishops, faced with what had be-come a deep "crisis of confidence in church leadership," formed a national committee to address this form of sexual misconduct.[48]

Religious leaders' lack of resolve in responding to the emerging pattern of sexual misconduct often has exacerbated the pattern's negative impact on fatherhood and authority. The striking simi-larity between the Roman Catholic bishops' slow and institution-ally protective response, for example, and that of other groups was noted by a leading national commentator on religion: "They suf-fered from the same reflexive group defensiveness that marks po-licemen and physicians as well as priests. They were enclosed in habits of clerical secrecy."[49] Evidence giving rise to allegations that the Roman Catholic Church frequently has overlooked and even covered up abuse of children by sending offending clerics to new parishes or to its treatment center in New Mexico, instead of taking initiative to root out injustice and protect the vulnerable, has been especially damaging.[50] Such evidence includes the resignation in March 1993 of Robert Sanchez, the former Archbishop of the Diocese of Santa Fe, where the treatment center is located, following accusations he had abused three women when they were teenagers. The aggressiveness of the church's self-defense in its effort to avoid high damage awards, including its repeated legal strategy of charging victims' willing consent, has mirrored the self-interest of businesses and other kinds of institutions and their leaders. Once again, while the church has, like any institution, a legitimate need to safeguard properly its own interests and those of its clergy, such legal aggressiveness has appeared to many to reflect greater concern with its own institutional and financial well-being than with justice and its pastoral mission: "Critics complain that the church has let lawyers determine its responses, treating victims as if they are potential legal adversaries rather than wounded faithful in need of support and healing."[51]

DOMESTIC VIOLENCE, MARITAL AND DATE RAPE

Along with sexual harassment in the workplace and the weakening of fatherhood, increasing domestic violence and marital and date rape have worked to erode the traditional meaning and status of masculinity. In the face of these disturbing trends, cultural belief that women can rely on men for physical and other forms of protection is crumbling. Moreover, contrary to the once common assumption that strangers pose the greatest threat to women, American women are now recognized to be most at risk for physical and sexual assault from their male partners and ex-partners.[52]

While women themselves can be violent, especially when abused, claims that men and women are equally violent in intimate relationships give way in the face of careful gender analysis of the data. When violence is defined as "physical aggression with the potential to cause physical harm, sexual aggression, forcible restraint, and threats to kill or harm," the data show that most violence in intimate relationships is perpetrated by men.[53] Expert estimates suggest that nationally as many as 4 million women may be assaulted by their male partners each year, more than 1.8 million severely. Moreover, women are more likely to be killed by their male partners than by all other types of assailants combined; contrary to stereotypes that associate such violence with minority populations, this is more true for white women than for women of other racial and ethnic groups.[54]

Marital violence is a major category of victimization for women across socioeconomic and age groups, although poor and younger women are especially likely to be the targets of marital as well as nonmarital violence.[55] Rape is a particular form of marital violence, occurring most frequently in tandem with other forms of physical assault.[56] Marital assault also takes the form of battering during pregnancy. Of pregnant women from all races, classes, and educational backgrounds who see obstetricians, as many as 37 percent may be victims of physical abuse.[57] Still another rising aspect of domestic violence, now estimated to be at least equal in prevalence to marital violence, is physical assault among dating and cohabiting couples. Here too, the risk to women of injury and death is much higher than to men. And the severity of both sexual and nonsexual physical assault is increasing. While it is a phenomenon that has only just begun to be studied, initial date rape studies suggest that college-age women, followed by women twenty to twenty-four, are most at risk for date rape (at an estimated rate of one in 3.6).[58] And a rising tide of harassment in the nation's high schools, junior high schools, and community facilities, of which young girls especially are targets, points to an emerging pattern in which abuse is seen as courting behavior.[59] Music popular among teenagers increasingly celebrates sexual domination of women and assault as male status symbols.

These patterns of intimate heterosexual violence, like sexual harassment and patterns weakening fatherhood, also have been symbolized by major public cases. None, of course, has received more national attention than that of O. J. Simpson, celebrity and former football player. Convicted of battering, charged with the murder of his former wife and her friend, and then acquitted, Simpson has given prolonged public visibility to domestic violence. Sol Wachtler, the nationally prominent and highly respected Chief Judge of New York State, and others also have turned the national spotlight on violence in nonmarital intimate relationships. The sixty-two-year-old Wachtler pleaded guilty, after a widely publicized arrest, to planning to kidnap his former lover's daughter. He described this plan as part of a lengthy campaign of terror against his lover designed to win her back. In words that help explain the national pattern of intimate violence against women, he presented this campaign as an effort to restore his masculine authority through fear by causing his lover "to seek [his] help and protection."[60] Among the other well-known cases of such violence have been those of the fighter Mike Tyson, convicted of date rape, and William Kennedy Smith, a young nephew of Senator Edward Kennedy (Democrat of Massachusetts), acquitted of the same crime. And in 1993 in Lakewood, California, a "respectable" middle-class community, eight high school boys, who were part of a larger, mostly white group called the Spur Posse, were accused of raping and molesting girls as young as ten as part of a gang competition they had devised imitating the conquests of professional athletes.

Feminists rightly call attention to the hatred of women and girls evidenced by these patterns of violence, and to the political, as well as physical and psychological, implications of women's victimization. But like other social analysts, they often overlook the effect male abuse is having on fundamental cultural beliefs about masculinity and the legitimacy of masculine authority. In contrast to the fairness and protection culturally represented as masculine traits, these patterns reflect men's predatory use of sex to dominate women. Because assault by male intimates destroys the dynamic of trust and respect, there is a direct connection between it and the erosion of male authority. This connection is well-illustrated by a woman who responded to a major newspaper story in 1993 on college rape and assault. She summed up the impact of the national patterns we have been examining, calling for an end to "boys-will-be-boys" tolerance of misconduct by males, especially privileged males: "[They] should have to leave college without their tickets to the board rooms and other corridors of power. They cannot be captains of industry, they cannot be football stars and they cannot be our admirals, senators, or judges unless they behave."[61]

THE CULTURAL CRISIS OF AUTHORITY

Analysts of all kinds tend to think of changes in the social realities of men and women in terms of changing sex roles or family structure. On one level, they are right. Changes in women's lives do underscore the need to reconstruct society's notion of the female social role. And the erosion of masculinity's traditional meaning underscores the need to rethink the male sex role, fatherhood, and traditional cultural assumptions about family structure. Given the changes in society and culture, it will not work to try to reverse the trend, as some advocate,[62] and attempt to breathe new life into the old model of fatherhood and its authority. New visions are needed of the basis for sustained heterosexual relationships, of the father's contributions to family life, and of ways for both women and men to combine parenting and wage earning. Yet on another level, even more than this is required. As a result of the changing meaning and status of masculinity, society must construct new models not only of masculinity, but of authority itself.

The cultural crisis of masculine authority is delegitimating male dominance, especially the dominance of white males, in the government and marketplace. The erosion of male authority is a crucial, if largely unidentified element in the steadily growing crisis of trust in American government analyzed by so many experts and commentators. As the traditional meaning and status of masculinity is disappearing, the white male public sphere—that dominant public which has defined, represented, and exercised authority in American life—is threatened as well. With the degree to which its justice and protection have been predicated on dominance being revealed, the cultural narrative of this public is losing plausibility and the capacity to prevent new narratives from emerging.[63]

Women are experiencing this cultural crisis of authority and playing a central role in it in ways that have not been widely recognized or well understood. Ironically, this role does not grow mainly out of feminism, what some see as women's attempt to supplant male authority. Rather, it grows out of the traditional cultural relationship between femininity and masculinity structured by beliefs about gender that have been dominant in the West since the early modern period.

Women have played a crucial role in maintaining traditional beliefs about masculinity and authority and the social arrangements shaped by them. The masculine promise to represent truth over self-interest and to protect has been a two-way contract. Men's authority in the home and in the world has involved not only women's subordination to that authority, but also their trust in the promise it represented. Women's trust, in turn, has depended to a significant degree on the framework of cultural beliefs about public and private that made this promise plausible—that made it "the way things were and the way they were meant to be." In the context of this framework of beliefs, evidence that the promise was being honored reinforced its plausibility. Even more fundamental, however, women's subordination prescribed by these dominant cultural beliefs has defined their proper relationship with male authority not simply as serving it, but as helping to construct it. The negative cultural association of women with authority, in other words, has operated in such a way that women have been deeply invested in the ongoing social and cultural process of *giving* authority to men and *believing* in male authority at the cost of their own.

It is in the context of women's traditional role that their new and newly noticed level of vulnerability to men, and that of their children, is such a potent force. Women are witnessing the effects of sexual harassment, the erosion of fatherhood, and domestic violence and marital and date rape in their own lives and in those of extended families and friends. Public cases *confirm* the growing personal and collective knowledge many have of the threats men can represent. Even against some women's hopes, it is women's current sexual, physical, and economic vulnerability to men that is eroding basic features of the traditional sexual division of labor: women's trust in the male promise, their subordination to men, and their function in the construction of masculine authority.

Thus the very dynamic of trust by which women's reliance on male authority historically has been generated, the cultural belief that men represent a guarantee of physical, economic, and existential security for women, is being undermined. For many women, therefore, the experience of equality is beginning not with, or not only with, a demand for equal rights, but with recognition that in public and private women cannot count on men to know, represent, or give priority to their best interests. Whether this recognition is viewed as a tragedy or a development long overdue, it is occurring now with a visibility and on a social scale broad enough to shatter long-held convictions to the contrary among women and in society in general.

In the process, many women are being thrown back on their own resources and into a new view of themselves and the world. Losing automatic belief in male authority and the maleness of authority, they are facing their own crisis of authority. Socialized to expect from men (fathers, lovers, husbands, other family members, political and religious leaders) the capacity and resolve to provide vision for individuals, institutions, and society as a whole, women have looked to men for reliable moral leadership in the meaning and purpose of individual *and* collective life. Today, in contrast, they are increasingly aware that American society has entered a new era. It is no longer guided by unquestioned belief that male authority transcends self-interest through both its distinctive capacity to *comprehend* the human and its unfailing *allegiance* to human interests.

CONCLUSION

"Illegitimacy," poverty, race, and mothers' entrance into the paid labor force are often special focal points of analysis of the decaying social and moral infrastructure of American life. Few recognize, however, the role in this values crisis played by the change masculinity is undergoing up and down the social scale. Erosion of masculinity's traditional social and cultural meaning is a major factor in the deterioration of interpersonal, family, and community attachments. It is a key element in the disintegration of "the American character" many analysts decry.[64]

Furthermore, erosion of masculinity's traditional authority is leaving the nation leaderless at precisely the points at which effective leadership is most needed. These points are visible in patterns of sexual harassment, the deterioration of fatherhood, and domestic violence and marital and date rape. Authority is eroding where it places self-interest ahead of commitment to doing justice; where it is embedded in and unable to reach beyond the particularity of its own reality; where it lacks both true dedication to the human as a collective enterprise and the capacity to discern humanity as it is expressed in plural forms and conditions; and where it places lower priority on compassion for the vulnerable than on profit, efficiency, or power.

Erosion of masculine authority, in short, identifies the challenge modern leadership faces as its *moral* task: adjudicating competing claims fairly in a social context in which traditional structures and values are deteriorating, as is the authority of the moral traditions that have shaped and sustained them. The capacity in a leader for moral criticism and self-criticism is crucial to this task. Only through the effort to discern justice as it emerges out of multiple perspectives, an effort disciplined by constant scrutiny of the play of power relations, including a leader's own, can values be reconceived in ways that gain new authority for the present and future.

While women are not the only resource for constructing the new social and cultural conception of authority that is needed, they are a major one. Men capable of critical distance on the deterioration of authority are major resources as well. However, because women's home and workplace experience allows them to see authority's failures more sharply than many, and because women are

comparative newcomers to full participation in the public world
outside the home, many have a special awareness of this urgent and
complex challenge. They see themselves confronting the dilemma
of simply being socialized to the traditional models of authority in
mainstream institutions or developing better ways of leading.
Poised on the brink between the public world and the private one
that is still their particular responsibility, many women already feel
deeply the desire to remake the values of public life. The crisis of
authority in American society presents a particular *need* for them
to do so. The question is where they will find help in rethinking
the moral framework that has shaped American society and in forging new public vision.

Neither the perspectives for reconstructing models of public authority nor the necessary resolve to undertake this task will come
to women automatically, by virtue of their being female. Women
show no "natural" capacity, even among themselves, to transcend
the particularity of their own experience. White feminists, for
example, often were blind to the fact that the Hill-Thomas hearings did not mark the achievement of solidarity between black
and white women many assumed. Instead, the hearings identified
black women's distinctive social predicament. They depicted the
impossibility for black women of choosing between feminism and
racial justice, revealing the complex race/sex problem separating
women of these two races.[65] We shortly will see, as well, that privileged women especially have much to learn from their own history
about where their efforts to work on behalf of the human, while
achieving much, also have fallen short of the goal of honoring
human diversity. Moreover, all women face more than the task of
constructing new models of authority. They also must learn as individuals to assert authority publicly, overcoming internal and ex-
ternal cultural prohibitions against their doing so. Assuming authority will be a challenge for most women.

The question is whether women, as they enter the paid labor
force in historic numbers, are learning to make a difference in reconstructing the cultural conception of authority and the values of

the public world. All too often, however, this crucial question, like the prospect of change itself, is preempted by central aspects of women's experience in the public world which are undermining their full participation. We turn next to examination of these barriers to women's full public potential.

CHAPTER FOUR

But It's Still a Man's World

With the majority now in the paid labor force, American women have taken their next major step into the public world after winning the vote. We might expect increasing opportunity in the workplace to draw women, as it draws men, further into informed participation in the public issues and processes of American life. A recent study demonstrates that paid work is a significantly better resource for developing civic skills (e.g., writing, speaking, decision making, planning and chairing meetings) and a predisposition to political participation than either nonpolitical organizations or religious institutions.[1] Highly skilled jobs especially provide a setting in which women can learn to speak with authority as they relate public issues and processes to the welfare of groups, institutions, and society as a whole. Women represent a tremendous new resource for institutional, civic, and political leadership in American society, and what is happening to them in the workplace is to a significant degree determining what difference their leadership will make in American society. Therefore, we need to ask to what extent they are finding at work the opportunity to progress toward their own visions of authority and its purposes.

Yet we tend not to think about women's paid work in these *public* terms. One reason is that much attention is focused on the problems women are encountering at every level of employment in institutional cultures fashioned and dominated by the power of men, especially white men. For even as social forces are eroding the masculinity of authority, male power continues to be the overwhelming pattern in contemporary American institutions, especially at the top. While there is much about women's work experience that is not negative, it is presenting them with problems so persistent and amply documented they have given rise to a new vocabulary: the "sticky floor," the "glass ceiling," the "mommy track," and the "second shift."

These terms reflect the degree to which the American workplace is not transforming but adapting and sustaining the traditional sexual division of labor and the authority of men. They also reflect the barriers to women's workplace advancement that exist across all sectors of the economy.[2] These barriers stem from the continuing gender-based structure of paid work in America, a structure whose effects disadvantage poor and minority women especially.[3] Both these barriers and the new ways in which the workplace is institutionalizing the traditional sexual division of labor mean that attention is focused mainly on two issues: whether women are gaining *access* to labor-force opportunity equal to that of men and what it takes for women to *juggle* paid work with their family responsibilities.

The second reason we tend not to think of women's paid work as a major step into the public world is persisting cultural beliefs about public and private that not only continue to associate women with the private world, despite their work outside the home, but also designate the market as a "private sector" within the public. The full significance of women's paid work for them and for American life thus remains hidden, allowing the country to witness the revolution taking place in women's lives as if little structural change were taking place in society. As a consequence, traditional beliefs prevent the nation from giving adequate attention not just to women's economic and workplace rights, but also to the public value of their leadership potential and to the fate of their unpaid family and community labor.

Political scientist Judith Shklar's examination of citizenship in American society offers additional insight into why we fail to recognize that paid work is bringing women further into the public world: historically, the distinction between "public" and "private" has been drawn from the perspective of privileged men, for whom earning has seemed private.[4] Yet citizenship, defined originally in the Republic in terms of the experience of these men, was predicated on their unstated social right to self-directed earning. This right was denied to black women and men by slavery. It also was denied to white women by the social and cultural norm of their economic dependence on men. As Shklar argues, the long quest of American blacks and white women for inclusion in the status of citizen demonstrates that earning is *public*. Along with the constitutional right to vote, economic independence is a crucial part of the ethical foundation of citizenship: "To be a recognized and active citizen at all he [*sic*] must be an equal member of the polity, a voter, but he must also be independent, which has all along meant that he must be an 'earner,' a free remunerated worker."[5]

Shklar's argument helps us recognize that women's paid work has important implications for their citizenship. In gaining the social right to earn, women are gaining access to citizenship on a new level and a new moral standing in society. Shklar also argues against the governing cultural belief that the market is a "private sector." Defined from the perspective of white men, "private" traditionally has been a term used to designate civil society, areas of the rights-bearing (white male) citizen's autonomy in relation to the power of the state. Hence, the family and religion, seen as sites of affective and moral freedom, have constituted the private sphere and the market has been a private sector. Yet however important it may be to distinguish the marketplace from the state, this designation masks the market's *public* nature:

> In America [civil society] has generally been treated as the sphere of private choices, but the legal structure, meaning, and character of these transactions are public, and they reflect the whole republic. Economic exchanges and entitlements are ultimately subject to public sanction, and so are the activities of the many voluntary organizations that have always

been a feature of American public life. Earning and spending are hardly private. . . . The individual American citizen is in fact a member of two interlocking public orders, one egalitarian, the other entirely unequal.[6]

To Shklar's insight, we must add that the market is public in a further sense too. It is made up of social institutions that are themselves public spaces and actors. These social institutions and the work-lives Americans lead within them not only are shaped by the nation's public life, but also help to shape it. The influence of myriad for-profit and nonprofit institutions—corporate, financial, government, manufacturing, medical, cultural, educational—operates not just through political lobbyists on Capitol Hill, but even more directly through the daily life and work of these institutions. The direction and quality of American life are affected by them, perhaps most fundamentally by the institutional demands, policies, and cultures that guide employment of their personnel. Through these, institutions help determine the destiny not only of individuals and social groups, but also of social structures like the family. Furthermore, institutions' compensation practices, by playing a major role in focusing and distributing the talent of society's leaders, help determine the dominant values and priorities guiding the nation.[7] And the missions that private-sector institutions define for themselves are just as important as the public policies government puts in place. It matters how institutions develop and deploy their products, material resources, and social power, and whether their own welfare is pursued in a way that overlooks their obligation to serve society or takes this obligation seriously.

In light of the grave problems that currently beset American society, it is important to acknowledge this public role of the private sector. Conservatives want it acknowledged in order to advance their agenda emphasizing free enterprise over government intervention. A progressive agenda, however, also must recognize that the private sector shapes many of the social values and patterns of American life. Looking at the private sector's public role allows us to take a more realistic, broader route as we explore the collective social good and how it may best be served. Service of the public interest can only be strengthened when we understand the public role institutions of all kinds play, especially "private" ones.

We must think in new ways about the workplace as a powerful force that helps shape the nation's life and also as a significant arena for citizens' public activity in addressing central aspects of America's values crisis. We can begin by examining how the gender-based structure of the workplace is both contributing to this crisis and affecting women's progress toward full public participation.

NOT THE IDEAL WORKER

Many argue and more would like to believe that American women encounter no problem of exclusion or discrimination in the world of paid work—that equality for women is either already here or just a matter of time. In fact, experts assessing women's work situation demonstrate that they face fundamental structural impediments at every employment level. Again, these impediments can be traced to embedded cultural beliefs about public and private. These institutionalized beliefs, adapting as women's domestic responsibilities expand to include paid work, still regulate women's progress in the public world. They have not been eradicated or superseded by the principle of gender equality, despite its progress in cutting a new path for women into many positions from which they were once barred. Most of all, these beliefs continue to support a model of human endeavor in the public world that is, as women often discover to their surprise, not gender-neutral, but male.

Historically, men have not only predominated in the world of paid work, but their lives and labor have set its terms, making the ideal worker male.[8] The basis of this gendered structure of paid work in America is the traditional sexual division of labor that links the structures of "the" family and the market. In a society whose institutions have been shaped by belief that women's main work is childbearing and childrearing, and that the world of endeavor and authority outside the home is men's preserve, women remained marginal to wage labor as it evolved in the nineteenth century and much of the twentieth. Their culturally prescribed work as homemakers overshadowed other work they did in or outside of the home, including work some did for wages. The ideal of women's work has been defined by the dominant cultural expectation, born in the early modern period, that all women will become wives and mothers, and that their true vocation lies in doing so.

It has been widely assumed, as the work norm for women has shifted in the last two decades to combine paid and unpaid labor, that husbands would take up an increasingly equal share of parenting and homemaking labor. To some extent, this has happened. Economist Juliet Schor found in 1991 that, looking at both the unemployed and employed, the average man had taken on almost three more hours a week of cooking, cleaning, and childcare than he was doing two decades before.[9] Despite such evidence that some husbands are doing more, however, both housework and childcare remain chiefly women's responsibilities. The gendered structure of work survives today within the home, as well as outside it.

The most time-intensive, traditionally female household tasks (meal preparation and cleanup, washing dishes, housecleaning, and washing, ironing, and mending clothes) are still defined by husbands, who do only a modestly increased amount of them, as women's work. These increases are evident in nonprofessional, dual-earner couples working sequential shifts, particularly where a husband is home alone and the wife is working a day shift.[10] Sequential shifts also increase the likelihood that husbands will help with childcare, although especially in the evening and at night. Between 1988 and 1991, the percentage of fathers providing care for preschool children whose mothers were working outside the home increased from 15 percent to 20 percent, with the largest percentage of fathers doing so to cover for mothers working a nonday shift.[11] In professional dual-earner couples, however, husbands' share of household labor shows modest growth not because they have increased significantly the hours of this work they do, but because *wives* do significantly less (standards for cleanliness are lowered, domestic help is hired, and meals are eaten out).[12]

Women in all social groups, that is, still not only do a disproportionate amount of house and child labor compared with their husbands, but also are in charge of seeing that it gets done. Research shows, for example, that in couples with a more egalitarian gender ideology husbands actually increase their household labor only as a result of their wives' changed expectations of them, not of changed expectations of themselves (husbands, instead, simply expect their wives to decrease *their* hours of household labor). Furthermore, when couples have children, wives' household labor grows too, increasing disproportionately in relation to that of their husbands, so that their husbands' share actually is reduced.[13]. It is at this point in privileged families, as fathers' entitlement allows them to continue to delegate their daily family responsibilities, that mothers often leave the workplace or marginalize themselves in it.[14] So while signs that men are doing more give some experts hope for future equal sharing of both housework and childcare, many, like Schor, warn against underestimating the structural barriers to equality:

> Despite this rise, it is premature to conclude that we are on the fast track to gender equality. . . . Most of the increase in men's domestic labor has been caused by the fact that many more men are out of the labor force. . . . Among men who are employed, the increase is far less—amounting to slightly more than one additional hour per week.[15]

Given this fundamental way of dividing society's work into unpaid and paid, female and male, work *not* related to reproduction and care has been structured as the responsibility and prerogative of men. This is why, as women increasingly entered the paid labor force early in the century, they were marginalized within it on the basis of their reproductive role (in combination always with their race and class, as well). They were marginalized first of all in terms of occupation. Until relatively recently, women entering the world of paid work were almost completely segregated in certain sectors of the economy (e.g., business and health) and certain occupations (e.g., secretarial work and nursing). They also were relegated to bottom- and mid-level jobs within sectors and occupations. And because the wage structure of paid labor has been gendered as well, women also have been marginalized with regard to wages. By the early twentieth century, men's economic entitlement to the better jobs was institutionalized, based on the belief that they, as husbands and fathers, needed to earn a wage adequate to support a family. Given the race and class hierarchy among American men, the most highly valued, powerful, and lucrative jobs, and the credentialing system leading to them, were accessible overwhelmingly to privileged men. As a result, privileged men's capacity to earn a "family wage" has been protected as, in recent decades, the wages of men toward the bottom of the labor market have stagnated and declined.

Furthermore, even in the same and comparable jobs, women systematically have earned less than men. Up and down the employment scale, the primary value of men's work culturally, together with the fact that women's family responsibilities keep them from being the ideal worker, has resulted in pay discrimination and women's economic vulnerability.[16] More than thirty years after passage of the Equal Pay Act, white women still earn only 75 percent of what white men earn, while black and Hispanic women, respectively, earn 65 and 58 percent.[17] And while there has been significant progress in the last two decades in decreasing both the earnings gap between men and women and occupational segregation, changes have come about as a result of other factors besides the concerted efforts of those seeking to eliminate discrimination. For example, what narrowing of the male/female wage gap has taken place is the result, in large part, of decline in recent decades in men's wages. Furthermore, women often have gained new or greater access to occupations, such as the ordained Protestant ministry and book editing, as men have left them and the occupations' status and earning power have declined.

The full meaning of the gendered structure of paid work in

American society, however, is revealed especially by the situation of employed mothers, who make up the majority of women in the paid labor force today.[18] The range of their responsibilities makes them a sharp contrast to the ideal worker, the central figure in what Schor calls today's "on-demand system of employment."[19] Shaping as it does the social infrastructure—the lives of individuals, families, and groups—this system is perhaps the chief way in which the market economy shapes American life. The high demands it places on workers, together with its assumption that the ideal worker can count on a supportive flow of domestic services from his spouse, marginalizes women and mothers in the workplace.[20] The ideal worker is male, that is, because, in addition to associating him positively with authority and market skills, the culture's sex-gender system leaves him unencumbered:

> At the core of the system is a notion of an ideal worker without primary responsibility for children: a worker absent from home a minimum of nine hours a day, five or six days a week, often with overtime at short notice and at the employer's discretion. Underlying the expectations for the "ideal" worker is the rarely challenged assumption that the accepted avenues of adult power and responsibility inevitably are incompatible with caregiving.[21]

Of course, the ideal worker is free of more than primary responsibility for children. He is also unencumbered by responsibility for sick, disabled, or elderly relatives, by homemaking responsibilities for others or himself, and even by aspects of his own personal care he can delegate to others. He takes his job as top priority, works long hours that grow longer as he moves up the occupational hierarchy, is available at his employer's demand at any time outside of regular work hours, lives in a face-time culture where he needs to be *seen* "giving his all" to work, must be willing to travel and relocate to suit the organization's needs, and must be constantly present at work to be supervised face-to-face.[22]

Because market work is organized around men as ideal workers and asks women to conform to a life-pattern society has defined as male, trying to conform puts women in double jeopardy. Not only are they still expected to provide a flow of domestic services for others, but they also do not have a "wife" to provide the flow that would allow them to meet the ideal worker standard. The result of men's social availability to conform to employer demands is that mothers, as a rule, are pushed to the economic margin of work. More than this, they are pushed to one side of accepted institutional routes to adult *authority* in American society or pushed off these routes altogether.[23] Because the ideal worker model applies especially to white-collar jobs, the top levels of management in American institutions remain overwhelmingly male.

Yet as Schor's study of work time found, it is not only those at the top levels of management and the professions who are overworked, but Americans at all levels and in all occupational and income groups.[24] In low-wage jobs, the ideal worker is also male. While such jobs offer more meaningful control over time, since they offer standard schedules and freedom from random work-demands on private time, the difficulties with which they present workers reflect demand problems similar to those encountered by the ideal worker in top jobs.[25] Increasingly, as Schor points out, since low-wage jobs do not pay enough to support a family, workers must be able to hold several jobs and work overtime. Because they do not have the right to refuse overtime requested by employers, high and quasi-permanent overtime creates difficulties for many. And those at the lower end of the occupational hierarchy may be assigned irregular or inconvenient schedules.

COMBINING DOMESTIC LABOR AND "BREADWINNING"

In short, institutions send the message that women are not the ideal worker chiefly by structuring paid work to exclude the possibility of workers fulfilling daily commitments to family and community. The ideal worker is supposed to delegate to others, traditionally his spouse, not only daily caregiving and childrearing responsibilities,[26] but also the social interactions and networking necessary to sustain the ties, interests, and well-being of families as parts of communities (e.g., helping friends in need; attending children's school events; volunteering in religious, educational, and community programs; or initiating community improvement efforts). Deviance from this ideal worker norm is a major source of the practical problems encountered in the workplace by women, especially mothers, who have daily caregiving responsibilities of any kind. In light of both their continuing cultural association with domestic labor and the cost of delegating this labor, most women face the challenge of combining domestic labor and wage earning.

The way women resolve the predicament of handling this conflict of paid work and family is widely described in the language of choice.[27] But seeing each woman's solution as an expression chiefly of individual preference overlooks the fact that a woman's resources and those to which her social position gives her access sharply distinguish the realm of choice within which she operates. Privileged women, for example, whose status provides them with financial and social capital, have more "choices"—including sometimes the "choice" not to work—than the majority of American women who must support or help support themselves and their family. Yet the implication of the language of choice is that most women, especially married women, have a similar and unlimited range of options. This language presents each woman as an "ungendered actor in the republic of choice"[28] who decides whether to enter the paid work force and marginalize herself within it to accommodate her domestic responsibilities (a choice often characterized as the "mommy track"); to become a superwoman who is both ideal worker and committed homemaker; or to return to full-time homemaking. Moreover, in a culture that still believes a "good" woman is a "good" mother, the language of choice also obscures the fact that it is used commonly to measure how women choose to *meet* this expectation and whether or not they do.

Viewing the effort to combine paid work and homemaking as a matter of women's individual choice, in short, masks the structural reality of society's sexual division of labor. In fact, as Joan Williams points out, the rhetoric of choice allows Americans to maintain their investment in equality between men and women while overlooking the way it conflicts with traditional gender roles: "[W]omen are really equal, goes the argument, they just make different choices."[29] But by presenting all individuals, regardless of gender, race, and class, as independent, rational actors free to pursue their self-interest, the language of choice obscures the limitations most women of all social groups experience *as women*. In fact, all women share the constraint, even if it is one against which they rebel, of having grown up with the cultural expectation that they will live lives encumbered by commitment to and accountability for the physical and personal well-being of children, husbands, and others. The "selfless" choice to accept this encumbrance is the norm that Western culture has held out for all women's lives; selflessness, paradoxically, is the dominant cultural conception of the route by which women *find* their selves. As a result, the marginalization of women in the paid labor force has been justified by the claim that women "choose" the commitment to family that precludes the earning power and the opportunities men enjoy. Why the world of work is organized so that this commitment need preclude both, for women *or* men, is a question foreclosed by this focus on women's individual choice.

Furthermore, by masking the way in which the conflict of domestic and paid labor belongs not to individual women alone, but to women as a group, the language of choice also masks how this conflict belongs to society as a whole. It obscures, that is, not only society's predetermination of the "choices" available to women, but also the nation's stake in how women choose. Because women contribute their family and community labor to society, as well as to their individual families, in other words, this labor's fate as a *social* good depends on whether or not women choose to be, like men, ideal workers.

Currently, their "choices" constrained by their continuing identification with the private sphere, most women end up, typically at great personal cost, assuming disproportionate daily responsibility for family life. As a result, the group that stands out among overworked Americans is married women who are employed, especially mothers.[30] A conservative calculation is that employed mothers work anywhere from twenty-five to forty-five hours a week in the home (childcare and housework) on top of forty-plus hours on the job; most studies find they average a total of more than eighty hours.[31] Despite their overwork, inevitably, women are spending less time at home on domestic labor, which is a source of guilt for many.[32] Yet their overwork from combining domestic labor and breadwinning has even deeper social significance than the problems related to equity, health, and quality of life for women that rightly have received experts' attention.

Their current situation puts women in a moral bind because they are in limbo, unable to meet the full demands or aspire to the full possibilities of either workplace or home. Even if they accept less demanding status in the workplace, exhaustion often prevents them from meeting and balancing the needs of family members in a way that delivers the quality and happiness of family life they are expected culturally to provide. Most American women, in short, can be neither ideal worker nor "good" mother, the two standards for adult work embedded in traditional beliefs about public and private. Caught between these two models of adult life, they are neither here nor there, living without a culturally ratified pattern for the meaning and value of their female lives.

This experience of not fitting the established social or cultural structures of domestic or paid work causes many women to feel great personal anxiety and guilt. It also, however, gives them a compelling interest, sometimes unformed but nevertheless deeply felt, in the broader social significance and potential of their plight. Many wish to ask whether being an ideal worker is ideal for anyone or for society, and why society is not structured to support *combining* paid and unpaid work as the adult norm. Before many women can pursue their interest in the broader social significance of their plight, however, their time and energy are drained by working a double shift. Moreover, combining domestic labor and wage earning is but one major aspect of a larger climate in the workplace that sets up further barriers to change.

A CLIMATE OF DISCOURAGEMENT

Many women love their jobs and numbers of them are treated fairly and well by employers and colleagues who value their performance. Nevertheless, it is common for women to encounter in the workplace, as a result of their gender, a climate of discouragement. Coming on top of the overwork of the double shift, this climate compounds to varying degrees women's sense of being on foreign and sometimes even hostile ground. This sense comes with the stress of negotiating institutional cultures that have been shaped by men's authority to define and direct human affairs. For women of color, who differ from the norm by race or ethnicity as well as sex, the challenge of negotiating these cultures and the discouragement are multiplied. Employment brings them not only the stress of adapting to a male culture, but also that of straddling the gap between their own culture and the European-American culture that dominates most institutions.[33]

The discouraging climate women encounter on the job is created by both implicit and explicit factors. Whereas men, especially privileged men, enter and move up in a work world that recognizes them as suitable inheritors of its traditions, from construction to the presidency, women are entering field after field with the handicap of being newcomers who must make an effort to fit in. As women, they are denied the basic sense that they belong in occupations, professions, and levels of authority long the preserve of men. Signals that they are newcomers still emanate from myriad points in the culture of workplaces—from the small number and distant location of women's restrooms, to exclusively or overwhelmingly male portraits of past leaders on the walls, to the mysterious rules of male fellow workers' patterns of formal and informal on-the-job interaction, to the sheer numerical dominance of men.

Overt attempts to resist women's progress in the world of paid work are more explicit indicators of their status than such environmental signals. Here discouragement turns direct and individual.

One of the ways in which American women's work lives are still least like men's is that women of all racial groups face patterns of gender-linked treatment that men do not face. These include problems such as discrimination in pay, hiring, and promotion, and sexual harassment, at which we already have looked, as well as relegation to the "mommy track" and careers stalled by the "sticky floor" or the "glass ceiling."

In all of its facets, this climate of discouragement has the effect of protecting a workplace structure and culture that supports the norm of the male ideal worker by *undermining* women's work. The discouraging climate regulates women's movement into the paid labor force, setting up subtle and not-so-subtle barriers that keep large numbers of women from confident, undiminished engagement in their work's substance and slow the pace of their advancement. Moreover, the effort to surmount these barriers, whether it is a psychological, legal, or strategic response to discrimination, often keeps women distracted and drained of energy. Discouragement seriously affects women's economic, employment, and personal well-being. Its impact runs the gamut from keeping them off balance and eroding their self-confidence, to denying them equal opportunity or equal treatment on the job, to encouraging many to leave for new jobs or full-time homemaking (in the comparatively few cases where doing so is economically feasible), to even forcing some to quit (a frequent result of discrimination complaints).

This climate is further evidence of persisting cultural beliefs about public and private that at once identify women's "real" work with the home and deny women economic independence and association with authority. Where conscious or unconscious resistance to women's progress in the world of paid work exists, these beliefs are used to justify traditional assumptions about what women's social roles are and should be. There are few better illustrations of the power of these beliefs to prevent women from reaching parity with men on the job than the "glass ceiling," that intractable and ubiquitous lid on women's advancement into the higher echelons of institutional leadership.

First named almost a decade ago, the "glass ceiling" refers to those barriers to upward mobility unrelated to ability that are experienced by women of all racial groups (and by minority men), especially "those in professional and managerial positions who have the potential to achieve high-status positions of authority."[34] By 1992, according to Bureau of Labor Statistics, white women held 37.1 percent of executive, administrative, and managerial positions, while 3 percent of these were held by black women and 1.9 percent by Hispanic women.[35] Despite the fact that a large number of women with earned credentials and education equal to those of men are in the managerial pipeline, twenty-five years after women began to move into management only 3 to 5 percent of the senior-level positions in major corporations are held by them; only 5 percent of the women who hold these jobs are women of color.[36] The senior managerial ranks of American business and many professions are still overwhelmingly male and white.

Indeed, the problem of the "glass ceiling" is so pervasive nationally that the U.S. Department of Labor established a separate commission to study strategies for breaking through it. Social scientists advised the commission that the "glass ceiling" needs to be understood not as one point at the top beyond which women do not advance, but as a whole series of points along the way in a woman's career that disadvantage her.[37] A number of studies point to the role of sex and race bias in keeping women out of positions that would prepare them for advancement to the top by giving them more responsibility, supervisory authority, visibility, and opportunity to contribute at the center of an institution's or corporation's mission.[38] Experts also point out that the vast majority of employed American women will never even have the opportunity to encounter the glass ceiling because the "sticky floor" of low-paying, low-mobility jobs keeps them trapped at the bottom of the labor market and the economy. Low-wage employment is the primary cause of the high poverty rate for families of wage-earning single-parent mothers.[39]

The "mommy track," another product of cultural belief that women bear responsibility for families that they should not delegate, helps to keep women out of the mainstream of advancement on the job, justifying creation of career paths for mothers that relegate many to an institutionally secondary pathway. This cultural belief is behind employers' common conviction that women will choose to limit their career options in order to reduce the conflicting demands of job and family.[40] Some women, indeed, do accept secondary professional and economic status as an alternative to conforming to the male work norm. As a result, in a field such as law, for example, it is often professionally experienced mothers who end up off the established pathway to winning seniority. Set to one side in positions that give them the reduced hours and pressure necessary to fulfill their domestic responsibilities, women who "choose" these positions give up the possibility of full partnership and profit sharing. In her recent study of women in the law, political scientist Mona Harrington summed up the social and professional rules that together limit the occupational success of women in many fields:

> Either they go by men's professional rules while shouldering the main burden of families and thus living under constant, punishing pressure, or they gain exceptions for themselves from men's rules and are thus not taken seriously as fully authoritative colleagues.[41]

On the one hand, this climate of discouragement that women experience has the potential to develop in some a strong motive for institutional reform and, as we shall shortly see, it often does. On the other hand, this climate more commonly distracts women from the project of developing visions and strategies for significant change, whether that be redefining the ideal worker and the structure of work itself, challenging workplace barriers to women, or addressing other social issues related to an organization's environment and mission. In short, the discouraging climate women encounter often depletes their energy for criticizing and changing public values. Even more, reminding women of their status as new-comers, it frequently can serve to strengthen in women the focus on fitting in that is already dominant in many workplaces—a self-centered focus on access, advancement, and financial goals. Most effective of all, in terms of undermining change, the climate of discouragement allows only a few women to advance to positions at the top where they can gain the degree of authority that gives them the best opportunity to change institutions. This climate also helps to ensure that the few who do arrive at the top have struggled so hard to get there that they may interpret their success in purely individual terms and condemn others for not being able to achieve what they have achieved. Women who reach the top are likely to have lost the motivation or energy for change they may have possessed.

WOMEN'S MORAL PREDICAMENT

Women's advancement in society appears to many to be primarily a matter of women "simply" overcoming their traditional exclusion from the public world. It is just a matter of time, the argument goes, until qualified women gain access to institutions of all kinds historically dominated by white men, until all women become full political, economic, and civic participants in public life. These developments are seen frequently as involving little institutional change or moral complexity. It is often assumed that the desirable goal is for women to fit as smoothly as possible into the established dynamics and pathways of the public world made by men. Women will leave behind their particular perspective and values and adopt the generic "human" values of public life formerly held by men alone. However, women's continuing cultural association with private values and responsibilities, and the climate of discouragement they often encounter, leads many to experience their situation at work as far more complex than this.

Women, especially mothers, face worrying and exhausting daily dilemmas related to the hard realities of pay, of juggling breadwinning and domestic commitments, and of negotiating family discord, workplace discrimination, and discouragement. Severally or together, such practical difficulties leave many women wondering whether their jobs are worth it: whether they are leading to better positions and, given the trade-offs, whether it is feasible and desirable to sustain the daily family logistics their work lives require. Meeting economic need is, for all but a comparative few, the paramount criterion in making this assessment. Semiskilled and unskilled welfare mothers, for example, cycle in and out of jobs looking for those that offer any slight edge in helping them provide for their children. As a recent study shows, this is because the jobs to which they have access in the low-wage labor market not only do not lead to other jobs that help them get ahead financially, but also pay poorly, rarely offer benefits, are physically demanding, require odd or irregular schedules, and leave them three times more likely than other workers in this job sector to be laid off.[42]

Yet when women of all kinds question their paid work, more is involved than simply practical concerns. The dominant cultural signals that motherhood is women's "real" work still reinforce in most women the expectation that motherhood rather than their paid work will serve as the central locus and source of their lives' meaning. To be sure, the circumstances and practice of motherhood vary dramatically by class, race, and ethnicity. Nevertheless, from the bottom to the top of the economic and social ladders, a strong cultural message has led women to perceive themselves and be perceived by society as living lives whose meaning is anchored by motherhood. A recent study of black teenage mothers found, for example, that these young women have been socialized both by the larger culture and by their immediate black culture to achieve independence, adulthood, and meaning *through* motherhood, increasingly single motherhood.[43] In contrast, because women's unpaid domestic labor and the traditional social emphasis on male "breadwinning" has allowed fatherhood to coexist easily with paid labor, most men have been more likely to see paid work as the anchor of their identity. Men, entitled by the traditional sexual division of labor, have believed it to be their right and responsibility to function as ideal workers.[44]

Most women, traditionally denied this right and responsibility, are situated culturally to bring a broader and more complex set of criteria than men to evaluating paid labor and its place in their lives. Straddling the private and public puts disadvantaged and privileged women alike at the intersection of the values of both worlds, encouraging them to weigh one set against the other. This is prompting many women to ask which values from both worlds carry the most meaning for their own lives, for the quality of other lives for which they are responsible, and for society. As they welcome not only the income, but also the engagement and satisfaction paid labor brings, many women also are likely to recognize the costs to family and community commitments this labor often represents. In the context of these costs, overwork, lack of opportunity, discouragement, and outright discrimination begin to weigh especially heavily.

What many women of all social groups are encountering in the workplace, in short, is a moral predicament. Paid work raises for them basic questions of meaning and value about their own identity, responsibility, purpose, and destiny in the workplace and more generally. For most, however pressing these questions are, economic necessity means they must remain secondary; few women are in a financial position to attempt to resolve them by moving to a more desirable position, starting their own enterprise, or leaving paid work altogether. Yet to a much greater degree than their male peers, colleagues, supervisors, and friends, women at all levels are encountering in paid work and institutional life a strong stimulus to deep personal reflection about *why* they are doing what they are doing. Too frequently, social critics analyze this reflection only in psychological terms, as if it were merely about mothers' guilt. But it is about a much more fundamental dis-ease than this.

The predicament many women encounter has to do with the effect on their sense of self of being thrust into a morally unsatisfactory position between two worlds. Many are concerned about where they are headed and who they are becoming; about how their paid work is affecting their unpaid personal and community commitments and the people they love; about whether this work is contributing to things they think are important in society; and about how to make this work incorporate more of the things in life that matter to them. These concerns are underscored by the fact that large numbers of women have entered mainstream institutions, including the professions, in the last two decades, just as acquisitive, self-centered values were becoming prevalent. They have encountered an ethos, especially among leading professionals, that emphasizes personal gain at the expense of the public interest and civic involvement. As Derek Bok's study of this ethos concludes:

> The principal failures of the past two decades—lagging productivity, shrinking savings, mounting deficits, growing poverty—all reflect an overweening desire to spend on ourselves and an inability either to care sufficiently for others or to keep from burdening future generations.[45]

Central to the values dilemmas women confront, therefore, is the challenge of whether or not they will *accept* the values that have come to dominate in the workplace, values that emphasize pursuit of self-interest and present human interaction as guided by an economic logic that gives priority to exchange and efficiency.

In most fields, there is abundant firsthand evidence that some women do not find it difficult to allow their own paid work to be shaped by these self-centered and materialist values. In fact, such women may never perceive the challenge at all. In the face of this evidence, it would be hard to claim that women as a group are possessed of a distinctively virtuous nature, one that disposes them to resist the ambition to succeed according to established norms and to earn the financial and other rewards of success. Moreover, whatever their economic circumstances, women, like men, are subject to the inducements and pressures to participate in the American culture of materialism that grew so strikingly in the 1980s. Many succumb to the consumerism that is the special disease of the mostly white middle-class in America. Not only the socializing power of modern institutions, furthermore, but also economic pressure induces numbers of women to conform to the existing values and norms of workplaces. Large numbers are trapped into working longer hours, to have some hope of maintaining their standard of living, by a national economy geared to an "insidious cycle of work-and-spend."[46] And this economic pressure on women has increased significantly in recent years as the earnings of male workers have fallen. The income of wives and mothers in managerial and professional jobs has become necessary to ensure that many families remain in the middle or upper classes, while the income of the far larger population of women in one full-time or multiple part-time, low-paying jobs is essential for many families to stay off welfare.[47]

For many women, however, whether or not to accept the prevailing workplace values that emphasize self-interest over public interest *is* a central challenge. A number would be led to question corporate values simply by their own individual makeup and histories. But they and many others are encouraged to be critical of the ethos of the public world especially by the expectation that they will conform to the male ideal worker model, accept secondary work status, or go elsewhere. For many women, in other words, the experience of feeling and being treated as "different" in the world of paid work defines a predicament that has important moral dimensions. Whether these dimensions are inchoate or sharply focused in the minds of employed women, most have a sense of them as pressing. Moral concerns impinge daily on their awareness as they negotiate the practical dilemmas we have been exploring.

We shall turn shortly to the main evidence for these concerns. But first it is worth noting here that their presence is particularly visible in the behavior of women executives because of the options these women have. For example, research shows that women at the top, more likely now than a decade ago to have children, often plan to leave their hard-won senior positions to seek other opportunities, rather than stay until retirement. Acutely aware of the barriers that block women's advancement, many of the few who break through the "glass ceiling" are burned out by the personal costs of both their experience on the job and their disproportionate load of family duties.[48] There is even some evidence that women on the pathway to senior status in legal and financial firms are especially likely to leave their positions because of the materialistic and individualistic values dominant at the top of their professions.[49]

The moral predicament women are encountering, however, involves more than the conflicts of value and meaning that arise from straddling the private and public worlds. It involves an even deeper moral problem stimulated for women, and therefore for the country, by changing social realities. This problem, the relationship between virtue and womanhood, has been, as we saw earlier, fundamental both to American culture and Western culture in general. Arising out of the ancient cultural assumption that women occupy a secondary moral status in society, it has been resolved from early modern times until the present by the domestic solution that defined the "good" woman as the married mother relegated to the home. Now the cultural problem of what constitutes "goodness" in women has been *re-opened*. The traditional domestic solution has lost the power to represent the reality or capture adequately the meaning of most women's lives. This is due chiefly to two things: the changes marriage as an institution is undergoing and the challenge to the traditional sexual division of labor represented by the unprecedented scale and access of contemporary American women's paid employment.

Women of all social groups are acutely aware of the crisis of the relationship between virtue and womanhood because it involves them directly. While many may be attracted by the hope that it is possible to go back, to revive the traditional domestic solution, doing so by *stretching* it to incorporate women's increasing participation in the public world is precisely the situation that many others find so inadequate as a way to sustain the values they wish to preserve. Still, because the moral dimensions of their predicament receive so little attention from progressive analysts of modern women's situation, including many feminist commentators, women who recognize the need to move forward are getting little help with the task they perceive, even if only dimly, of forging a new cultural meaning and moral status for womanhood.

RESPONDING TO THE PUBLIC ETHOS

Now we can see, in answer to the question we posed at the outset of this chapter, that most American women are encountering in the workplace significant barriers to the development of their own visions of authority and its public purposes. Ironically, by undermining in various ways women's progress toward realizing their full potential as participants in the public world, the gendered structure of paid work also is creating an important opportunity for them. The barriers women encounter are for many stimulating moral criticism of the public world and many of its values.

Women's perception of the need for moral criticism of American life and moral resolution of their own predicament is especially evident in the way many turn to the cultural rhetoric of gender difference. This rhetoric reflects the traditional cultural belief that women are morally different than men, that they possess distinctive nurturing, relational, and egalitarian traits. Many hold this belief today, whether they argue the traditional view that this difference is natural, inscribed in women's biological makeup, or the view more common in the late twentieth century that it is socialized, a result of nurture rather than nature. In either case, the belief in "difference" fuels the argument that women, by acting *like women* as they move into the world outside the home, will change public values instead of adopting them. They will instill in the public world the distinctive values and virtue of the private realm. Specifically, it is commonly argued that as women enter positions of authority in society and politics, they will bring new integrity and humanity to institutions, strengthening public sensitivity to social welfare obligations. Such popular claims find support in academic studies, hotly debated by scholars, which argue that women possess distinctive ways of reasoning morally, of knowing, of managing and leading, of thinking, and even of speaking.[50]

Sensing the moral dimensions of their workplace predicament, and its broader implications for American life, heightens many women's need for an authoritative moral response to the public ethos they are encountering. The cultural rhetoric of gender difference, ready at hand as it is, helps many women build workplace identity and confidence in a public world that still accords them secondary status. Asserting the distinctive value and values of femaleness, this rhetoric offers an alternative perspective on women's identity and on society that carries cultural weight. Many women use it to explain and signal their rejection of prevailing values and their affirmation of those that ought to guide women in public institutions. Women politicians in both parties provide highly visible examples of how this rhetoric is used in women's analyses of their significance as workers. For example, Madeleine Kunin, former Governor of Vermont and Deputy Secretary of Education in the Clinton administration, writes in her autobiography of learning that women in politics need to rely "on our female instincts and let them surface, realizing that this [is] why we [are] there, to be different."[51] Likewise, arguing that women have special capacities and the responsibility to bring them to the public world, Elizabeth Dole, President of the American Red Cross and Secretary of Labor in the Bush administration, in a 1993 speech to Radcliffe College alumnae, advised women in the workplace to ask "'Why can't a woman be more like a woman?' rather than 'Why can't a woman be more like a man?'"[52] Both Kunin and Dole reflect the common view that the values that characterize women's behavior can and should change the public world.

Such beliefs about women's domestic "nature" and its translation to the public world are reassuring to women, as well as men, in the face of the profound social change represented by the majority of American mothers working outside the home. In the nineteenth century, traditional cultural beliefs about women's distinctive traits served a similar function. They justified women's activity in the world outside the home at a time when women were expected not to be active in public matters or settings at all. Then clergy could be counted on, as some can today, to spell out this social expectation and the cultural values women put at risk by claiming public authority. So, for example, in 1837 the General Association of Massachusetts ministers admonished women working for the abolition of slavery:

> We invite your attention to the dangers which at present seem to threaten the female character with wide spread and permanent injury. . . . [W]hen she assumes the place and tone of man as a public reformer . . . she yields the power which God has given her for protection, and her character becomes unnatural. . . . [W]e cannot, therefore, but regret the mistaken conduct of those who encourage females to bear an obtrusive and ostentatious part in measures of reform, and countenance any of that sex who so far forget themselves as to itinerate in the character of public lecturers and teachers.[53]

Women reformers, responding to the central issue in such admonitions—the nature of "the female character"— legitimized their public reform activity by appealing to the very thing that the ministers thought should keep them home: their supposed peculiar virtue as mothers and homemakers. These women successfully claimed, however, that their God-given devotion to helping others gave them a *duty* to engage in public life to improve its moral quality. Thus, by characterizing women's actions as selfless, belief in women's difference went a long way toward quelling spoken and unspoken fears about their seeking or achieving power in the public world, inspiring and allowing women to accomplish much there.

Today, a similar thing is happening. The rhetoric of difference continues to be used to provide legitimacy for women whose action in the public world raises fears about changing cultural norms of authority. Beliefs about women's different nature provide justification for claims about women's value in public settings, while denying that anything fundamental has changed. For example, women executives reported in a recent influential study that women have a distinctive interactive leadership style that "comes 'naturally'" and is based in sharing power and information, in contrast to men's hierarchical and power-seeking style.[54] One of the most vivid illustrations, however, of appeal to the power of beliefs about gender difference is Senator Patricia Schroeder's (Democrat of Colorado) strategic defense of Hillary Rodham Clinton. At a Denver forum on health-care reform in March of 1994, introducing Clinton and seeking to support her original prominence in the administration against those attacking it, Schroeder claimed that the First Lady "only wanted power to *help* somebody, not to be somebody."[55]

Yet the rhetoric of gender difference is used to do more than justify contemporary women's appearance in new numbers, new places, and at new levels of authority in the public world. It speaks to contemporary women's accurate sense that they need a moral language to *respond* to the moral dimensions of both their own predicament and the country's. Many women are not persuaded by arguments that the rhetoric of difference promotes a cultural stereotype of them, limiting their efforts to achieve equality or to gain public authority, precisely because such arguments do not address their moral concerns.

Women employ this rhetoric not just because it is familiar or still culturally authoritative, but because it seems to many to hold reliable and desirable truth. It seems to hold a vision and promise of how women can make a difference. Moreover, this rhetoric seems to do so despite modern biology's knowledge that moral traits have no simple biological basis and that no direct link can be established between human biology and behavior.[56] And it seems to do so, as well, despite refutation of the alternate claim that women's distinctive values are a product of nurture, of socialization to a set of values culturally associated with motherhood and the private sphere. The "truth" of this rhetoric also seems impervious, that is, to argument that there is no automatic correlation between internalized values and actual behavior that allows us to predict the values that will characterize women's thought and action.[57] Whether based on nature or nurture, the power of the rhetoric of difference persists because, as women's use of this rhetoric attests, many espouse the values it associates with them; they have, or see themselves as having, an investment in them. The rhetoric appears to many, in sum, to be a good moral response to the personal and social predicament they perceive.

Once we recognize the important moral concerns of women and take them seriously, we can ask a far less common, but equally important question: Is the rhetoric of gender difference adequate to the purpose for which many women use it? Is it equal to the task, that is, of providing moral criticism of American life today and resolving the moral predicament in which women find themselves? I want to suggest that it is precisely as a moral strategy that the value of this rhetoric is most limited and that the most important criticism of it can be made.

Instead of providing the moral insight and guidance women seek in order to address the profound social change taking place, this rhetoric masks crucial dimensions of this change. Most important, it actually keeps women from recognizing and addressing *moral* questions regarding their agency, claim to authority, and public effectiveness. By carrying a program and strategy for public improvement that are implicit, that is, this rhetoric functions most often to short-circuit women's own development of both. For example, the claim that women are nonhierarchical offers an implied vision and model of change that all too often *takes the place* of women's developing new public vision, goals, and strategies for effective institutional and social change. This is due in large part to the fact that the rhetoric's criticism of self-interest as an organizing principle in public life and its suggestion of the value of incorporating greater attention to affiliative and communal needs is not fully articulated or developed.[58] Moreover, the model of change implicit in this rhetoric suggests that change will occur as a function of women's mere presence in public settings in a critical mass. Thus, this rhetoric encourages a simplified view both of what it takes to bring significant change to structures as large and complex

as modern institutions and of the power of these institutions to resist certain kinds of change. At the same time, by emphasizing
women's distinctiveness, the rhetoric of difference undermines
women's readiness to construct values alliances across, as well as
within, gender lines.

In short, while belief in difference quite rightly identifies values
to which culture and society have oriented many contemporary
women, the logic it promotes actually helps undermine these values. It does so mainly by obscuring the need for women to claim
the authority to criticize existing values and structures of public institutions, to assess how domestic values espoused by women translate into visions for changing these settings, and to develop alliances and strategies for implementing change. In order to respond
to their very real moral predicament, women at all levels in the
workplace need to become critical evaluators of the moral dimension of traditional beliefs about public and private, of their own
lives and work, and of the lives of institutions. If they wish to set
different courses than those which public institutions are offering
them and the nation, they will need to rethink both the missions
and social obligations of institutions of all kinds and the relationship between them. Setting new courses will involve all women in
learning to claim public authority, whether as citizens or officials,
for their new visions of the good for individuals, institutions, and
society as a whole.

CONCLUSION

The moral predicament women face presents an opportunity rich
with possibility and rife with danger, both for them and for the nation. It signals an important moment in which many women are
hesitating on the verge of being socialized to the existing norms of
the public world or to a reconfigured secondary role and status
within it. In this moment, struggling to gain a critical perspective
on social and cultural patterns which have significantly shaped
their lives, women can begin to formulate a new agenda for American society and give shape to new public visions.

Women's moral predicament raises larger questions of meaning and value about basic aspects of the structure of American life, including society's definition of adult paid work, the relationship of this work to families and communities, and the very nature of adult responsibility and authority. The political and religious right answers these questions by reasserting traditional social arrangements, whose demise is well-documented, as the only arrangements congruent with nature's plan for human life. But *progressive* analysis is missing from the current debate about the crisis of American values. The challenge progressives face is to recognize and address the transformations that have taken place in social arrangements in order to make structural provision, at the heart of society, for men's and women's family and community commitments and the unpaid work needed to sustain them. Whether women take the lead in calling the nation to meet this challenge depends on whether they seize the opportunity to reflect self-consciously and self-critically on the larger social significance of their daily struggles.

This brings us to the real task that confronts contemporary women, that of developing new public vision and implementing it effectively. This task receives comparatively little attention because traditional cultural beliefs about public and private do not associate women with the capacity to formulate vision for society as a whole. Where will women find encouragement and energy for this task? Where will they find a moral resource for assessing their predicament and its larger implications that is more adequate than the shorthand of gender difference?

Women will find such a resource where they least expect to: in the public achievements of nineteenth- and early-twentieth-century American women reformers. These are still widely unknown outside of academia and until recently were all but obscured within academia as well. Nineteenth- and early-twentieth-century women and their public agendas were rendered largely invisible by traditional histories focused on public life as a sphere of male actors and activity. The twin assumptions that public activity is what men do and that women are domestic not public actors had produced the truth they presupposed: traditional scholars of American society and politics did not expect to see women on the stage of public life and did not find them there. Historians of women in recent decades have challenged these accounts, recovering nineteenth- and early-twentieth-century women's public tradition.

Even once they know it is there, however, modern American women might not turn to this public tradition, thinking it irrelevant. At first glance, it does not appear that the experience of women reformers who were overwhelmingly Christian, white, middle-class, and not employed outside the home, has much light to shed on the situation of modern women, in all their racial and ethnic, religious, and economic diversity, most of whom are in the paid labor force. In fact, however, the experience of this historical group has much to say to both modern women and the nation. First of all, the sheer scope of what these women reformers accomplished in public life, with few resources other than initiative and resolve, is inspiring. More than this, many women today share a commitment similar to theirs: a commitment both to equal rights and to institutionalizing in the public world concern for the welfare of others and commitment to fostering the public good. Because the work of these reformers over the course of more than a century is the major instance of this commitment in American history, it serves as a crucial resource for positive lessons and negative ones as well.

Most of all, it is because these reformers' actions and words constitute an explicitly *moral* discourse about their own and the nation's social predicament that they are so valuable for contemporary women. In particular, their discourse challenged the set of dominant cultural beliefs about public and private in America that were then still couched in overtly Christian language, not yet having taken on their more secular modern form. This discourse offers modern women an important guide to the complex moral prescriptions in these beliefs that they are *still* confronting in the structure of American life and institutions. Thus, the moral concerns of women reformers hold insights relevant to modern women. Moreover, in creating the cultural expectation that women are "social housekeepers" who will clean up the world outside the home, these reformers refashioned the traditional beliefs contemporary women have inherited. Critical assessment of the way women reformers and their leaders construed the moral dimensions of their social situation and their efforts at social reform can help modern women understand more fully the moral dimensions of their own public participation. Such assessment can help women today break out of existing patterns of thought about public and private, weaken the hold of these patterns on society, and develop new and progressive vision for American life.

In short, if modern women are to sustain for themselves and the nation private values many hold dear, they must move forward to change the public world of American institutions. What will it take to do so? What should this change look like? The moral discourse of nineteenth- and early-twentieth-century women reformers, who put similar goals on the map of American public life, has much light to shed on the answers to these questions. But before we can explore what positive and negative lessons this discourse has to offer, we must first ask why it and the relationship between women's struggles for rights and for social improvement have been ignored even by many feminist historians. Understanding how women reformers and their social situation have been interpreted will help open up to us in important new ways not only the past, but also the present and future.

CHAPTER FIVE

Recovering Women's Public Tradition

We are prone to think that historically women have not claimed the authority to speak about American public life, that they are on the verge now of doing so for the first time. But this is wrong. White and black "organized women" of the nineteenth and early twentieth century built a major tradition of public vision and activism through which they asserted their right and responsibility "to speak for the welfare of the whole society."[1] This tradition, which can inspire and offer guidance to modern women, was obscured almost entirely by mainstream histories. In recent decades, historians of women have begun to make it visible. And yet, because not all of what organized women were saying fits these historians' idea of a feminist public agenda, even this new history has kept us from hearing fully these voices from the past.

The interpretation that initially dominated American women's history linked the public agendas of both nineteenth- and early-twentieth-century reformers and contemporary women in a way that gave priority to their struggles for equal rights. This interpretation reflected basic assumptions about the proper destiny of women in American democratic society, defining from modern feminist perspectives the goals that should guide women's public participation. It shaped what has been the governing approach to understanding not only women's past, but their situation in the present. Indeed, it is still popularly assumed that the movement for woman's rights is the only significant tradition of women's public achievement in the past.[2] Fed primarily by mainstream histories and photographs, our imagination pictures marching women carrying suffrage signs, their large hats shading intent white faces, emerging from their homes onto the public stage in order to demand the right to vote. We have been taught by leading historians of women to think that more than anything the struggle for equal rights constituted then, and constitutes now, women's claim to full participation in public life.

Ironically, this focus on rights fit in fundamental ways the set of dominant traditional beliefs about public and private in American society whose descriptive accuracy and prescriptive desirability is challenged by many scholars of women's history. This rights focus emphasized access to the white, male public arena over women's broader civic agenda. It devalued the range and significance of the historical public efforts of women reformers of elite groups, while failing almost completely to represent those of black, ethnic minority, and wage-earning women.

In fact, human welfare achievements, of which emphasis on equal rights was a part, were the most prominent aspect of nineteenth- and early-twentieth-century women's public leadership. Only quite recently, however, have several important studies begun to illuminate the major traditions of effective public initiative for social improvement developed by white and black reformers.[3] Women reformers forged these traditions despite being excluded from formal citizenship, positions in mainstream institutions, or direct access to the resources of those institutions.

Unlike many modern historians of women, these reformers did not see their struggles for civil, legal, economic, and educational rights as distinct from their other efforts to improve the social condition of women or from their goal of general social improvement. Twin commitments to rights and welfare guided the public efforts of both white and black women as they organized separately at local and national levels. The two commitments were integrally linked. To the reformers, women were simultaneously a priority in their own right and agents crucial to larger purposes.

Thus, through much of the nineteenth century and into the

twentieth, black organized women joined their focus on women to their work on behalf of equal rights for the black race, as did numbers of white women, at midcentury especially, in the antislavery movement. Race "up-lift" was the language in which both black and white reformers articulated their concern for improving the quality of life in American society, in particular in its rapidly emerging cities, where industrialization multiplied misery. Black women worked to lift the black race out of oppression and poverty and thereby, as they saw it, to uplift the human race in general. White women also spoke of improving the moral and social condition of the human race as a whole, commonly assuming that in improvement too their own race would continue to set the human standard.

Over and over again through the decades, organized women of both races defined public priorities, offered social services, identified issues of justice, created momentum and consensus for legislative and policy change, and created new local and national institutions:

> In the early days women built orphan asylums and homes for aged widows and spinsters; by the 1930's the landscape was covered with libraries, schools, colleges, kindergartens, museums, health clinics, houses of refuge, school lunch programs, parks, playgrounds, all of which owed their existence to one or several women's societies.[4]

Equally as striking as the quality of leadership, creativity, political skill, and persistence that produced their public achievements was the sheer initiative women demonstrated in banding together in thousands of local associations and national networks to tackle particular social problems.

The following brief list gives a vivid flavor of the types of associations they established: the Society for the Relief of Poor Widows with Small Children; the Female Moral Reform Society (to reform prostitution and the legal and moral double standard it represented); the Colored Female Produce Society (to boycott slave-made products); the Boston Fragment Society (an elite white women's multipurpose benevolence association) and the Daughters of Africa (a working-class, black mutual-aid society); the Female Benevolent Society (for abandoned women); the Brooklyn Female Bible Society; the Association for the Relief of Respectable, Aged, Indigent Females; the Female Anti-Slavery Society; the Northern Ohio Soldiers' Aid Society (to supply Ohio soldiers in the Civil War), the Colored Ladies' Soldiers Aid Society (to aid black soldiers), the Hebrew Ladies Soldiers' Aid Society; the Female Bethel Society (to aid destitute widows and children of seamen); the Ladies' Temperance League; Female Protective Unions (organizations of sewing women to seek protection from wage exploitation) and the Ladies' Helping Hand Association (to teach working girls sewing and needlework); the Women's Foreign Missionary Society (Methodist) and the Women's Baptist Home Mission Society; the Woman's Health Protective Association (public health); the Young Women's Christian Association; the Women's Educational and Industrial Union; the New England Woman's Club; the Woman's Association for the Betterment of Public School Houses in North Carolina; and the Women's Trade Union League.

The programs and institutions built by organized women were aimed at improving the quality of human life. They focused on a range of social problems in addition to poverty, including "slavery, education, alcohol abuse, prostitution, women's wages, child labor, industrial pollution, occupational health and safety, the depletion of natural resources, juvenile justice."[5] And, while some modern scholars of civil society argue that community ties and consciousness are often a *by-product* of social activities organized for purposes other than strengthening the social fabric,[6] these reformers *set out* to increase the sense of community responsibility they believed was the key to social progress. As they did so, the institutions they created to serve the priorities they identified set in place many of the democratic and humane resources of American communities. Today we assume these resources were always an integral part of the conception of American government, but they were not. Scholars are just beginning to recognize that the public achievements of these women and the politics that produced them laid the foundations for social policy and the American welfare state.[7]

Yet to recover this full public tradition of nineteenth- and twentieth-century black and white women reformers, and the distinctive visions of American society that drove it, we must go further even than most recent scholarship that demonstrates the public significance of these women's human welfare work. We must challenge the limited conception of women's moral agency in claiming public authority that still guides many histories of women. We also must recognize the fundamentally progressive elements of the moral discourse that shaped and were expressed in women reformers' actions and words. This discourse played a crucial role in motivating women to organize on a massive national scale to help women, children, the poor, and others in need. It galvanized white and black women into civic action on behalf of their own visions of social and racial priorities at a time when, even more than now, public effectiveness was defined in terms of the agenda and actions of white male citizens and officials. What made the difference when women made a difference in public life, through their myriad voluntary associations, was their vision of how the moral and social order of the nation needed to be improved.

Before we can explore critically, on its own terms, the progressive moral agency women asserted in both their welfare and rights initiatives, however, it is necessary to examine the assumptions that shaped the once dominant focus on equal rights that obscured this agency. Understanding these assumptions will not only help to correct our view of the past, but will also revise the way we think about women and American public life in the present. Many of these same assumptions continue to color interpretation of the public purposes contemporary women might pursue. I refer to assumptions that the importance of rights outweighs and is distinct from that of social responsibility as a public agenda for women; that becoming full public participants is a legal, economic, political, and even psychological challenge for women, but not a moral and cultural one; and that religion is always conservative and an instrument of women's oppression.

ASSESSING HISTORICAL INTERPRETATION

As we have seen, much of the history of American women has been depicted in relationship to the priority scholars placed on women's rights and on women organizing to challenge established power and radically transform their lives.[8] There can be little argument with this emphasis. The suffrage, increased civil and political rights under law, was as a "symbol and guarantee of all other rights" an achievement crucial to progress.[9] Neither can there be argument with histories that emphasize the evolution of women's economic rights; important progress for women is charted too by scholarly focus on their paid work and decreasing labor force discrimination. However, every definition of progress involves judgments about what constitutes it and what does not. These judgments were the historical lenses that brought women's rights to the center of our vision and pushed other historical data to the margins.

In addition, the placement of the suffragist and her public activity at the center of interpretation of the nineteenth- and early-twentieth-century women's movement involved multilayered value judgments about what *kind* of woman represents progress. Most scholars of women's history think that they do not and should not concern themselves with what constitutes a "good" woman. Furthermore, those who place emphasis on rights see the case for equality as one that is largely self-evident and avoids these other questions. Yet whether they recognize it or not, as they interpret historical data scholars inevitably are making judgments about who women should be, what their social roles and destiny should be, what the nature of their agency as human beings should be, and how race, ethnic identity, and class affect all these things. They do so in the context, furthermore, of judgments made in past and present by the dominant culture about the same set of issues: Who and what is a "good" woman? Rather than attempting to avoid these unavoidable issues, historians need to be even more self-conscious and self-critical about evaluating these interacting layers of judgments.

Scholars of women of color in America have unmasked a number of the judgments about womanhood that have focused historical lenses on marching suffragists. They criticize this concentration on the public status of white women reformers for its implication that these women represented all American women and their progress.[10] This criticism has helped reveal the extent to which much initial interpretation of historical women took the white, male public sphere as its standard. Assuming the importance of access to this particular public arena helped determine for many scholars which women's history carried the significant story of women's progress as a group. Their historical perspective, which viewed women's alternatives as claiming their natural difference from men *or* claiming equality, focused on women's gaining access to opportunities and legal status equal with those of men in American society. Furthermore, these historians defined women's progress into the public arena as necessitating above all their movement away from domestic confinement, which historians viewed as the cause of their sexual inequality.[11]

It is ironic, therefore, that this view of progress continued to reflect in one basic respect dominant cultural beliefs the nineteenth century helped to fashion about how women differ from men. It reflected the values hierarchy that in that period strengthened the cultural link between the emblems of women's secondary status: religion, morality, and motherhood. Many histories of American women are shaped by the assumption that gaining equality required women to leave behind these emblems of their difference from the male standard. It is this assumption which drives many scholars to distinguish rights feminism from human welfare feminism and to associate religion, morality, and motherhood with the latter.

Thus, before we read any one of a number of influential histories of nineteenth- and early-twentieth-century women, we must recognize that they represent implicit judgments about what it is important for us to see and not to see. The history of nineteenth-century women originally was presented as the history of the modern women's rights movement. Many historians "raised the quest for suffrage and the claim of equality as the standard for the nineteenth-century woman's movement as a whole, and classifie[d] anything else as a type of 'domestic feminism,' an inferior variety which mounted no challenge to the male hierarchy."[12] Embedded in this historical interpretation was a particular model of change and public values that did not view rights and civic responsibility as equally important or compatible, but gave the former priority over the latter. This framework of interpretation distinguished between the "protofeminist" (voluntary), "less successful" women's movement and the "genuine" (equal rights), "successful" feminist movement.[13] Women's challenge to men and male dominance represented by the search for legal equality was presented as a more liberal and radical call for change than their agenda of other public priorities, which began with helping women, especially women in need.

Although this view of the choices facing organized women as "difference *or* equality" is consistent with the main philosophy of the modern women's movement, this was not the way these reformers looked at themselves and their world.[14] Rights and difference were mixed in their philosophies, not neatly dichotomized. These women's experience was complex, but it has been simplified by being interpreted in terms of established cultural meanings of public and private. As a result of this still influential dichotomy, much that was new about what women reformers envisioned and did continues to be overlooked. How did we arrive at a view of historical and contemporary women that construes their alternatives in terms of public *or* private, equality *or* difference, and rights *or* social responsibility?

We must recognize, first, that American historians are part of the culture whose history they write. While their viewpoints reflect a certain diversity, their fundamental assumptions have been shaped by the same beliefs about public and private that have shaped the society they chronicle. This is equally true of feminist historians, even though they are critics of the gender inequality that characterizes American culture and society. These historians have been pioneers in challenging the definition of history as properly a male-centered account of public events and figures. Indeed, the traditional cultural distinction between public and private that has shaped American society and its historical interpretation was one of their primary discoveries in the process of recovering the history of women and reconstructing our view of the past. Feminist historians showed us that this distinction is less a fully accurate description of the way society has worked than a set of beliefs about the way it ought to work. Furthermore, the fact that they need to recover data about women's lives testifies to a fundamental feature of this set of traditional beliefs: the asymmetry that places higher value on men and public life than on women and private life.

We might expect, therefore, that historians of women would have registered early on the *full* scope and significance of organized women's public tradition, recognizing their human welfare achievements as formative influences on the nation's social and political life. And yet, that significant attention has been given to these achievements only in the last several years illustrates how deep the cultural roots of our beliefs about public and private run. These beliefs helped make the struggle for equality *the* priority in women's history because they make the rights-bearing individual the norm for participation in the American public sphere. Influenced by these beliefs, scholars viewed attack on gender inequality as women's most important public activity, and looked historically for the emerging feminist consciousness that was the antecedent to modern feminism (as they defined it).[15] Although they had left behind much of the influence of male-centered historical models, these scholars assumed that gaining rights, along with access to the formal political system, constituted women's significant public agenda. They also assumed that women reformers could never be real public actors without the formal citizenship and access these rights confer. Many feminist historians, therefore, identified women reformers' human welfare efforts with humane values in American society, but not with civic authority, political effectiveness, or public vision.

In short, instead of critically assessing women reformers' efforts on their own terms, many scholars evaluated them in terms of the male standards of the dominant cultural conception of the public sphere. These standards reflect deep skepticism about religion, morality, and motherhood. This skepticism *still* colors much inter-pretation of both the rights and human welfare movements of nineteenth- and early-twentieth-century women, and it sustains the view that the two movements were more different than alike. Moreover, this skepticism continues to obscure the full public sig-nificance of women's social improvement activities because they were religiously based and motivated, presented in the language of nineteenth- and early-twentieth-century morality, and carried out largely by white and black married mothers, who lacked the legal rights and status of citizens.

RELIGION

Historians of women increasingly have recognized the roots of or-ganized women's voluntary associations and moral reform in their religious affiliations. Nonetheless, because religion has played a powerful role in the historical subordination of women, many his-torians who emphasized equal rights regarded religion as a barrier to women's progress. They expected true feminists to share this view, tending to see women like Elizabeth Cady Stanton, who ap-peared to them to have rejected religion, as the leading edge of wom-en's progress. Indeed, in writing the chronicle of this progress, these scholars often employed rejection of religion as a chief standard in evaluating women reformers and their public activities. They as-sociated a secular orientation with women reformers' efforts to ad-vance women's rights, while associating religious motivation with reformers' initiatives that did not break free of belief in women's "difference." Thus, many scholars contrasted Stanton, who scath-ingly (and brilliantly) criticized the Christian church for its teaching that women are morally inferior to men, with Frances Willard and her followers, who remained within the institutional fold.

Assuming that religion is predominantly a conservative force from which women must and will be rescued by modernity allowed scholars to close their eyes to the complexity of the religious character of *both* radical and conservative reformers' public activity. Hence, the dominant historical interpretation established the pattern of avoiding serious investigation of white middle-class Christianity or of the broader social and cultural impact of religion across class, race, and ethnic boundaries—from the black churches to Roman Catholicism, Judaism, and the largely female religion of Spiritualism.

This interpretation reflected a simpler analytical pattern that fit scholars' predisposition to dismiss religion in analyzing women reformers and their society. In this pattern, nineteenth-century mainstream evangelicalism often was allowed to stand for Protestantism in general and was equated with the conservatism of the modern Christian right. Overlooking the possibility of liberal religion, historians of the movement for woman's rights also often interpreted the waning of the revivals after midcentury as a sign that religion itself had become a waning social force. This still influential pattern of analysis projects onto the past a characterization of national politics typical in the present. It sees the modern political configuration of secular liberals and radicals and the religious right as appearing by the second half of the nineteenth century. In a recent study, one scholar of women makes this explicit:

> Indeed, what is striking . . . is how like our own times the relationship of morality to social change had become. Liberals and radicals, those concerned with ameliorating or transforming societal conditions, turned to the state—and to a secular rhetoric—for their legitimacy and appeal. When those who adopted the evangelical voice appealed to government, they did so with the intent of institutionalizing religious control over an increasingly secular nation.[16]

Thus, many scholars still interpret religion as a hallmark of individuals and public efforts undermined either by conservative, sentimental (ineffective) piety or by theocratic disregard for separation of church and state. They justify their minimal investigation of religion's historical role by the assumption that liberals and radicals who advanced the public interest and power of women in the past (as in the present) left religion behind. And they find confirmation for this assumption in the growing dissociation of religion from both masculinity and the public sphere in the nineteenth century.

This lack of depth in the treatment and appreciation of religion as a significant factor tells us more about the values of modern scholars than about the lives of historical women. These modern values have been reinforced by the separation in academic life between historical and religious studies. This separation encourages many feminist scholars in religion, whose strength lies in critical assessment of value and meaning, to stop short of social and historical analysis of the public and political implications of their theoretical formulations. At the same time, it encourages many feminist scholars in other humanities fields and the social sciences not to pursue the moral and explicitly religious dimensions of their analysis of American public life.

Yet biblical religion—traditions, especially Christianity, that draw on the texts of the Hebrew Bible and the New Testament— shaped the lives and public achievements of black and white nineteenth- and early-twentieth-century women reformers. Furthermore, while religion may have been on the wane after midcentury as a significant institutional force in the male-dominated public sphere, it drove *women's* reform goals from the antebellum period through the reforms of the Progressive era. Kathryn Sklar, who more than most historians attends to religion as an important variable in the activism of nineteenth- and early-twentieth-century women, argues that until 1920 moral and religious traditions had "colossal significance" for women's political culture.[17]

However, as a result of scholarly attempts to minimize the role of religion, especially as a constructive element in women's politics, this significance is poorly understood. Despite the common effort to distinguish between women activists who accepted established religion and those who rejected it, the line between reformers who have been labeled "rights" and "difference" feminists was not as clear as it has been made out to be. Radical "rights" feminists, including Stanton, were religious, even if deeply critical of Christianity; "difference" feminists, including evangelicals, were not always religiously conservative, even if unwilling to leave the church. Furthermore, the religious worldviews of women reformers who first mobilized under the banner of temperance and those who made equal rights their priority from the start led both groups to claim equal rights for women on the basis of their full moral accountability in the eyes of God. It is not possible to contrast radicals who drew chiefly on "secular" rights traditions with conservatives who drew on a Christian one.[18]

Similarly, neither group of reformers can be distinguished neatly from the other with regard to belief in difference. For Stanton, women's claim to moral equality with men did not mean sameness. She believed in difference to some degree, as she illustrated by her argument that giving women the vote would bring the nation the benefit of women's unique contribution to regenerating society:

> It is this underlying faith of women in human nature, this love of the weak and forsaken who most need it. . . . The day is dawning in which our creeds and codes are to be essentially modified by this diviner element destined to work to radical reconstruction in society.[19]

And despite the fact that Willard argued chiefly in terms of the special contribution to be made to the public world by wives and mothers, it was moral *equality* she claimed. What really distinguished Stanton's position from that of more religiously conservative women was not rejection of difference, but her desire to engage head-on the cultural paradox regarding women's moral nature that religion had played a powerful role in fashioning. Unlike more conservative women reformers (and modern feminist scholars), Stanton believed women's equality depended on *uprooting* the Christian teaching deep in American culture that sustains women's moral inferiority by claiming that their socially constraining roles as wives and mothers make them morally superior.

While radical and conservative women reformers differed on this question of challenging organized religion,[20] they shared a basic orientation to rights and to society as a whole that came in large part from their deep "religious sensibility." A liberal Protestant sensibility influenced mainstream antebellum women reformers' rights thinking and linked it to a broad public agenda:

> The content of their rights thinking was informed by a deeply religious sensibility which stressed the interconnections between rights and responsibilities, between civil and domestic relations, and between the workings of the state and of the home. Suffrage did not automatically take pride of place in the panoply of rights women sought in the period before the Civil War, but stood as one goal among many, and not the most important. Further, rights consciousness was originally rooted in domestic concerns for many women, who saw them as a means of achieving protection for themselves and their families while pursuing the ends of social justice.[21]

This religious sensibility, fundamentally liberal in its concern for rights and for the vulnerable in society, continued throughout the nineteenth century and into the twentieth to influence both the rights and social welfare activism of the majority of reformers.

For numbers of white, middle-class women, religion may have been the sentimental, otherworldly piety accentuating the split between sacred and secular that some scholars argue it was. And there is no doubt that biblical religion reinforced the norm of women's exclusion from the developing "secular" state and marketplace. Nevertheless, religion was not for all women merely a social constraint or a set of passively accepted doctrines. It inspired many with the goal of the perfectibility of human beings preached by the evangelical revivals of the first half of the nineteenth century. The legacy of this teaching echoed down the decades, encouraging numbers of women to continue to exert the "prodigious influence" they had first discovered when the revivals inadvertently expanded their role outside the home.[22] For these women, religion was a tool to be fashioned and used in service of this goal. It was something women reformers not only received, but also shaped themselves.

Many scholars miss women's role as interpreters of religion because they understand religion as almost categorically conservative politically, and also as mainly institutional and increasingly marginal in a secularizing society. Taking a clergy-centered view of religion, scholars are likely to overlook the degree to which women reformers' relationship to religion was not defined and controlled by men or by male theological meanings. Some historical accounts, for example, judge whether religion was a major stimulus to reformers' work based on the degree to which Protestant *ministers* supported or restrained women's public efforts. Furthermore, women's unofficial theological role is overlooked as a major variable in nineteenth- and early-twentieth-century history because the majority of scholars not only focus on male-led religious institutions, but also identify theology with men and their published, systematic doctrinal expositions in the Calvinist tradition.

Ann Douglas, a scholar of Victorian literature, reinforces this approach to nineteenth-century religion in her influential study *The Feminization of American Culture*.[23] Douglas argues that this century witnessed the "loss of theology" with the loss of public authority previously enjoyed both by Calvinist doctrine itself and by male clergy respected for their intellect as well as piety. Many historians of women have accepted her theoretical framework with its uncritical repetition of the Christian and American cultural norm that identifies masculinity with truth and public authority. As a result, historians have been led to interpret religion's increasing association with women and the private sphere, by the second half of the nineteenth century, as a sign of its waning social influence. Douglas's identification of "real" theology with male leadership, male statements, and male texts overlooks the reformers' theology because it was expressed by *women* in *action* and *speech*. In fact, women reformers' theological vision, which was as evident among rights activists as others, amounted not to a "loss" of traditional

Christian theology, but to a practical and public criticism and re-construction of it. Some scholars fail to recognize this because they accept the boundaries to women's moral agency set by traditional male theology.

As a consequence, scholars of women often miss the fact that for organized women religion was not simply a motivation for social reform, but a resource for formulating the vision to guide reform. Across a religious and political spectrum, both radical and conservative white and black women reformers and their leaders *reinterpreted* the meaning of religious symbols and values, expressing their theological perspectives in action that reflected varying degrees of independence of mind and will. Although they differed significantly in whether they saw a need to reform established religion, all reformers were engaged in this process of reconstruction, taking from religion their sense of women's rights *and* responsibilities as human beings before God. Employing biblical principles of justice to criticize both society and religion itself, they arrived at positions that were not completely divergent, but rather gave different emphases to rights and responsibilities and expressed differing theologies.

The most radical women's rights advocates, such as the Spiritualists, found a framework for their actions in a profound religious sensibility, and religion gave them the terms for the fullest expression of their radicalism.[24] They took from religion the moral standard against which even male supremacy itself might be evaluated and found wanting, condemning "the authority of any human being over any other human being because it usurped the authority of God by interfering with the autonomy of a moral agent."[25] Indeed, Stanton, like other Spiritualists quite willing to reject established religion, in particular Christianity, nevertheless consistently placed herself and women's fight for suffrage in the tradition of the sixteenth-century Protestant reformers Luther, Calvin, and Knox.[26] Her protest against Christian misogyny, which she likened to their protest against the oppression of Rome, opposed any authority that attempted to insert itself between the individual con-

science and God. And she condemned men's effort to subordinate
women in the name of a higher standard of justice, which she referred to constantly as "the Spirit of all Good," "God," "our ideal
great first cause," or most frequently "the God of justice, mercy,
and truth."[27] Herself a sophisticated religious thinker, Stanton recognized the power of religion in American culture in shaping
women's lives. She adapted the Protestantism of those earlier reformers to women's situation, arguing in the *Woman's Bible* the need
for women to reinterpret biblical text by the light of their own reason, not of the church's authority.[28] Her moral and political claim
was that divine truth, properly understood, called into question all
forms of oppression.

As we shall see, women reformers who were more religiously
conservative shared with radicals this sense of women's direct accountability to God. Accountability authorized the moral autonomy that all reformers demonstrated in the independence of their
public actions and that was sharply criticized by the clergy and
other men. Likewise, conservatives and radicals alike took Christian beliefs about motherhood as a fundamental starting point in
their reconstruction of traditional Christian theology, although
radicals like Stanton soon moved beyond identifying women with
the maternal role. Thinking and acting theologically, they used
motherhood as a metaphor to assert their God-given responsibility
and right to act, translating motherhood into a warrant for the civic
authority denied them by religion and society. Among white
women reformers, those who were less radical with regard to the
reform of religion made motherhood the focal point of their reinterpretation and social application of religious meaning.

Missing the significance of the reformers' religious vocabulary
and biblical references as a medium of self-expression, however,
many scholars mistake use of both for failure to challenge the subordination represented by the private sphere. Their assumptions
about women and religion lead them to believe that only *non*religious and *non*domestic language signals the historical emergence of
women's full public agency. Yet even when it was religiously and

politically conservative, organized women's employment of this language was not rote repetition of fixed doctrine or symbolic meaning. It represented instead an assertive *appropriation* of religious authority and social power. Women reformers across the political and religious spectrum used religious authority as both guide and shield in their efforts to claim the right to shape public reality.

Frances Willard, head of the Woman's Christian Temperance Union and a woman as prominent and revered in her time as Eleanor Roosevelt was later,[29] illustrates best the error of interpreting even the religious language of more theologically conservative women as de facto conforming. Willard was one of the foremost figures to rework the meaning of motherhood in order to mobilize women to address alcohol abuse, poverty, domestic violence, and a range of other social ills, as well as to claim their rights. It was she, most of all, who gained wide social acceptance for *mothers* as public actors. Her political effectiveness in mobilizing large numbers of women nationally was due in large part to her ability to reinterpret mainstream Christian teaching. Undoing significantly the work of the sixteenth-century humanist and religious reformers, Willard used motherhood as a metaphor to establish the new norm of women's social responsibility and agency *beyond* the home, taking a major step toward claiming public authority for women. She did so also by reinterpreting the traditional Christian notion of family.

To be sure, Willard focused much of her energy on working for women's rights within the family and on strengthening the family as a social institution. While she, like most liberals and conservatives of the time, did not support divorce,[30] she called for reform of the power structure of the traditional family, seeing equality between spouses economically and in all other respects as the key. Nevertheless, as her own achievements in the last decades of the nineteenth century demonstrate, Willard played a central role in establishing a national and international family of women linked together in the World Woman's Christian Temperance Union through their commitments to a range of social reforms. "Infus[ing]

traditional institutions and values with new content," Willard redefined home and family to build a political movement of women.[31]
She formulated and acted on the fundamental ethical principle that
home was not any particular location or family structure, but an
attitude toward the human family: "one of welcome, care, respect-
fulness, and affection."[32] Equality between men and women was to
be the hallmark of the family, church, and state women were remaking. Willard's presidential address of 1887 exemplifies how she
reinterpreted biblical text to articulate this public vision:

> Under the curse, man has mapped out the state as his largest sphere, and
> the home as woman's largest; under the blessing, man and woman shall
> map out home as the one true state, and she who, during centuries of train-
> ing, has learned how to govern there, shall help man make the great, cold,
> heartless state a warm, kind, and protecting home. . . . The White Rib-
> bon women would invade the masculine . . . hierarchy of church and
> state; and ring out in clear but gentle voices the oft-repeated declaration of
> the Master whom they serve: "Behold, I make all things new."[33]

Thus, Willard found resources within the Christian tradition
not only for criticism of the patriarchal family, but also for a larger
sense of family that relativized traditional family loyalties and
authorized women's political activity. She, like reformers often
viewed as more radical, was skilled at using biblical exegesis to support her views. In all probability, therefore, in light of her particular interest in the figure of Jesus Christ, Willard was intimately
familiar with New Testament texts that depict him as consistently
challenging the idea of traditional family loyalties, demanding freedom from the restraints of his own family to serve God and the
wider universal family. At one point, Christ sharply reproves his
own mother and brothers with the words "Who is my mother?
Who are my brothers?" Repeatedly, he warns his followers that
discipleship is an alternative to traditional family structure and that
salvation depends on willingness to leave one's family behind.[34]
These are words in which Willard found vision for her private life
too; as historian Carolyn De Swarte Gifford, the editor of her jour-

nal, points out, instead of marrying, Willard created for herself a family of related and unrelated women. Thus, critical biblical perspectives on the family provided Willard with the authority to call for correcting injustice within the traditional family *and* for freeing women to pursue their duty to social loyalties beyond their immediate families.

In short, religion provided the symbolic resources through which many women found latitude to express their own view of themselves and their world. It offers an important source of insight, therefore, into the changing subjectivities and social agency of nineteenth- and early-twentieth-century women reformers. When historians overlook this, they also miss the access that analysis of religion provides to these women's capacity to think in *social* terms and to their social vision. Viewing religion as personal piety, as many historians do, renders invisible the explicit and implicit social dimension of religious ideas, values, and symbols. In the principles it sets forth to guide individual conduct and the prescriptions it contains for the proper ordering of human relationships, from the household to the world, biblical religion fosters a fundamental orientation not just to the personal and private, but also to the collective and public.

Kathryn Sklar recognizes this public dimension of religion. She writes about Florence Kelley that, like other Progressive reformers of the early twentieth century such as Jane Addams, Julia Lathrop, and Grace Abbott, her vision of social relations was self-consciously based in "religious values that rose above self-interest and advanced a vision of the social whole as greater than its parts."[35] Sklar sees that religion shaped the social vision and politics not just of Progressive women, but of organized women all the way back to the early nineteenth century.[36] It oriented them to speak for the welfare of society as a whole. Religion gave them the conceptual and moral resources, the powerful common language, and the collective sense of responsibility they used to build alliances with other women across the nation, sometimes even across racial, class, and ethnic lines, and also with men. For these reasons, and because the separate religious associations they formed provided women with an avenue into the public world and skills to negotiate it, religion was organized women's school for democratic citizenship.[37] What historian of religion Evelyn Brooks Higginbotham has written about black women reformers at the close of the nineteenth century was true for many white women as well:

> More than mere precursors to secular reform and women's rights activism, black women's religious organizations undergirded and formed an identifiable part of what is erroneously assumed to be "secular." The black Baptist women's convention thrust itself into the mainstream of Progressive reform, and conversely such clubs as those constituting the secular-oriented National Association of Colored Women included church work as integral and salient to their purpose. This complexity precludes attempts to bifurcate black women's activities neatly into dichotomous categories such as religious versus secular, private versus public, or accommodation versus resistance.[38]

MORALITY

While most historians of women pay comparatively little attention to religion, some are concerned with the broader moral dimension of women's nineteenth- and early-twentieth-century reform activities. Yet, following the pattern set by the initially dominant rights-centered interpretation, few explore seriously the moral universe these reformers inhabited. They tend to be interested in morality for a particular reason and in a limited way. Scholars of women's history often understand morality, like religion, as by definition conservative in content and role. Accepting the cultural definition of morality as one of the chief emblems of the private sphere, many see it as functioning only to constrain women and their activity. Often, they focus on morality mainly to make this point, as the following words of one historian illustrate:

> [I]n the early and mid-nineteenth century, the tightly joined terms of femininity and morality supplied the language of conformity with respect to gender roles, sexual behavior, and political beliefs. . . . [E]ven those who sought to transform the material conditions that made women and men

socially unequal believed enough of the ideology of female propriety and female difference to serve the interests of the more conservative among them.[39]

This evaluation substitutes criticism of one aspect of the dominant morality in nineteenth-century society for more thorough consideration of morality's relationship to women's lives. Such a narrow, negative view of morality is common among scholars who want to criticize the idea that, as wives and mothers, women possessed a distinctive, biologically based moral identity that made them inherently virtuous. Many scholars are particularly interested in criticizing this idea because they assume that progress for women involves their dissociation from the private sphere and their journey toward equal rights and political involvement in the public sphere. But scholarly criticism of the idea of women's special virtue also often accomplishes a related aim. As I will show, such criticism throws into question the purity of women's motivation to help those in need. By casting doubt on women's social welfare activities, it then can assign these activities secondary status in historical accounts.

In challenging claims about women's moral purity and the cultural beliefs that lay behind it, scholars often implicitly make the case that individuals' morality always is shaped by their social location. This intellectually sound position undergirds the argument that the race and middle-class status of white women reformers profoundly influenced their morality. Yet many scholars discredit women's motives for social reform by explaining them almost exclusively in terms of their class and race interests. In this way, an important argument about the nature of morality becomes the ground for downplaying its integrity and avoiding the moral complexity of these women's lives. At the point where serious analysis of the interaction of these women's values with their social situation and interests might begin, many scholars instead conclude that, because in most of these reformers morality was not *pure* motivation for the good, it was nothing more than the sum of social variables and interests. Thus, much scholarship reduces the central values with which most discussions of morality and nineteenth- and twentieth-century women are concerned—charity and benevolence —to a "charity legacy" of condescending poor relief donated by "Ladies Bountiful." The public significance of women's reforms is undermined when they are characterized as reflecting primarily desire for social control of the poor and native-born and of immigrant racial and ethnic minority populations.

This scholarly judgment presents women reformers, especially after midcentury, chiefly as instruments of middle- and upper-middle-class identity and power.[40] Borrowing the class-centered approach developed by mainstream historians of early-nineteenth-century male benevolent activity and of the later evolution of American social policy and the American welfare state, scholars of women's history often explain away morality. Linking class, morality, and women, and overlooking the larger historical and cultural moral pattern that gave rise to True Womanhood, they go so far as to assume that the feminine domestic ideal was a class tool that originated with the nineteenth-century middle class.[41] This class-based interpretation of both women and morality reduces morality mainly to a social standard of respectability, defining it as the special "virtue" middle-class women represented. While they are right to draw attention to the social power of respectability in reinforcing the status of middle-class women over wage-earning women, many scholars do so by dismissing moral complexity. The simplified moral pattern they see is that, in the name of respectability, privileged women were discouraged from challenging cultural beliefs about the family that narrowed their lives and cost them economic (true) independence. In turn, these women taught young working-class women submission to these restrictions by schooling them in the values and behaviors of gentility. Respectability thus undermined wage-earning women's radical politics aimed at improving their work and hence their economic condition.

Reducing morality to an instrument of middle-class women's interests also reveals a tendency in some women's history to depict wage earning as women's main avenue to public participation and

power, thus narrowing our idea of both. The emergence of
women's economic independence is presented often, with rights,
as the primary sign of their progress and their value to the nation.
For example, taking this independence as her priority, historian
Alice Kessler-Harris analyzes the values of privileged women in
the past chiefly as they contributed to holding in place the patriarchal family, its structural impact on labor patterns that marginalized (and still marginalize) women, and the gender structure of the
economy. She concludes that only in recent years have economic
and social conditions, by challenging traditional values and making
women's paid labor a norm, created "a new woman, an individual
whose dynamic ability now has to become part of any equation for
America's future."[42] Kessler-Harris's emphasis on the importance
of women's paid labor in helping to fashion the fate of the nation,
and the fact that she leaves unmentioned the ability, moral agency,
and public significance of their *unpaid* labor, implies that this labor
is a lesser contribution.

Thus, morality often is used by scholars in the service of particular economic and social explanations of the past. Historical approaches based on theories of social control analyze morality in a
larger interpretive framework in which it already has been given a
fixed place and function in relationship to other social variables,
notably class and race. To point this out is not to challenge the notion that both women and morality played a prominent role in the
construction of class and race privilege. Rather, it is to argue that
reducing middle-class reformers' motives to the politics of dis-
guised self-interest runs the risk of appealing to the ancient suspicion in Western culture of women and their moral agency.[43] In
short, while class and race are certainly two of the contexts in
which values should be placed to evaluate their historical meanings
and functions, values cannot be *reduced* to class and race. Values also
cannot be simply abstracted from the broader contexts of the moral
traditions that helped fashion them and employed in the work of
class and political analysis. Were scholars to give morality priority
and attention equal to that they give other social variables, for ex-

ample, they would need to recognize that benevolence is a moral value with a centuries-long history of meaning in Christian culture. While women reformers drew on this meaning in a way that was indeed shaped by their social situation, that situation itself was not the *origin* of the value of benevolence. The complexity of meanings benevolence had for white and black reformers becomes visible only when the outcome of analyzing morality, race, and class together is not preordained by models of historical explanation that define religion as epiphenomenal.

Recognizing the larger moral landscapes that help shape society means recognizing also that morality is not *only* middle-class. Ironically, when many historians define morality as middle-class and deny genuine moral commitments other than condescending pity to white, middle-class Protestant women, including reformers, they deny full moral agency to all women. This seriously misreads lower-class, black, and Jewish nineteenth-century women, as well as others.[44] It misreads the fundamental orientation toward the moral they received as women through both biblical religion and a dominant culture that defined their particular moral status and arena of action.

Morality in its broadest sense—a basic orientation to meaning and value—was the language of the overwhelming majority of nineteenth- and twentieth-century women. Whether they drew on biblical religion—the primary moral source for most—or other moral traditions, women reformers made this orientation evident in the way they identified social problems, conceptualized social goals, and fashioned strategies for change. It should not be a surprise, therefore, that wage-earning and minority women might *share* some of the same moral values and language of nineteenth-century white, privileged women. For example, in 1868, Emily Peers, a wage-earning woman expressing doubts about suffrage, articulated the belief she held in common with many middle-class women that the vote would be a poor trade for women's moral force as an instrument for real social change: "custom, more tyrannical than law, would remain, and once possessed of the ballot, a moral force—a woman's truer weapon, would, I fear, be lost."[45]

Emily Peers's words point to a standard of judgment and a vision of society that she, like middle-class women quite different from herself, employed as a result of her social experience as a woman. Her idea that effective politics involved changing social values reflected a worldview heavily influenced not only by moral and religious traditions, but also by women's exclusion from formal power. The way Peers's conviction about the importance of changing values related to the actual conditions of her working-class existence and to other views she held was obviously not the same as the way it related to the existence and views of a middle-class woman. But in holding to this standard, Peers was like many other women who believed that public progress depended more on transforming the conscience of individuals than on the vote. As women reformers engaged increasingly in public debate with state and national legislatures in the course of the century, most came to believe also in the power of the law to bring about change,[46] but few— including Stanton, as we shall see—gave up their belief that effective legal reform also depended on reforming individual and social values.

A final feature of the still common negative view and inadequate exploration of morality in women's history is the distinction many historical accounts make between moral and social reform. DuBois established this distinction when she identified the roots of the modern women's movement in the midcentury Garrisonian split in the abolitionist movement.[47] It was there, in her view, that the politics of women's rights took shape, leaving "traditions of pietistic female benevolence" behind in favor of social reform efforts that involved lobbying politicians, constitutional and legislative change, organizing rather than agitating, and secular rather than moral rhetoric.[48] This prevalent distinction dismisses moral rhetoric as a utopian and less effective language of social change, while implying that social reform, having crossed the boundary between sacred and secular, private and public, was somehow without moral content. It is yet another case, in other words, in which many historians of women judge women's actions on the basis of standards of the male public sphere. Insofar as women reformers in the past employed the established male methods of the formal political system—what historians of the Progressive era reforms call "state resources and remedies"[49]—they are judged positively as moving women toward participation in the "real" politics of social change. Insofar as they do not, women and their activities are devalued and deemed not fully public.

Male standards also help shape descriptions of women's reform activities. Many scholars still describe organized women's human welfare efforts as depending on the strategy of moral suasion and *suppress* the link these reformers drew between their efforts to change values and to influence legislation. Accounts minimizing this link argue that at midcentury female benevolence was superseded by the growing association of social welfare with political, professional, scientific, and institutional strategies, leaving many women behind in local benevolent societies. There, these women are depicted as being pushed "further from the symbolic and real centers of power for social change" by their continuing use of the language of moral superiority and public motherhood.[50]

Yet this is not, to take the key example, an accurate description of women in the Woman's Christian Temperance Union, the largest national organization of women reformers. Contrary to the common presentation of the WCTU as "primarily an evangelical movement devoted to moral suasion," it came consistently to combine moral discourse about change with a focus on legislative remedies —including the ballot for women—and by 1874 was strategizing to affect mainstream politics.[51] When historians do recognize this, they often discredit the WCTU's social reform work in another way, characterizing the organization as undertaking legislative and political strategies for the purpose of establishing Christianity as the state religion.[52] A more accurate and less biased historical account would identify and criticize the concrete instances in which the WCTU indeed moved in this direction, such as its attempt to legislate observance of the Christian Sabbath, rather than dismissing its public reforms wholesale. It would point out that without the help of the WCTU, the constitutional amendment granting women suffrage would never have been passed.

In fact, contrary to the dominant picture presented by scholars of women's history, even as the place of religion in society underwent change from the mid nineteenth century into the early twentieth, women reformers' use of moral rhetoric to influence public opinion and affect mainstream legislative politics continued to be crucial to their effectiveness in both equal rights and social welfare efforts. In their struggles for social improvement, these women, unlike many of their historians, did not dichotomize morality and politics.[53] They recognized the importance both of moral change and alleviation of misery at the individual level *and* of legal and structural social change. In both the woman's rights and temperance movements, morality and politics were mixed, albeit with firmly differing orientations toward institutionalized religion and differing emphases in regard to women's grounds for claiming equal rights.

Furthermore, as sociologist Theda Skocpol argues, the success of the innovative social policy agenda championed mainly by white women reformers in the second decade of the twentieth century, which laid the foundation for the American welfare state, was dependent *still* on women's political use of moral rhetoric. Neither weak nor ineffective, moral argument was a central aspect of women's distinctive political style and crucial to the political process. Argument was an effective agenda-setting tool, convincing justices, civic leaders, and the educated public that mothers and children were worthy of public protection.[54]

In summary, histories frequently implicitly depict women reformers as escaping the limited moral agency ascribed to them by traditional cultural belief only by asserting their claim to equal rights. Even in the case of rights activists, scholars often fail to recognize reformers' distinctive moral perspectives on social welfare.

But scholars who emphasize rights obscure almost completely the distinctive public welfare vision of other white and black women reformers and the *progressive* aspects of its moral content, thus obscuring too new possibilities for the present this vision could help us recognize. By making compassion suspect as a motive for social improvement, many scholars lose the opportunity to recognize its constructive social power and to underscore how that power needs to be strengthened by constant criticism of compassion's aims and effects. By emphasizing the role of morality in social control, many also fail to explore what might be learned from the positive role that values played in the construction of alliances among women, and between women and men, to address social problems.

In short, many scholars still understand women and morality largely in the terms defined by dominant nineteenth- and early-twentieth-century cultural beliefs about public and private, rather than in those defined by women reformers themselves. By discounting the centrality of women's full moral agency and vision to their public leadership in the past, such scholarship undermines recognition of the central importance of both in the present.

MOTHERHOOD

Finally, skepticism about morality is closely linked to skepticism about motherhood, a third major pattern in interpretation of nineteenth- and early-twentieth-century women reformers. Ironically, while many scholars criticize the connection drawn between motherhood and morality by traditional cultural beliefs, they commonly make the same connection themselves.

If the language of religion and morality was the first language of organized women, motherhood was the second. One of the striking characteristics of the public activities of black and white women reformers is the language of motherhood and family in which they often were couched. Because that language reflected the cultural ideal for women articulated by dominant cultural beliefs about the domestic sphere, it helped explain and justify women's activities outside the home. The best example is the WCTU, which em-

ployed the language of public motherhood and female moral superiority to forge a major national and international political wom-
en's movement. Motherhood was at the heart of WCTU women's
identities and their politics—their slogan was "organized mother
love."[55]

Many historians, however, following the lead of those who emphasized rights from the outset, are not persuaded by reformers'
public application of the language of motherhood. Judging progress by the movement of nineteenth-century women into the mainstream, watching for signs that women were picking up the political consciousness and language of the public sphere, for many the
language of motherhood, like that of morality and religion, seems
to signify that women were not really public actors. These scholars
often simply accept the premise that women in the past, especially
mothers, inhabited a domestic world of narrow concerns and private responsibilities that left them unprepared and poorly positioned for significant or effective public action. In this respect too,
ironically, much women's history has found itself sharing some of
the deepest assumptions of the very beliefs about private and public it has done so much to challenge. Thus, a number of historians
interpret the work of women for social improvement not as a significant public achievement, but as voluntary (hence, later, volunteer) work.

Some scholars who write about organized women in the first
two decades of the twentieth century, the start of the Progressive
era, continue this criticism of earlier manifestations of white reformers' maternalism. A number argue that in this period maternalists used middle-class motherhood to set the social standard by
which mothers of other races and classes were measured, making
motherhood one of the chief means by which the native-born
middle-class consolidated and asserted its cultural and economic
dominance. While this is undoubtedly true to some degree, it is not
the full story of those who constructed a political strategy based on
motherhood. Yet a number of scholars are skeptical of the link between mothers and politics. This skepticism is well represented by

historian Linda Gordon, one of the leading scholars of the American welfare state. Gordon is critical of maternalists for initiating public policy (the mothers' pensions that were the forerunner of Aid to Dependent Children in 1935 and our modern AFDC) that asserted the social value of women's unpaid domestic labor instead of challenging the male "breadwinner" norm by recognizing many mothers' need to work for pay.[56]

At heart, what bothers Gordon is the way she sees class and morality coming together with motherhood in maternalism. Because maternalism drew on the moral authority of middle-class mothers, she believes that its public vision was chiefly one of social control and moral improvement of the poor. So, for example, Gordon contrasts the female welfare advocates of the early twentieth century and their maternalist strategy of putting children first with male social insurance reformers, advocates of monetary benefits to protect working men and their families. She conveys her suspicion that the moral commitments of even unmarried, educated women leaders—"such as Jane Addams with her noble disdain for greed and exploitation and her longing for higher forms of community than the market could produce"—amounted to a desire for moral control:

> They inherited the charity legacy, with its direction toward the "helpless" and innocent victims, and the "rescue" tradition of nineteenth-century moral reform, with its interest in control and regeneration. Children fit all these categories: helpless, "innocent," controllable, malleable.[57]

Gordon's preference is for what she sees as the more value-neutral public approach of men. She describes men's approach as coming from outside the (female) tradition of moral reform and employing clear-cut bureaucratic criteria that prevented caseworkers from inserting judgment and stigma into interactions with clients.[58] Shaped by beliefs that associate morality and motherhood with "private" and value-neutrality and men with "public," Gordon's analysis may well misread the historical data. Skocpol disputes her claim that male advocates of social insurance were not as concerned as female welfare advocates with applying standards of deserving-ness in determining eligibility for benefits.[59]

Not all historians focusing on the Progressive era are as critical of maternalism as Gordon. A growing number recognize mater-nalism as an effective public strategy that, despite its disturbing tendency in some hands to elevate "good" mothers over "bad," did make an important difference. They attribute to maternalism the agenda and political success of both white and black organized women at the peak of their public achievements. So, for example, in her study of the reform activity of white middle-class women from 1900 to 1930, Molly Ladd-Taylor credits the maternalist rationale with leading to public programs and legislation to help protect children and poor mothers in particular, but also the needy in society in general: "Women reformers and the members of moth-ers' clubs believed that, as mothers and potential mothers, they were naturally more sensitive than men to the needs of the power-less and were therefore responsible for protecting them."[60] And black women, while they shared with white women use of mater-nal metaphor for their public efforts, gave it a *distinctive* meaning in the context of racism. Race up-lift was the explicit purpose behind the range of black women's "social housekeeping" initiatives. Be-cause the experience and status of motherhood had been fractured by slavery, their maternalism constituted an aggressive assertion of that purpose. Nevertheless, black women did not share the social and symbolic power of white motherhood, which set the cultural standard. As a result, their public initiatives, especially their strug-gle for rights, had little hope of achieving the degree of progress achieved by white women.[61]

Yet even scholars who see reformers' maternalism as in part quite positive stumble because of the link they draw between mo-rality and motherhood. Many who see maternal qualities as pro-viding the motive and explanation for important civic action tend still to conflate women with their motherhood. They overlook the larger framework of values women drew on in developing their civic vision. The exception to this pattern are those historians who offer glimpses of the vision of reformers that went beyond narrow maternal concern for mothers and children. Ladd-Taylor, for example, emphasizes that clubwomen who supported mothers' pension legislation had a vision of "a society which used its resources to promote the health and welfare of its citizens."[62] And Sklar argues that work and unemployment were the focal points of women's larger vision and of their attempts to address a range of social ills.[63]

Yet, most frequently, historical treatment of motherhood tends, like traditional cultural beliefs about public and private, to circumscribe women's moral agency, defining it in terms tied to their biology. Reducing mothers to the dominant cultural view of them, most historians see motherhood more as a biological state than as a social institution women consciously might make into an avenue to a distinctive vision of self and society. Thus, many scholars overlook the full nature and meaning of women's public agency and activity. This is less true of historical accounts of the maternalism of black women reformers, which are somewhat less likely to limit black women's moral agency. In part this is because racial consciousness and community commitment are seen as motivating black clubwomen's work long before, and after, the deterioration of race relations and the founding of the National Association of Colored Women at the end of the nineteenth century.[64] Equally important, however, black maternalists' larger vision and the subjectivities that generated it are more likely to be recognized by scholars who analyze them because black reformers based their claims clearly on motherhood as *work*, rather than as a natural state.[65]

In short, although rejecting women's relegation to the domestic sphere, by accepting the link that nineteenth-century beliefs drew between mothers, morality, and biology, many scholars of Progressive reformers still deny to a significant degree the subjectivities of women whose race and privilege identified them most closely with this cultural ideal of womanhood. Some scholars quite rightly point out that middle-class reformers conflated *themselves* with motherhood by basing their claim to respect and power on it.[66]

Others blame this conflation for identifying women with differ-ence, providing the basis on which they won "a kind of social cit-izenship" but not equality under the law.[67] Still others come closer to getting behind historical women's motherhood-based claim by arguing that it was a political strategy.

What is called for, however, if these reformers are to be under-stood fully, correctly, and in a balanced way is *deeper* critical as-sessment of the continuing power of traditional cultural beliefs to shape our view of women's moral status and agency. In a culture where women have been valued primarily for their motherhood, we must resist the unwitting reduction of the female self to moth-erhood or of female moral agency to maternal traits. If we are to understand organized women on their own terms, we must recover and examine the full moral discourse that reflected their social lo-cation and shaped their civic action and achievements.

CONCLUSION

The reductive and even dismissive treatment of religion that char-acterizes the dominant interpretation of nineteenth- and early-twentieth-century organized women has a high cost. Lack of a more complex view of religion prevents us from recognizing the centrality of moral agency to these reformers and to the situation of American women in this period. Oversimplification obscures the paradox that the dominant culture defined women's moral sta-tus as at once inferior and superior, despite Stanton's warning about the crucial role this paradox plays in American women's sub-ordination. Most important of all, inadequate attention to religion leads scholars still to overlook the progressive vision of public life that animated both rights and human welfare activists and has im-portant implications for the present.

Taking seriously the universe of religious and moral meanings these women inhabited, and critically assessing its role in their public achievements, will help us see how they revised the moral knowledge embedded in traditional beliefs about public and pri-vate. It also will help us recognize how our view of women and society today continues to be bounded by these beliefs. Important lessons for moving beyond these bounds can be gleaned from exploring the *full* moral agency organized women expressed in their progressive public vision and priorities. We turn next to examine what made these women a public force on their own terms.

CHAPTER SIX

The Difference Women Made: Reconceiving the Public Agenda

Organized women's full public vision has been obscured not only by scholars' preconceptions about what should constitute women's public agenda, but also by scholars' preconceptions about who first successfully championed society's responsibility for the welfare of all Americans. Most scholars of American public life focus primarily on male actors and working-class activism when accounting for the emergence of social-welfare policy. They do not hear the voices of white and black organized women. Yet for more than a century of public effectiveness during which they did "the nation's work," to borrow Florence Kelley's phrase, organized women generated their own public vision, an agenda that began with the disadvantaged. Drawing primarily on two established discourses about the public order—biblical religion and democracy— and in the case of black women, a philosophy of racial advancement as well, these women forged their priorities for the welfare of American society as a whole.

Critical analysis of religion enables us to hear their voices more clearly. This analysis, by bringing into sharper focus the issues of meaning and value that shaped women's public discourse, will help us restore women's rights struggles to the wider public vision of which they were an essential feature. In particular, it will help us see that in the eyes of reformers, society had a moral dimension and a moral project that were central to its existence. Both were to be addressed through all facets of social life—especially the economic, legal, familial, educational, medical, and environmental. When reformers defined progress for women, they defined it as *more* than access to the existing public world. To them, progress was public effectiveness grounded in a reconception of the public world and its issues.

Because organized women lacked the authority to institutionalize their reinterpretations of male religious and republican discourses, the main text from which their public vision must be read is their public action and speech. Understanding this text requires understanding that women reformers drew an explicit connection between private values and public life. Refusing from the start to vault "from the private into the public arena leaving the wall intact,"[1] they challenged existing public values with their social objectives. We may well want to question, from our contemporary perspective, some of the values they chose to assert in public and even the way they asserted them. Nevertheless, to understand the public vision that animated these women's efforts to shape their society, we must discover how for them "social, political, and religious beliefs combine[d] to form a comprehensive understanding of reality."[2]

When white and black organized women connected the social, political, and religious in their public action and speech, they were expressing their subjectivities. Taking seriously, as their starting point and ours, the frameworks of meaning and value on which they drew will allow us to recapture more of the worldview of these reformers and to gain a sense of why they were trying to make the difference they made. By listening carefully for how women reformers of this period understood themselves and the society they were trying to improve, we can uncover new perspectives not only on the past, but also on women's predicament in the present and on the nation's values crisis.

A NEW PUBLIC VISION

Although it was an agent of women's civic, legal, economic, and political marginality, and of the racism which doubly burdened

women of color, biblical religion also had positive value for organized women. It was not simply a set of Christian or, for a minority, of Jewish doctrines these women believed, but a landscape they
inhabited. Offering a map of human and divine reality, religion set
forth a fundamental geography of personal, social, and universal
order that had unrivaled authority and worth for most women.
Furthermore, this geography was inherently evaluative. It oriented women to making judgments (according to their reading of
divine standards) about the way individual and collective human
life was and the way it ought to be.

This is the reason women reformers could critically appropriate
the symbolic resources and authority of the Bible in order to challenge gender, race, and other fundamental norms of their society.
Sophisticated leaders and religious thinkers, both white and black,
from the Grimkés, Willard, and Stanton to Virginia Broughton
and Mary Cook, brilliantly employed the multivalent symbolic resources of religion to build large-scale reform movements. Drawing on biblical resources and authority, these leaders used their political and oratorical skill to forge public vision that criticized the
moral basis of separate-spheres doctrine and the values, priorities,
and institutions of the public sphere itself.

Even though fundamental social divisions of class and race
among women remained intact, the biblical symbols of meaning
and value they had in common allowed women of varied political and even religious stripes to come together. In their separate
women's associations, they attempted to reach across social divisions in humanizing efforts of unprecedented scale. As Ann Firor
Scott and others point out, these initiatives, however flawed, made
a difference on important social issues that government on its own
was neither recognizing nor addressing. Most often allying with
others like themselves, women in associations across the country
made common cause with one another on behalf of women, children, and men who were often quite different.

While the public vision that drove these women's initiatives was
by no means uniform, and changed and evolved from the early

nineteenth to the early twentieth century, important common emphases in it are discernible over time and across racial, class, and regional divides. Salient among these are new notions of the female self, a commitment to common humanity, an understanding of justice as tied to human welfare, and a sense of civic action as both a right and an obligation.

CLAIMING MORAL EQUALITY

We tend today to think of the self in terms of individualism, that idea of the (male) self arising out of the Enlightenment that has given us the notion of the rights-bearing individual at the center of American public life. The alternative to this social norm has been a self conceived in terms of the "feminine" traits traditionally opposed to those of the autonomous, rights-bearing "masculine" self: relational, nurturing, caring. At the heart of the public vision which organized black and white women expressed, however, was a *new* conception of the female self, a conception that differed significantly from both these public and private norms. This progressive conception was forcefully articulated by leaders of organized women from diverse perspectives and social circumstances along the political and religious spectrum. The symbolic complexity of biblical religion gave ample room to both white and black women to respond to it in varying measure without having to break with organized religion.[3]

This new female self cannot be represented adequately in terms of either individualism or its opposite. Beginning within a biblically derived framework of meaning and value, the self represented and promoted by women reformers was first and foremost an ethically formed self, a self identified always with and by its values. Nineteenth- and early-twentieth-century women did not separate the "I" from the values they saw as constituting their selves. Being, for them, was inconceivable apart from the personal and social commitments and purposes which give the "I" its meaning. Most important, for both white and black women leaders, being also was inconceivable apart from the central *value* of the female self.

This claim was more fundamental and systematic socially than their claim to legal equality. The assertion that God created women equal with men challenged the moral basis of the cultural doctrine of separate spheres. As we have seen, this doctrine, while appearing to confer moral superiority on women, was predicated on the moral superiority of men. Although most modern scholars have overlooked this paradox, it was not lost on women reformers. Their leaders addressed themselves primarily to it, pointing out that the domestic code actually institutionalized a cultural view of woman as morally weak by restricting women's sphere of moral activity.

Both white and black leaders emphasized that this cultural view of women's inherent moral inferiority was anchored in male interpretations of biblical text. Because the authority of the Bible for nineteenth-century women reform leaders and their society was tremendous, it was critically important for them to challenge these traditional interpretations, especially of the Creation and the Fall, and to demonstrate how they misrepresented God's true intentions for women. It was to these texts, therefore, that women reformers turned to begin their reconstruction of the cultural conception of woman. The most systematic effort in this regard was Stanton's major project of writing a feminist interpretation of the Bible, the *Woman's Bible*. This project was crucial in her view because, while religion had helped fashion the cultural pattern of injustice that subordinated women, it also offered powerful leverage on the injustice of state and society. Stanton recognized that women's moral standing in society lay at the core of what had to be changed and that formal politics alone was an inadequate tool for changing it. She saw that social values and beliefs, powerfully expressed in and influenced by biblical images and symbols, would continue to block structural change in society sought by legal and other means. However, Stanton and other leaders gave priority to reinterpreting biblical and Christian traditions not only because the Bible was crucial to persuading a wide public, but also because of its central meaning (however much they might contest that meaning) in their own lives. While many organized women moved away from the original biblical understandings that shaped their youth, the Bible still gave them their bearings in the world. For this reason, the crucial step in asserting public authority was claiming the right to reinterpret sacred text.

Women leaders found support for their claim regarding the simultaneity of the creation of men and women in the text of the first creation story in Genesis (1:27–28).[4] It challenged the common interpretation that men were created first and morally superior to women.[5] For her part, Willard was prone to cite Galatians 3:28, "There is neither . . . male nor female, for you are all one in Christ Jesus."[6] Reformers also forcefully rejected the notion that it was Eve who caused the fall of humanity through her disobedience, the original sin identified by mainstream Christian teaching that was the basis for women's subordination. As a consequence, for Stanton and for Willard and others too, the individual's first responsibility was not a life of repentance for sin, but of moral development and growth.[7] Reformers saw in biblical text the charter for women's personal and social progress and responsibility.

The Grimkés were the first to bring women's claim to moral agency to the fore in their public speeches and writing, anchoring the association of the female self with values and asserting the value of the female self. Defending woman's right to campaign publicly for the abolition of slavery, it was the Grimkés who claimed for women a full moral agency that was historical and political. This claim was advanced by Angelina Grimké when in 1837, rejecting the idea that men had higher moral rights and duties than women, she argued that woman's moral responsibilities could not be limited on the basis of the "mere circumstance of sex":

> When human beings are regarded as moral beings, sex, instead of being enthroned upon the summit, administering upon rights and responsibili-

ties, sinks into insignificance and nothingness. My doctrine then is, that whatever it is morally right for man to do, it is morally right for woman to do. Our duties originate, not from difference of sex, but from the diversity of our relations in life, the various gifts and talents committed to our care, and the different eras in which we live.[8]

The key to authorizing women's participation in public affairs, their role in the "great work of reformation," as Sarah Grimké called the antislavery and other reform movements, was rejecting not woman's sphere, but her restriction to it and her exclusion from the public sphere. The Grimkés directly challenged the widely held belief that women were unequipped to represent truth or exercise power on its behalf in public.[9]

For nineteenth-century reformers, women were condemned by being denied not simply legal equality, but the status of *full* moral being. This denial determined the meaning and value of their activity in all matters private and public. Without full moral status, women had no public duties and even their private duties, relations, and influence as wives and mothers were corrupted.[10] It was *moral* inequality that these women saw as the root of sexual inequality, something which some modern feminists who think about the sources of sexual inequality mainly in economic and legal terms find hard to accept.[11] Sarah Grimké recoiled not at the domestic duties of women, not at gender difference, but at the different moral status and character assigned men and women. She rejected the idea that women did not also have a higher duty to truth and justice which they were obliged by God to pursue unrestrained. In the context of her own early self-centered life spent "among the butterflies of the fashionable world"[12] and of her later commitment to abolishing slavery, she protested the sinful state of moral childishness to which society relegated women:

> Man has inflicted an unspeakable injury upon woman, by holding up to her view her animal nature, and placing in the background her moral and intellectual being. Woman has inflicted injury upon herself by submitting to be thus regarded; and she is now called upon to rise from the station

where *man*, not God, has placed her, and claim those sacred and inalienable rights, as a moral and responsible being, with which her Creator has invested her.[13]

The Grimkés identified the wall separating private and public spheres as a moral barrier women had been taught to believe they had neither the capacity nor the responsibility to break through. They defined equality not in a narrow legal sense, but as an intellectual and moral agency that involved woman's duty and right to participate in public matters. The sisters saw legal equality as a necessary, but not sufficient, basis for realizing equality. For them, moral equality was the source of human dignity and responsibility that brought full social standing.[14] A woman participating in public work, Sarah wrote,

> must feel, if she feels rightly, that she is fulfilling one of the important duties laid upon her as an accountable being, and that her character, instead of being "unnatural," is in exact accordance with the will of Him to whom, and to no other, she is responsible for the talents and the gifts confided to her.[15]

The Grimkés articulated a notion of woman's moral agency that was also essential to the self-conceptions of other leading women reformers, including Willard, Stanton, and black intellectual Anna Julia Cooper, and to their conceptions of the female self. Many historians of women have tended to merge moral equality with the principle of equal rights, and to distinguish between early feminists who learned the principle of equal rights from their participation in the abolitionist movement and those they label "moral reformers" who are said to have found equality too radical a claim and rejected it.[16] But as their actions and words demonstrate, women reformers, from religiously conservative to radical, expressed a comprehensive conception of self, not a narrow political one.[17] This comprehensive conception was based on the moral claim to full humanity in God's eyes. While religiously more conservative women might indeed have found criticism of the Protestant Church and its clergy too radical, they nevertheless developed a strong sense of their own moral responsibility as individuals. In the first half of the nineteenth century, the series of Protestant revivals known as the Second Great Awakening had infused into society a powerful focus on the *agency* of God and men by emphasizing the relationship between faith and social regeneration.[18] While revival leaders had not meant to empower women to seek new social roles, women reformers found in this call to agency a familiar summons to moral duty coupled with a welcome new authorization for public action.

In fact, many organized women who resisted criticism of institutional religion may have done so because their sense of moral duty in the world was nourished and supported by the church. As Willard observed, it was not necessary for women to oppose institutional religion to gain from the temperance crusade knowledge of their power and a wholly new sense of their own agency.[19] Methodism, for example, to which Willard and the majority of WCTU members belonged, was a denomination fundamentally oriented to social justice activity—to home and global mission. And clergy at times played a positive moral role in the lives of women reformers. When, for example, Willard declared her intent to lead a Christian life, she did so as a result of her great admiration for the antislavery Methodist bishop who preached an 1859 revival. It was he who drew the link for her between moral agency and intellect, pointing out that she might rely on her mind to discern what was just in setting her life on a moral course.[20] He encouraged her to understand the claim to moral agency in terms of dedication to becoming a person of moral strength. Her journal shows that this was her central project: "To develop character, she attempted to bring her disparate faculties—intelligence, will, emotions, conscience—under her control, and direct them toward living a moral life."[21] For black Baptist women too, strong criticism of the black church's sexism did not weaken an equally strong sense of belonging. Black women leaders found support and inspiration in black (male) pastors noted for their leadership on behalf of race up-lift and even on behalf of black women. Walter H. Brooks, Nannie Burroughs's pastor at the

Nineteenth Street Baptist Church in Washington, D.C., was such a figure, one of the chief race leaders in the National Baptist Convention and an early champion of black women's education and theology.[22]

In advancing this claim to moral equality, radicals and conservatives alike sustained a belief in women as both equal and different.[23] Moral difference between men and women and their separate spheres, not difference in general, was the problem women reformers addressed. They did not protest women's different duties in the home, but women's exclusion from education and agency with regard to the great moral challenges of the public arena. Reformers were profoundly concerned with asserting woman's moral duty and right to serve truth and justice, and the implications of this for both her public action and her moral guidance of the home. For most women reformers, again including the most radical, the moral equivalence of women and men coexisted quite easily with the notion that they were different in other respects and even that women's maternal nature gave them particular moral strengths. But it is important to note that, like the Grimkés, reformers saw motherhood as altered by women's claim to full moral agency. This claim removed a mother's morality from the realm of nature and made it a matter of moral *consciousness*, even in relation to her maternal and family duties. No longer was she subject to the cultural view of her morality as biological, automatic, and secondary.

In reformers' comprehensive conception of the self, individualism was inseparable from moral responsibilities and commitments, even for someone as passionately concerned as Stanton with individual rights. Women rejected moral difference from men, after all, for the purpose of asserting equality of moral duty, not just of moral status. Equality never meant a radical individualism without commitments. Stanton, over the course of her life, as she moved increasingly away from traditional Christianity and toward her own religious synthesis, expressed in varied forms her view that moral responsibility is central to women's selves. As she put it in 1890 in a speech to the National American Woman Suffrage Association:

> The moment we begin to fear the opinions of others and hesitate to tell the truth that is in us, and from motives of policy are silent when we should speak, the divine floods of light and life flow no longer into our souls. Every truth we see is ours to give the world, not to keep for ourselves alone, for in so doing we cheat humanity out of their rights and check our own development.[24]

But it was in her words on women and the "solitude of self" that Stanton expressed most eloquently her view that the struggle for moral agency was the key to women's social equality. The significance of solitude was that women, like men, are responsible not only for their own physical well-being, but especially for the moral meaning and contribution of their own lives. Because, like all individuals, they must face existence and death alone, they cannot be made dependent morally or otherwise on others. So she began in an 1892 address to Congress:

> The point I wish plainly to bring before you on this occasion is the individuality of each human soul—our Protestant idea, the right of the individual conscience and judgment—our republican idea, individual citizenship. In discussing the rights of woman, we are to consider, first, what belongs to her as an individual, in a world of her own, the arbiter of her own destiny.[25]

Stanton, like other reformers, believed a woman could not sidestep accountability for moral decision and action, the duty central to every identity. The meaning of humanity and of justice for Stanton was that each individual's soul is her own with which to make of life what she can and will. Furthermore, this moral capacity is the key to independence—"the power of the human soul, taught of God, to make for itself a world that no mortal hand can mar, nor foot invade."[26] For this reason, she argued, denying women or any human being the moral and material means to encounter that solitude on their own is the most fundamental kind of social injustice and barbarism.

In the most basic sense, then, this new female self set forth by Stanton and even by more conservative reform leaders was related primarily not to children, family, or society, but to the ultimate source of value and meaning in the universe—whatever individual women called that source. The stuff of this relationship, not vague but substantive, was what gave all other relationships their shape and character. Neither was this new female self static in its conception. There was a strong directionality expressed by women reformers in their orientation toward individual and social improvement. The new female self was identified fundamentally with moral development and progress—the potential of human beings reaching for the good.

This orientation to improvement was inseparable from the self's essence, and constituted the very purpose of the life of the self. Organized women existed in the context of what black Baptist reformer Nannie Helen Burroughs called "righteous discontent" with the gap between the way things were in the world and the way they ought to be.[27] It was in the context of this discontent that these women expressed a notion of the female self as responsible for the destiny both of itself and of the human condition in general. They found in biblical religion resources for an explicit, tough-minded criticism of social reality and a set of standards for society's improvement. Emphasizing women's moral agency, white and black women leaders forged from these resources social, economic, and political national agendas.

THE MORAL DIGNITY OF ALL

A second feature of the public vision expressed by women reformers based in predominantly religious associations, in groups that grew from religious roots, and in groups formally independent of religion but connected to it by informal networks was this vision's *collective* focus. Critically appropriated from biblical religion by both religiously conservative and radical reformers, the notion of a common humanity gave rise to not only their emphasis on rights, but also their emphasis on responsibility. Those focused on women's rights, on black civil rights, and on women's social obligations all acted on the premise that human beings share a common moral dignity and destiny.

Black and white women reformers, in different ways, saw human beings as inhabiting a moral universe in which women, because of their nature and their subordination, had a special role to play. Their view that women were the key to the progress of the human race began with awareness of what it would mean for regeneration of the whole to raise women to equality, given their sheer number. As Willard put it, a focus on women was "uplift for one-half the human race."[28] In Stanton's view, as theologian Mary Pellauer points out, the human race as a whole had been dragged down and thrown into chaos by the subjugation of its female half. Elevating women to whole personhood through individual rights —the vote—would, in Stanton's words, add the power of half the human race to its endeavors:

> Man is but half a complete being, with but half an idea on every subject, and yet he has undertaken to govern the world according to his fragmentary ideas, never dreaming that woman's thought, everywhere, was necessary to his success. Need anyone wonder at the disorganization of the state, the church, and the home under a dynasty so incomplete and one-sided?[29]

It was the view especially of the more conservative WCTU that equality would allow women to make their distinctive contribution to the rest of society. Although by the 1890s the WCTU added to its public philosophy the claim that women were due the vote on the basis of their humanity, its primary argument was that the vote would allow them to fulfill their responsibility, bringing their particular moral qualities to public life. Emphasizing that it was womanliness, what women *were*, that made the difference, Willard claimed that women "came into the college and humanized it, into literature and hallowed it, into the business world and ennobled it."[30] She used this logic to move many middle-class, often quite orthodox Christian women and men in a more liberal political direction.

Stanton, however, also offered a version, with important variations, of the same argument. She did not believe that it was yet known how the sexes differed by nature, precisely because both men and women had been distorted by the subjugation of women: "In the education and elevation of woman we are yet to learn the true manhood and womanhood, the true masculine and feminine elements."[31] If there was a way in which she identified women as having distinctive qualities, it was through motherhood, which bred in them special capacities of mercy and love, but she also referred to the distinctive nature of women's thinking.[32] Stanton viewed society as a kind of moral economy. Balancing the masculine and feminine elements would balance and purify distorted national politics, not so much because women were morally superior to men (although she at times described them as representing the "diviner element"), but rather because their association would bring out the "noblest sentiments of both."[33] Just like religion, American democracy had been distorted, Stanton argued, by the fact that half of the nation had been excluded from life according to its principles. The nation's principles would not be realized until women were equal with men and equally responsible citizens.[34]

Like most of her colleagues, and many modern women too, Stanton's commitments to justice did not save her from a perspective bounded by her own cultural limitations. Speaking against the constitutional amendment that would extend suffrage to black men before white women, Stanton revealed that she thought in terms of a global racial hierarchy. She argued that women would save not only the Republic and the Saxon race whose creation it was, but in doing so, all races:

> All must see that this claim for male suffrage is but another . . . violation of the republican idea. With the black man we have no new element in government, but with the education and elevation of women we have a power

that is to develop the Saxon race into a higher and nobler life, and thus, by the law of attraction, to lift all races to a more even platform than can ever be reached in the political isolation of the sexes.[35]

By their racism, Stanton's words confirm the case black women reformers made for why the public world needed most of all to hear their voices. Black women saw themselves as having a special role to play in regeneration of the black race, and hence the human race in general. As Cooper pointed out, "[t]he vital agency of womanhood in the regeneration and progress of a race"[36] was common wisdom; less common was understanding of the pivotal role of black women. Noting that the black race could not be "purified from without," Cooper argued:

> Now the fundamental agency under God in the regeneration, the retraining of the race, as well as the ground work and starting point of its progress upward, must be the *black woman*. . . . the black woman of to-day stands mute and wondering at the Herculean task devolving upon her. . . . No other hand can move the lever. She must be loosed from her bands and set to work.[37]

Demonstrating how belief in separate spheres worked itself out in terms of the experience of black women, Cooper went on to display the logic, based on very different experience, that black mothers shared with white mothers:

> A stream cannot rise higher than its source. The atmosphere of homes is no rarer and purer and sweeter than are the mothers in those homes. A race is but a total of families. The nation is the aggregate of its homes. As the whole is the sum of all its parts, so the character of the parts will determine the characteristics of the whole.[38]

Whatever black women might have in common with white women, however, Cooper made it clear that black women's need to fight both the racism of white society and of white women, as well as white and black sexism, meant that it was they who were at the heart of change in American society and politics.[39]

THE LINK BETWEEN MATERIAL
CONDITIONS AND JUSTICE

While women reformers' commitment to the moral development of humanity as a whole might appear at first to be an abstract goal, the opposite was true. Organized women from the early nineteenth century forward emphasized that humanity's progress depended on the fulfillment of concrete physical needs, to which human beings had a right. Antebellum women reformers, in sharp contrast to the Founding Fathers, developed the notion that rights follow from the essential, *physical* fact of humanity and that this physical reality is basic to the goal of human striving to meet the highest potential:

> This concept of rights as following physical function ordained by natural laws is at odds with the idea of inalienable rights as settled during the struggle for independence. But it provided far greater scope for claims to economic and social justice than the revolutionary model, which effectively limited feminists to claims to political rights.[40]

This early understanding of the physical basis of human welfare, development, and potential continued to be one of the most striking and consistent aspects of organized women's public vision and work into the twentieth century. To be sure, addressing material needs was less of a focus for suffragists, who began after the Civil War to focus chiefly on the narrower goal of legal rights for women. Yet Stanton herself saw relief of suffering and improved physical conditions as crucial to the highest human aspiration, the development of what was noble and true, and the right of the individual to happiness.[41] This focus on alleviating misery through both direct care for individuals and structural change is represented especially well by Jane Addams, who in the 1880s was starting the Hull-House Settlement in Chicago to address the suffering caused by industrialization and urbanization. Twenty years later, in her autobiography, Addams identified the impulse to improve the physical condition of "our common humanity" as basic to women reformers' social welfare and rights activity.[42] While she valued higher education immensely, she feared that because it focused on acquisition of knowledge it threatened to make her and other young women lose "that simple and almost automatic response to the human appeal, that old healthful reaction resulting in activity from the mere presence of suffering or helplessness."[43]

Women's own familiarity with suffering, the suffering of injustice and childbirth, was often cited by women leaders as the basis for their particular ability to empathize with and respond to human suffering in general. When women reformers rejected the "curse" brought upon Eve in Eden, for example, they were rejecting the positive value that Christianity traditionally had placed on women's suffering in marital subordination and childbirth. Reformers were intent on using women's moral knowledge that suffering means the physical and moral degradation of human beings through pain and loss of dignity. They sought to address this moral degradation on the physical level, as well as on the level of rights and opportunity, recognizing the link that often existed between the two levels. In an 1888 opening address to the International Council of Women, as elsewhere, Stanton argued that it was their own physical and political suffering that had given women a deep sense of injustice and moral insight into the universal principle of justice.[44] She was articulating a theme that ran throughout the human welfare and the rights work of nineteenth-century white and black organized women.

What most white women could not see, however, was that seeking justice for themselves and others also meant learning about the limits of their own understanding of justice. In her 1892 book, *Voice from the South*, Anna Julia Cooper attempted to get these reformers to recognize that they were preoccupied with the rights of privileged white women and blind often to their own participation in racial injustice. She sharply reminded white leaders of the broader scope of their responsibility:

For woman's cause is the cause of the weak; and when *all* the weak shall have received their due consideration, then woman will have her "rights," and the Indian will have his rights, and the Negro will have his rights, and all the strong will have learned at last to deal justly, to love mercy, and to walk humbly; and our fair land will have been taught the secret of universal courtesy.[45]

However imperfectly for white women, reformers' concern for justice was at the heart of their public vision. More than providing women with motivation and justification for their public initiatives, religion provided them with resources for a public vision of justice. White and black women, from their different perspectives, were guided by a notion of justice that criticized subjugation of human beings in body or spirit. With the goal of justice setting the standard for relations between individuals and groups, organized women visualized social reform as promoting both the moral growth of individuals and the regeneration of basic social relations to meet this moral standard.

INDIVIDUAL CIVIC ACTION

A final characteristic of organized women's new public vision was its emphasis on the individual's obligation to civic action. For these reformers, community was not first a concept, but a *practice*. They brought democracy and Protestantism together in a way that generated a remarkable and sustained level of civic initiative and responsive action. Focused on building a sense of common humanity, transforming injustice into justice, and improving the material condition of those in need, their civic action was guided by three major religious values: philanthropy, charity, and benevolence.

While it is important to learn from the ways in which white women reformers' notion of the goal of justice was provincial, it is anachronistic to understand their intentions, or those of black reformers, on the basis of modern, secular meanings of these values. All three, but especially philanthropy, represented organized women's reading of the Christian commandment to love one's neighbor as oneself. For them, philanthropy did not mean the optional, condescending concern for those in need that scholars depict. After touring Rome in 1869 on an extended trip abroad and seeing how full the world was of the misery of poverty, Frances Willard spoke of philanthropy as a deep fellow-feeling:

> Whoever can fail to feel the fires of a quenchless philanthropy kindling in his breast as he contemplates such scenes is either too frivolous for thought or too hardened for emotion. For myself, whatever I have not learned here, Rome has taught me an intense love & a tender pity for my race.[46]

Charity had a related meaning. It too referred to the Christian injunction to love, but more precisely it meant acceptance of the human as a fundamentally *common* enterprise. For organized women, charity was an act of positive faith in and a spirit of openness toward the human—a recognition of moral community. Like any principle, charity might be employed to serve good or ill. Willard, however, testified to its potential for challenging her own moral provincialism. She acknowledged in her journal her pleased surprise at the "nobleness & right-heartedness" of people she met who were not members of any church: "It enlarges my charity—my faith in mankind as such, my catholicity—my cosmopolitan spirit. And this is a *gain* surely."[47] Although Willard, like other white reform leaders, was not free of racism, her achievements in building political alliances among disparate national and international groups, and between Protestants, Catholics, and Jews, certify that the spirit of charity could discipline reformers to be more open to difference of various kinds.

While philanthropy and charity referred to the value placed on cultivating sensitivity to others, especially their need, benevolence meant *doing* justice. Anthony reflected women reformers' self-consciously revisionist emphasis on doing over believing when, at midcentury, she protested the church's focus on creed and dogma in her diary. She was particularly frustrated by Protestantism's greater concern with abstract theology than with "conditions" and making a difference on earth:

Thus it is belief, not Christian benevolence, that is made the modern test
of Christianity—when will the world wake from its stupor and look *truth*
strait [*sic*] in the face.[48]

Anthony was articulating a characteristic theme of organized
women. They aspired to a practice of Christian benevolence that
meant not incidental kindness to social inferiors, but accountability to the universal law of doing justice. This was the principle of
benevolence that undergirded women's rights claims and to which
Cooper appealed in trying to enlarge white women's grasp of justice:

[W]hen the right of the individual is made sacred . . . then is mastered the
science of politeness, the art of courteous contact, which is naught but the
practical application of the principal of benevolence, the back bone and
marrow of all religion; then woman's lesson is taught and woman's cause
is won—not the white woman nor the black woman nor the red woman,
but the cause of every man or woman who has writhed silently under a
mighty wrong.[49]

NEW PUBLIC PRIORITIES

Public vision characterized by these shared emphases motivated organized women's activities and was reflected in their priorities. Fed
by their moral imaginations, the power of their vision and its reach
challenges the modern understanding we have of moral values as
private, individual, and necessarily conservative. Rooted as they
were in religious narratives of oppression overthrown, in symbols
of just authority, and in accountability for the progress of the race,
these women were not satisfied with the conditions of human life
they witnessed around them and reached, undaunted, for such
goals as equality, freedom, and community. Constantly citing the
prophetic public authority of female biblical figures like Deborah,
Huldah, Hagar, and Esther, they imagined that fundamental social
change was possible. And even though the surprising degree of
openness and idealism many white women displayed was matched
by a high degree of embeddedness in their own privilege, they still
achieved much that was good.

From their earliest moral reform efforts to their progressive legislative achievements of the 1920s, the power of organized women's moral imagination identified approaches to social improvement that consistently challenged the moral structure of society and social relations, whether through efforts to meet concrete need or promote social legislation. Applying the moral standards of human dignity and progress as their guide, both black and white women set their particular agendas for action with the bold purpose of righting social arrangements gone, or going, wrong.

Women and Women in Need. The most striking illustration of these women's moral imagination was that they identified women themselves, especially women in need, as their major priority. Recognizing women as a social group, asserting their rights, and seeking to improve their welfare was new. Organized women strove to bring attention, legal reform, and social resources to eliminating women's secondary status in society. Major focal points of their struggle included civil rights, "home protection" (temperance), maternal and child health, employment, pensions, education and culture, and protection from violence.

This priority alone is proof that organized women's critical reinterpretation of religious and republican traditions made new public vision out of traditional values. There was no historical precedent for making women an item on the public agenda, let alone at the top of it. By asserting the full moral dignity of women as a social value, they were claiming, in the face of the established public authority of privileged men, the authority to redefine the democratic social order. They also were upending in the United States the inherited pattern of centuries of religious and cultural subordination of the female in the West. By linking their rights to the welfare of the black race and the human race as a whole, black women made the most radical claim of all.

This departure of identifying women as a priority, as innovative as it was, did not bring with it social thinking that was different in all respects from the norms of the time. Some women reformers did champion radical reforms of women's political, legal, economic, and sexual rights. However, many did not intend to push the boundaries of contemporary thinking about gender too far. For this reason, especially in the face of often fierce male opposition, black and white organized women alike typically justified their public activity on behalf of women with the reminder that the family—women and children—was their special province.

Nevertheless, they saw themselves, in Ann Firor Scott's apt phrase, as "natural allies" with one another, in national associations, and with the women in need they were trying to help:

> Few comfortable well-to-do people in any time or place, and of either sex, seriously try to think of a society different from that in which they find themselves. The wonder is not that so many women were unwilling to risk their own position for principle but that a few were and that a considerable number spent their whole lives trying to change things for women not at all like themselves.[50]

To be sure, the majority were white middle-class women who remained creatures of their time, "only occasionally manag[ing] to look upon black or Asian women as anything more than possible recipients of their good works."[51] Yet on rare occasions, the biblical framework that gave organized women a shared language even provided the basis for a new and "unlikely sisterhood," allowing some to cooperate across class, race, regional, and religious lines on shared agendas for social change.[52] Within the Baptist tradition, for example, white northern women worked with southern black women in the 1890s to address black educational needs and poverty. These women managed to swim against the tide of increasing racial segregation at the close of the nineteenth century in the tradition of evangelical abolitionism:

> Their neo-abolitionist rhetoric stressed the importance, centrality, even primacy of woman's role in solving the nation's race problem. As such, "woman's work for woman" served to connect women who would otherwise have never met at all, much less forged a sisterhood that traversed regional, class, and racial boundaries.[53]

Sisterhood lay in another direction as well. When the Jewish Women's Congress and the National Council of Jewish Women were established in 1893, its leaders saw it as an organization to "represent the modern Jewish woman side by side with her non-Jewish sisters."[54] These new groups were greeted enthusiastically by one of the leaders of the General Federation of Women's Clubs who was an energetic pioneer of municipal reform and a Christian:

> Jew and Gentile no longer exist. We stand hand to hand, heart to heart. . . . We ask no longer of any woman, what do you believe, what is your sect, . . . but are you a clubable woman, are you willing to go to work with us. And if she says yes, she is of us.[55]

When women recognized that they were natural allies, a new notion of individual and collective responsibility for human welfare was born in the United States. Based on a new, if far from perfect, vision of national community, it grew out of the recognition not only by privileged women, but also by wage-earning and even poor women, that they inhabited the same moral universe with women in need.[56] It was a recognition that women's destiny and cultural status in some sense tied them together, and it led women reformers to identify as a new public priority ideas about who deserved help in society and why, about the relationship between helper and helped, and about the value of that help and that relationship to the nation.

Mothers and Mothers in Need. Reformers' second priority was mothers. Asserting the value of motherhood meant recognizing motherhood as both a public value and a social institution deserving public support. At one level, organized women were recognizing the gap that existed between motherhood as a religious and republican ideal and the vulnerable condition of many mothers. At another level, however, by making mothers a priority organized women were addressing the way society was structured. This was particularly true of black reformers, given the racism of the republican tradition that held black mothers firmly beyond the pale of the legal rights and social recognition granted white mothers. The marginality of black motherhood meant black reformers' actions had even more profound significance. By claiming the social status as mothers denied their enslaved female ancestors, black women were also laying claim to new standing in American society for African Americans in general.[57] And while most white women accepted the ideal of mothers' unpaid domestic labor taking precedence for them over paid work—something for which modern feminists often criticize them—what was unprecedented was organized women's *rejection* of the traditional principle of the social organization of motherhood: the relegation of responsibility for motherhood as a social value to the home and its exclusion from the public sphere. One of the most radical initiatives of nineteenth- and early-twentieth-century women was their rejection of the idea that this central social institution might exist as only a private, individual responsibility and not a public one as well.

Organized women sought to make motherhood a public value in various ways. One of the most basic, spanning the century from the earliest reform efforts to the 1920s, was their focus on prostitution and sexual exploitation of women. These efforts, no doubt, were for some moralistic crusades for sexual purity, but they represented something more as well. They addressed the sexual degradation of women and the licentiousness of men and women as a threat to the social fabric. With regard to prostitution, as elsewhere, middle-class women were keenly aware of the link between their lives and those of the women they sought to reform and help. They too lived with and resented the effects of the sexual double standard,[58] and they recognized the *economic* vulnerability that was connected to all women's sexual vulnerability. Moreover, reformers' efforts to change sexual social behavior were aimed at asserting the dignity of women, stopping sexual exploitation of women and children, and winning equal rights under the law for prostitutes so that their male patrons also might be held accountable. To read about reformers' achievements with regard to social practices of sexuality is to realize, as in so many cases, that it was women's efforts that introduced standards in a number of areas that today we take for granted. In addition to the regulation of prostitution, for example, they worked into the 1890s and beyond for state by state legislation to prevent the sexual exploitation of minors. By 1894, as a result of the efforts of the WCTU, the age of sexual consent was still ten in only four states and had been raised to sixteen in twenty states.[59]

A second indicator of reformers' systematic approach to their concern about motherhood was the temperance movement itself. One of the chief threats to all mothers and children in nineteenth-century America, in the context of rapid industrialization, was the prevalence of extreme alcohol abuse. Like concern about prostitution, temperance reform began early in the century and continued throughout it. It was aimed at protecting women and children from abuse, physical and emotional, suffered at the hands of drunken husbands and fathers, as well as from the effects of poverty resulting from paychecks spent in saloons. Poverty, one of the root concerns of the WCTU, was attributed to alcohol addiction, but addiction also was seen as a result of patterns of social injustice. The WCTU realistically linked women's welfare and rights with the need to protect the welfare of their families and communities. When Willard led the organization in 1881 to endorse what she strategically called the "home ballot," she connected women's lack of power at the ballot box with their inability to address threats to the home and other patterns of injustice in the society and made voting rights the focal point of the WCTU's national work.[60] But another fundamental purpose of organized women's focus on women's rights was their effort to improve the status of motherhood. So, in 1896, a founder of the National Congress of Mothers (which in 1924 became the PTA) linked the lack of rights and dignity of mothers to the poor quality and character of national life:

> The race which is born of mothers who are harassed, bullied, subordinated, or made the victims of blind passion or power, or of mothers who are simply too pretty and self-debased to feel their subject status, cannot

fail to continue to give the horrible spectacles we have always had of war, of crime, of vice, of trickery, of double-dealing, of pretense, of lying, of arrogance, of subserviency, of incompetence, of brutality, and, alas! of insanity, idiocy, and disease added to a fearful and unnecessary mortality.[61]

Thus, the movement for women's rights gained much of its power from the argument that rights would reverse the subordination of mothers and make them a public force. By the early twentieth century, organized women had laid the foundation for a wide social consensus that mothers, based in the home, had a crucial role to play in improving and sustaining the physical and moral health of the country. Together, in the years leading up to World War I, married, middle-class women and professional reform leaders mobilized this consensus behind the twin notions that women were important leaders of social reform and that mothers and their children were a valuable public investment.[62] Progressive reformers were reacting to their perceptions that the social and cultural status of motherhood needed strengthening. They spoke out of a deep sense of the threatened state of motherhood, not out of sentimentality, when they sought "the greater honor and the greater stability of home life."[63] These later reformers drew on the traditions of nineteenth-century organized women when they recognized in the plight of the disadvantaged the potential economic vulnerability faced by all women dependent on a male wage and threatened by "the great and growing evils of non-support and desertion of children by their fathers."[64] They were seeing many patterns that have become prominent in American life by the close of the twentieth century.

By the first decades of the twentieth century, organized women's massive grass-roots mobilization on behalf of mothers drove a new national agenda: the protective legislation that launched the American welfare state. This legislation set in place, at the state level, pensions for mothers without a male breadwinner's income and established minimum wages and maximum hours to protect working mothers. It also established female-dominated federal public agencies—chiefly the Children's Bureau, established in 1912, and the post-war Women's Bureau, established in 1920, in the Department of Labor—and, through the Sheppard-Towner Act, made provision for maternal and infant health education programs. This protective social legislation was conceived and championed by the politics of a national association of organized mothers skillfully working to establish policy and programs that honored mothers:

> These upper- and middle-class women were trying to embrace as sisters, fellow mothers, the impoverished widows who would be helped by mothers' pensions. The originators of mothers' pension laws intended to include needy mothers in the same moral universe as themselves, providing them with regular and nondemeaning material assistance to make it possible for them to realize a version of the same basic ideals of homemaking and motherhood to which the ladies themselves aspired.[65]

Building motherhood's cultural meaning and value into a national responsibility, progressive reformers intended mothers in need to receive deserved support.[66] This ensured that the primary logic for mothers' pensions was not their poverty. Mothers in need were recognized as part of the larger universe of mothers and supported by a consensus about motherhood as a socially valued and politically significant institution.

In making motherhood a public value, organized women acted to make the cultural ideal of domestic rather than paid labor available to mothers in need and to prevent other vulnerabilities that poor families faced: child wage-labor, the government practice of intervening to take children away from widows engaged in paid work (often full-time) outside the home, or families' dependence on charities.[67] Their motive was improvement, to change what they saw as unfair social practices for families without a male wage, not to impose middle-class norms for motherhood on women in financial need.[68] Nevertheless, modern feminists often criticize maternalist reformers for promoting this legislation with a "limited vision of women's rights and responsibilities" and for failing to champion instead such things as childcare to support mothers' wage labor.[69] This criticism is not only anachronistic in its expectation that these reformers should have set and achieved policy goals even modern feminists and policymakers have not yet achieved. It also underestimates the issue at stake. In championing mothers, organized women also were asserting, as they had been for decades, the value for society as a whole of mothers' unpaid family and community labor.

Human Welfare and Rights. From the early nineteenth century to the early twentieth, the emphasis white and black reformers placed on women, mothers, and children existed in the context of their broadest public priority: human welfare. They felt what Jane Addams later called an urgent "Subjective Necessity" to focus on purposes of fundamental significance to human life.[70] None was more fundamental for women, from the earliest moral reform and anti-slavery movements forward, than the effort to restore individuals and society as a whole to the path of progress. The principle that drove them was belief in the responsibility of local communities and the national community for providing human beings with conditions that supported moral and material well-being—nutrition, housing, health, education and employment, literacy and cultural growth, and recreation. White reformers and black alike took the religious and secular ideal of the "common good" and developed their own understandings of it.[71]

These understandings are most evident not only in the rights-oriented legislation that organized women championed, but also in the actual structural change that their notion of welfare brought to American politics and society. Not only new institutions, but new *kinds* of institutions embodied their broad concept of social welfare. By literally institutionalizing their notion of collective responsibility for human dignity, well-being, and growth, these reformers revised and expanded the American idea of community and built significant aspects of communities across the century:

[W]omen found a way to shape community life and to influence American concepts of community responsibility and social welfare. Churches, orphan asylums, homes for the aged, juvenile courts, playgrounds, libraries, women's colleges, kindergartens, and well-baby clinics are only a few of the community structures that we now take for granted but which first were inaugurated by some women's association.[72]

Indeed, among the religiously less radical reformers, the ballot was valued as a right because it was a means to carry out women's moral obligation to achieve a range of economic and social reforms. The WCTU, which made temperance the center of its wide human welfare agenda in the second half of the nineteenth century, exemplified the welfare focus of many of the federated women's associations. By 1889, it was sponsoring through its headquarter branch in Chicago alone direct services that included "two day nurseries, two Sunday Schools, an industrial school, a mission that sheltered four thousand homeless or destitute women in a twelve-month period, a free medical dispensary that treated over sixteen hundred patients a year, a lodging house for men that had to date provided temporary housing for over fifty thousand men, and a low-cost restaurant."[73] Under Willard, the WCTU called for a broad program of civic and government-sponsored social reform that put it at the forefront of the Social Gospel movement emerging at century's end.[74] This movement, with its focus on urban labor, immigration, and other issues, built on the same principle of the relationship between individual and social regeneration that first had elicited organized women's commitment in the evangelical revivals earlier in the century.

ORGANIZED WOMEN'S PUBLIC ACHIEVEMENTS

Organized women's tradition of public leadership represents a major stage in the history of American women's claim to full public participation. Addressing the moral state of the American social fabric and improving it, these women made a difference both through what they accomplished and in how they fell short. Most of all, organized women challenged dominant American cultural conceptions both of women and of leadership. By establishing women's right to vote and the legitimacy of their activity outside the home on behalf of public goals, they significantly transformed the social roles of women, and the cultural images and status that underlay them. They did so in large part by drawing on traditional cultural beliefs and deploying them in a new way:

[P]aradoxical as it may seem, American devotion to the cult of domesticity may best explain women's political influence in the nineteenth century. American society embraced with conviction the idea of women's moral superiority, and as women moved into the public sphere they carried with them that aura of uncorrupted righteousness bestowed on them to justify the importance of their role as guardians of the home and nurturers of children.[75]

Thus, they established the norm of women's agency on behalf of local communities and the nation by extending to the public sphere the traditional expectation of their moral distinctiveness.

In doing so, organized women also transformed the social roles, and the cultural image and status underlying them, of mothers and motherhood. Reformers expanded the earlier notion of women's public and political function, "Republican motherhood," shifting the cultural norms as they went. As, to varying degrees, they claimed to be taking maternal values out of the home and into the public world, reformers made mothers not only public actors, but also confident, although otherwise unrecognized, public *experts*.[76] This sense of mothers' authority to assert expertise in matters of public policy related to mothers and children rings in their words and actions. So, for example, in 1913 the Vice-President of the Massachusetts Mothers' Congress replied firmly to a male expert opposing mothers' pensions:

You see, mothers in spite of the sociologists, feel themselves, for once, on their own ground in this matter; and in possession of all their faculties, will continue to think that, as far as children are concerned, not they, but the learned doctors, are in the amateur class.[77]

But women asserted expertise that had to do with the conditions and health of the broader community as well. Their logic was summed up neatly by Jane Addams in 1910, when she described the challenges to urban motherhood—ranging from sanitation and safety to immorality on the streets—that justified and required women's involvement in public affairs:

> If a woman would keep on with her old business of caring for her house and rearing her children she will have to have some conscience in regard to public affairs lying quite outside of her immediate household. The individual conscience and devotion are no longer effective.[78]

The third major accomplishment of organized womanhood was constructing an effective political culture based on women's social vision, organizations, and peculiar style. This culture expressed women's positive sense of themselves as different and separate from the politics and public agenda of men.[79] Both white and black women saw value in being outsiders to the (white) male political system; black women recognized themselves as outsiders too to the whole of white racist culture and society. Both groups of women expressed their sense that much was fundamentally wrong in society and relied on their experience of exclusion for insights and vision. By the early twentieth century, organized women could draw on their own political tradition and distinctive political style: a capacity for effective public education, wide-based lobbying, and persuasive moral rhetoric that spoke to fundamental, widely held social values.[80]

While there were significant differences between rural and urban women's initiatives, nothing captures the distinctive profile of organized women's politics better than an example of temperance activity in a village in upstate New York in 1874.[81] In an attempt to stem the practical costs of alcohol abuse to individual women, men, and children, women reformers set out during a year of concerted effort to decrease alcoholic consumption in their village, a noted Finger Lakes resort. Their first step was to temporarily halt service in the saloon of the largest hotel by praying as a group on its premises. Then they attended a meeting of the village licensing board to request that the hours of bars be limited and no new liquor licenses be issued in the village. All along, they worked directly to get merchants who sold liquor to stop. Next, they campaigned to convince men to vote for the temperance candidate in the village election, contributing a political presence by public fasting and praying on election day. When the reformers' candidate lost, men of the village who opposed temperance paraded through town with effigies of the women, which they proceeded to hang and then burn. Undaunted, the women organized a petition drive, communicated to the new board the opposition of the village to new and renewed liquor licenses, and succeeded in convincing the board to allow a new license only to the drugstore.

While such activity has seemed to many scholars so indirect and informal when measured against male norms for political effectiveness as hardly to be worthy of the label politics, it made women a political force to be reckoned with. They held their own view, that government ought to limit behavior that threatened communities, and by appealing to state government, which set broader liquor and other policies, often made it a crucial ally.[82] Moreover, through personal commitment, initiative, determination, and often physical courage, organized women at local and national levels acted in terms of the community as an entity—assessing community need, addressing directly all those bearing moral and formal responsibility for community welfare, and persisting until the priority they saw was met.

At heart, women's politics were a criticism of the power held by privileged men and the values it served. This criticism was focused particularly on institutions women saw as central to the health of society and social relations—including religion, democracy, motherhood, the family, education, and public health. Both black and white women boldly laid claim to central responsibility for helping to reshape the mainstream of society and politics. Their view that the government itself needed improvement, especially with regard to its claim to represent justice, was entirely logical, for they saw themselves as owing their standing in the public arena to a sover-

eign principle and symbol of justice greater than the state, a principle that conferred on them the moral equality the state denied.
One of the most telling examples of this critical political perspective that women articulated with growing momentum over the decades is the congressional testimony of reformer Florence Kelley in
1920 in support of the Sheppard-Towner Maternity and Infancy
Protection Act. Speaking of the public health crisis of infant mortality and of congressional opposition to spending that would address it, Kelley said:

> [W]hen we are told that this country is so poor and this Congress so ha-
> rassed by things of greater importance than the deaths of a quarter of a
> million of children a year, . . . we say to ourselves, "Surely we are not to
> take this seriously? . . . Why does Congress wish women and children to
> die?"[83]

Organized women's crowning accomplishment was thus to contribute the vision of social welfare to American society and government. By acting over the decades on their broad vision of the
public good, they began to make national politics over according to
their conception and their social priorities—making their social
policy into national public policy.[84] In this way, they played a significant role in transforming liberalism as a political ideology and
practice, encouraging government to understand that "the concerns of politics and of the home were inextricable."[85] As Ann Firor
Scott writes:

> Women certainly did not set out to build what we now call the "welfare
> state," but in the process of trying to solve one concrete problem after an-
> other in the face of the often implacable opposition of businessmen of
> many kinds and even of professional bodies such as the American Medical
> Association, they turned to the state and federal government as the only
> sources of countervailing power. In the process, they persuaded govern-
> ments to take on many of the responsibilities for human welfare that they
> had themselves originally assumed, as well as those for which they had
> developed the rationale. . . . [T]he work of women in their associations

over nearly a century and a half shaped the ideas, brought about the grass-
roots support, and gave our federal-state welfare structure much of its
characteristic form.[86]

SO NEAR AND YET SO FAR

If there is much to learn from what organized women accomplished
over the decades from the early nineteenth century to the early
twentieth when they won the vote, these lessons come into even
sharper focus with the abrupt *ending* of their public effectiveness
in the 1920s. This ending came, paradoxically, following the constitutional amendment on suffrage and reformers' successful establishment of federal programs and policies to protect women
and children. Contrary to expectations, gaining the right to vote
marked not a new beginning in women's political power, but a decline. To be sure, suffrage guaranteed women access to the mainstream of electoral politics—voting and officeholding. But access
did not de facto win women equality, for "the ballot proved a sterile
victory. The larger social and economic disabilities of women remained untouched, and the battle had to be fought all over again
two generations later."[87]

What suffrage did was fold women into the dominant male political culture. Joining the political mainstream encouraged them to
give up the work of constructing their own political culture in
which they had been so long engaged. Yet women's political impact
had not been automatic and would not be in the future, as was demonstrated by the failure of a female voting bloc to emerge once they
gained the vote. Without the continuing effort and strategy of their
organized politics, women had gained structural change of one
kind and lost their momentum for broader social-structural reform. Whether or not women actually believed that voting and formal access to political office were sufficient mechanisms for change,
their earlier political clout dissipated once they came to rely on voting as their primary political activity.[88]

This outcome helps us see that separateness was an ingredient
as essential to women's political culture as their ability to build

alliances with men. Exclusion from male politics and mainstream institutions originally had turned women back on their own re-sources—on their own dedication, energy, vision, creativity, sense of priorities, organizations, and leadership. Here women had found the power to act to make a difference. But they lost the vari-able of self-reliance, the political significance of which organized women may not have understood, when they gained the vote. And what was behind that self-reliance was even more important—women's sense of their own authority. It was this authority, which they painstakingly had developed collectively through years of ef-fort, that women handed over to the federal government.

It has been observed that in the 1920s women passed the social policy baton to government, so that "[g]overnment now carried moral authority and the obligations it implied" in terms both of eth-ics and social and economic welfare.[89] But this observation ob-scures how much was lost by women and the country in this pass-ing of the baton. To be sure, when social welfare became a national priority in the Depression, women reformers' work provided the models for the Roosevelt administration: the Social Security Act of 1935 included maternal and child health provisions based on the Sheppard-Towner Act and Aid to Dependent Children based on the mothers' pensions, and the priority of child-labor regulation was reflected in the Fair Labor Standards Act of 1937.[90] At the same time, however, women *gave up* belief in their own social and political authority. Seemingly, they failed to recognize the signif-icance of this authority in comparison with the vote. In exchanging separateness for belonging, they also lost awareness of the need to formulate and promote their own broad agenda for public reform. This was evident even in the behavior of the few women elected to Congress, as Jane Addams concluded in 1930, commenting on their voting patterns:

> Some of us feel that women in politics thus far have been too conventional,
> too afraid to differ with the men, too ill at ease to trust their own judg-
> ments, too skeptical of the wisdom of the humble to incorporate the needs

of simple women into the ordering of political life. . . . it is much easier
to dovetail into the political schemes of men than to release the innate concerns of women, which might be equivalent to a revolutionary force.[91]

It was not only, however, that women let slip through their fin-
gers the public authority for which they had made such a successful
bid. Other developments also contributed to undermining
women's progress toward establishing public authority. Not the
least of these was the backlash that grew in the mid-1920s against
the very maternalist policies and programs that had been successfully set in place.[92] In the face of this backlash, it was all the more
costly that the style of nationally coordinated politics women had
used to set mothers' pensions legislation in place was not as effective
in guaranteeing adequate funding of pensions state by state or in keeping their implementation on track with supporters' original intentions.[93] The challenge of "governing" required sustained political
effort of a wholly new kind; national alliances of women reformers
did not rise to meet this new challenge. Neither were women's politics able to address the ways in which administration of public policy by bureaucrats and social workers altered the value of honoring
motherhood that the legislation had been intended to establish as a
public value.[94]

Finally, the biggest challenge to women's bid for public authority came from the professions. The Children's Bureau, established
in 1912 and staffed by leading women reformers, was at the center
of a community-focused government effort. This effort involved
large numbers of women in fashioning government services and
many women doctors and nurses in developing an effective public
health program. Thus, it had significantly increased women's influence in government, health, and politics. Steadily, however, the
medical profession asserted control over the Bureau's approach to
its work; by the end of the 1920s that profession had successfully
medicalized (and individualized) women reformers' original economic and social orientation to maternal and child health.

By 1930, the White House Conference on Child Health and

Protection was dominated by the perspectives of medical special-
ists, instead of the women reformers and clubwomen who had
played key roles in the conferences of the 1910s and 1920s.[95] It was
the medical establishment, along with conservatives, that also got
the Sheppard-Towner Act repealed in 1929 despite its significant
progress in addressing rural women's health and infant mortality,
and by the 1930s mainly male doctors and psychologists directed
child-welfare policy at state and national levels:

> Their medical perspective replaced the earlier Children's Bureau model of
> community involvement in maternal and infant health care. There was lit-
> tle place for club women and social activists—or even women physicians
> —in the work of the new Bureau. Although all but three of the forty-eight
> state directors of child-welfare programs had been women when Shep-
> pard-Towner began in 1922, by 1939 three-quarters of them were men.
> Professionalism had triumphed over social reform.[96]

Along with this development came a devaluation of mothers and
motherhood. As Ladd-Taylor points out, by the 1930s motherhood
as a policy area nationally "had become the domain of physicians,
psychologists, and psychiatric social workers, who generally ignored mothers or blamed them for their children's problems."[97]
The fact that bearing and raising children were being taken out of
women's "exclusive control," with mothers being advised increasingly to depend on medical professionals,[98] meant that the social
and cultural *authority* of that work was being shifted from mothers
to the new "experts." It has been noted that in promoting the rights
and dignity of mothers, women reformers had challenged the patriarchal family.[99] By the 1930s, the male-dominated professions of
health, especially, began to reassert the patriarchal authority over
mothers that had once belonged chiefly to the father in the family.

CONCLUSION

In retrospect, it is remarkable that organized women made as much
progress as they did in bringing about political, social, and cultural
change. Because motherhood was the linchpin of the cultural be-

liefs controlling their social reality, it was particularly remarkable that they were as successful as they were in bringing motherhood out of the realm of the natural and private and into the public arena as a rationale for women's political activity and as a social institution deserving public support. What happened demonstrates how fundamentally new women's vision of motherhood, national community, civic responsibility, government action and obligation, and democratic values was. It demonstrates too how difficult it was for American women to achieve public power, let alone to achieve it on their own terms and that it was even more difficult for them to sustain it once they had gained access to male-dominated political institutions.

In short, as modern women face the continuing challenge of becoming full participants in American public life, contemplation of the public tradition of organized women should correct any tendency we might have to identify access as a sufficient goal. By its achievements and limitations, this tradition reminds us that culture plays a powerful role in shaping social reality and in determining what must be addressed to change women's social situation. This tradition helps us see that efforts at social change today must take into account a complex set of dominant cultural values and meanings linked to gender that still are shaping the social roles and status of modern American women in all their racial, ethnic, and economic diversity. At the heart of these values is the cultural belief that continues to deny women authority by denying them moral equality.

Engaging and transforming this belief requires that women assert their full moral agency in following a public agenda of their own. We turn next to consider where contemporary women should begin in developing new public vision and a new agenda to help address the crisis of values in American society at the turn of the twenty-first century.

CHAPTER SEVEN

Toward a New Public Vision

When we do not view nineteenth- and early-twentieth-century women reformers narrowly, as precursors of contemporary feminism or even of the welfare state, but allow them to speak in their own terms, we learn new lessons. Exploring the moral content of their public vision and the full record of their public achievements, we see beyond the established popular understanding of these women as suffragists or originators of women's volunteer tradition. We see, instead, that black and white reformers separately asserted women's full moral equality and agency, struggled for racial uplift, and established in America the idea of public responsibility for human welfare. They have much to teach us about women's public participation, the values of democratic society, and motherhood and social reform. These lessons are crucial to understanding our national values crisis better and to devising a sounder approach to addressing it. In particular, they encourage modern women to take initiative—to formulate their own vision both of themselves as public actors and of society and paths to its improvement.

Above all, these lessons from the past make us see in new ways the centrality of motherhood to sound new vision for the lives of contemporary women and for the nation. They correct modern feminist tendencies to shift the focus on women away from motherhood. Yet, most of all, the lessons we glean from the public traditions of organized women reveal the superficial nature of current conservative views of women's public contributions as mothers. Instead of developing a responsible grasp of the nation's grave social problems, these conservative views scapegoat poor "bad" mothers, especially black teenage ones. Motherhood, however, is central to sound new public vision in a way far more complex than that grasped by belief that female-headed, single-parent families are eroding the moral order of society and that "good" (i.e., married) mothers are the solution to this problem. Furthermore, motherhood's crucial role in women's public participation is far different from that implied by a narrow maternalist proposal that women's nurturing qualities define their public vision and activity.

I want to propose a new and larger view of the public role that modern women and motherhood have to play in shaping American values. Both the progress made by organized women and the limits of what they achieved help us see that the nation faces an unfinished agenda of moral and cultural, as well as social, change. Traditional beliefs about public and private continue not only to restrict the public participation of women, but to marginalize the daily unpaid labor of family and community welfare associated with women, preventing this labor from becoming a priority also of the public world. The cultural conception of motherhood embedded in these beliefs limits the moral status in society of women and of this labor. The result is an imbalance at the heart of the values and structure of American society, a far more fundamental cause of the nation's values crisis than the "social pathology" of people who fail to fit successfully into this social structure.

RECONSTRUCTING MOTHERHOOD

It is this imbalance that identifies motherhood as the starting point of a major agenda of cultural change that women in all their diversity and the nation must address if we are to resolve our values crisis. Beginning with motherhood is especially urgent, moreover, because of the growing gap between traditional ideals and social reality created by profound changes in American life. This gap imperils mothers and those dependent on them. It also imperils the values of family and community welfare for which motherhood has stood in society, raising the question of how best to support these increasingly threatened values and the labor that sustains them. For these reasons, reconstructing the traditional conception of motherhood and organizing new social bases of support for this labor is crucial both to women of all racial, ethnic, and class groups and to the nation.[1] This project should share top priority with equal rights for women and is essential to achieving them.

The reconstruction of motherhood must revise the sixteenth-century judgment sustained by traditional cultural beliefs that motherhood is *incompatible* with women's full moral equality and independence as individuals. Reconstructing motherhood requires rejecting the maternalist notion that women's moral agency is constituted by instinctive maternal ways of behaving and thinking that automatically shape women's thinking and action. If women are fully human beings and morally equal, their moral agency must be understood as going beyond instinct to involve conscious and self-conscious reflection: to involve "mak[ing] moral judgments, creat[ing] moral meaning, and claim[ing] moral values in preserving, resisting, and transforming relations."[2] Reconceiving the cultural meaning of motherhood means rejecting the premise that female morality is a secondary form—dependent, natural, and unconscious—that sets boundaries on women's moral agency. It means asserting that women's family commitments also are governed by moral consciousness and exist in the broader context of their priorities for society and for the world, and of their duties to both. In short, reconstructing motherhood begins by recognizing mothers as women whose individual values, although centrally influenced by their cultural association with motherhood, and most often by their experience of it as well, are not wholly or predictably defined by it.

Reconstructing motherhood makes concern about black, teenage single-parent mothers part of a broader social strategy, recognizing that these mothers are only the most visible indicators of a society in transition. The goal of this broader strategy must be structural change aimed at *weaving anew* the eroding daily patterns of mutuality in American life and the public bonds of social obligation. By enlisting women's commitment, skill, and vision in reshaping American values, reconstructing motherhood, coupled with continuing pursuit of equal rights for women of all racial, ethnic, and class groups, promises to set women on the path to achieving their full public potential for themselves and for the nation.

RENEWING DEMOCRATIC VALUES AND VISION

As they develop new public vision that makes reconstructing motherhood a priority, modern women can find in organized women's public vision important correctives to contemporary ways of thinking about women and leadership, citizens and public policy, and social welfare and American democratic values. Among these correctives are conceptions of both the individual citizen and public participation that combine rights and responsibilities, self-interest and altruism, and that define the "public sphere" as broader than government and its policy.

The public tradition of organized women, which emphasized the complementarity of government action and civic initiative, allows us to see how much modern American society has come to privilege the role of government policy at the expense of a strong and authoritative civic culture. Strategies for solving major social problems have increasingly come to be viewed as the province of federal, state, and local government and of policy experts, even by conservatives, whose strategy is to reduce the federal role. This state-centered orientation coexists with a deep cynicism about government on the part of the American public, one cause of which may be the public's resentment of its dependent role. With this orientation come three assumptions: that social reform depends on expert manipulation of large social forces and is beyond the ken of ordinary citizens, that experts' vision can be substituted for citizens', and that citizens' political activity should be chiefly focused on elections and responding to opinion polls.

While organized women proposed that government has a crucial role to play in social policy, however, their conception of policymaking was very different from that of the modern welfare state. Their achievements suggest that a crucial element missing from our modern vision of public life is a sense of civic accountability, authority, and expertise. These achievements throw into stark relief modern society's willingness to defer to policy experts, a willingness which reveals an undemocratic bias against individuals, groups, and communities as agents of social insight, initiative, and change. While growing self-interest has oriented many Americans away from public-mindedness, the emergence of a public policy establishment linking academia and government, which dominates response to social problems, has distanced citizens even further from active social and political responsibility. Public debate, one expert has remarked with specific reference to the 1993–94 national health care discussion, has come to be conducted by public officials in the language of this establishment, "an insider language, virtually incomprehensible to people."[3] Citizens have increasingly become outsiders in the democratic process, their participation reduced largely to observation, voting, or financial support for candidates and parties.[4]

Organized women help us see that the problem with the growing prominence of a public policy establishment representing the spectrum of political viewpoints goes beyond the social cost of the disempowerment of citizens. It has to do also with our modern conception of policy's role. The ineffectiveness of much policy can be traced to the notion that policy's purpose is "to fix what is broken" in society, a notion that tends to narrow experts' focus from the whole social system to the most visible lapses in it. Much policymaking is hindered by its premise that what needs attention is not the social system itself, but the people for whom the system most obviously is not working. The assumption implicit in this premise—that basic social structures are fundamentally sound—legitimates policymakers' lack of attention to the state of the social fabric as a whole. One often noted result of narrowing the focus to those Americans who are not succeeding in existing social conditions is that these people often are distinguished pejoratively from

the rest, based on the judgment that their "failure" is a product of
their own shortcomings (e.g., poor character). It is less frequently
noted, however, that making this distinction at the same time affirms the status quo, reinforcing the unexamined assumption that
the social problem being addressed may *threaten* the social structure, but is not a product of it.

By its nature, therefore, modern policymaking often affirms
policymakers' unreadiness to explore how the situation of disadvantaged populations, distinctive as it is in important ways, may
be related to patterns among the larger population that receive less
attention. Instead of maximizing the social learning of policy experts and public leaders, that is, our conception of policy and policymaking *short-circuits* this learning, impoverishing our definition
of social problems and formulation of policy solutions. Hence, as
we saw at the outset, the current debate on the values crisis can ig-
nore basic structural shifts in American life affecting Americans as
a whole. Widespread patterns of family change can be treated in
terms of the "breakdown" only of certain families. They can be
analyzed as a problem of deviation from an unquestioned social
norm to be addressed chiefly among disadvantaged, single, black
teenage mothers. The "immorality" attributed to these young
women acts to bolster belief in the status quo and to deflect perceptions that there are wider problems with it.

Even as they argue for strong government intervention, in
short, organized women's public traditions help us recognize that
the effectiveness of modern policy as a social instrument has limits.
By demonstrating the importance of organized civic action for social improvement, these traditions suggest that public policy by itself lacks the capacity to mend or change the basic social fabric of
American life. They call attention to the fact that women reformers
did not put the state alone at the center of public life as the ultimate
public authority. Because of this, these women's vision has been interpreted by some scholars as antisuffrage or antistatist. But it was
neither. Far from representing either naiveté about the hard realities of public life or rejection of the strong public authority of the

federal government, these women expressed in their decentering of the state their different conception of the citizen's relationship to the "public."

Today, by contrast, a sophisticated grasp of the important relationship between public policy and citizen initiative is missing from national debate over the desirable degree of government intervention. Organized women's example of citizen-initiated partnership with government suggests that the important issue is not simply what amount of government social intervention is desirable, but what *kind* of effectiveness government policy is capable of and under what political and social conditions. Their tradition suggests that there are particular things government can do in addressing the welfare of citizens and society and important things it cannot do. By the nature of their visions, priorities, and politics, organized women raised the question of what is distinctive about government intervention on the one hand and civic action on the other.

Here we begin to recover the full significance of organized women's public achievements for American democratic values. These women reformers, at their best, meant something by the notion of society's moral responsibility for people's welfare that was different in important respects from what "social policy" and "welfare" are widely taken to mean today. Like us, they could not refrain from thinking in terms of who deserved help and who did not. Yet at the same time, they had a sense of citizens' *shared* dignity and destiny. They emphasized citizens' obligations to one another and especially to those in need; citizens' individual and collective responsibility for the daily work of weaving, sustaining, and reforming the bonds of family and community that constitute a common universe of experience; and citizens' accountability to principles of justice and humaneness. In short, organized women viewed welfare as irreducibly *social*, involving a complex web of relationships. Their view corrects our modern view of welfare as a relationship simply between the state and individuals in need dependent on it. Furthermore, these women help us see that collective responsibility for human welfare arises just as much from collective dependence on the health of the basic social fabric as it does from altruism.

Organized women saw civic concern, initiative, and expertise not as something that supplements or facilitates policy, but as crucial to setting and achieving social welfare goals. For them, civic culture was something far more robust than what many today mean by "civil society." It was not a zone of citizen voluntary activity and autonomy in relationship to the state. This modern conception places government at the center and the civic in a marginal and responsive, rather than initiating, role. Such a weak and secondary civic role is evident in arguments for the revival of civil society that give little credit to citizens for social vision or commitment. Political scientist Robert Putnam, for example, emphasizes the importance of civic ties for economic prosperity and "as a vital backdrop" that increases the effectiveness of government, even suggesting that we can look to public policy to *create* civic culture or "social capital."[5]

In contrast to such modern views, black and white organized women envisioned civic culture as the struggle for justice and social improvement aimed at *changing* who constituted the public and what constituted the public agenda. For them, civic action was fundamentally concerned with the social and moral order of the nation. These women believed that citizens are equally important in unconsciously and consciously reproducing and changing basic social arrangements, as well as deliberately reforming them. Their politics of improvement demonstrated, until women won the vote, how civic voices might initiate and shape national social policy.

The public traditions of black and white women suggest, further, that especially in times of rapid social change, when the needs of many being left behind in society are particularly great, citizens can be ahead of policymakers in learning about what is happening in society and how to address it. Unlike policy experts' thinking about society, which is most directly influenced by existing policy and established patterns of social analysis, citizens' social learning is not as filtered through policy loyalties. It is often closer to changing social needs and patterns, and as a result at least as likely to be a source of insight for sound social solutions. One reason for this is that citizens' grasp of social reality, unlike that of much of the social scientific research that informs modern policymaking, captures the dimension of meaning and value so important both to the welfare of society and to people's perceptions of it. Furthermore, citizens can shed light on this values dimension from diverse perspectives, including those that are marginal in national policy debates dominated by privileged men. Just like data gathered scientifically, this values dimension requires critical assessment, but it is the purpose of a democracy to subject civic insight, as well as government policy, to public scrutiny and decision. Organized women's achievements help us see that civic insight has a central role to play in effectively addressing the need for social improvement.

Finally, these reformers also help us see that citizens are especially crucial in building and representing the *social will* to identify and address public priorities. No attempt to address social problems can be effective without this will, an important part of which is compassion, perhaps the most distinctive contribution citizens can make to social welfare. Never by itself a sufficient basis for public action, compassion is also not an unalloyed good. Yet when its goals and impact are subjected to the same scrutiny that any human motive requires, compassion is a crucial ingredient of public action. Without compassion, neither the political will to tackle grave social problems, nor that sense of local and national community essential to all solutions, can be generated. Compassion, along with persistence and creativity, is necessary to build the climate of hope essential to renewing the health of any community. In fact, it may be precisely the civic capacity to respond to human suffering, to recognize in the midst of diversity one's common humanity with others, that however imperfect lies at the root of any successful strategy for changing social attitudes and systems. And while policy can do many things, it cannot address the dimension of social welfare that requires communication of the personal and collective compassion of individuals, groups, and communities.

All of these correctives to current ways of thinking about American public life offer women an alternative vision of their public participation, its motives, potential settings, and relationship to government. Most of all, these correctives suggest an important possibility modern women can glean from the public tradition of white and black organized women, the notion of a welfare *society*.[6] Reformers' achievements moved in the direction of a new vision of society, not just of government. They made responsibility for the vulnerable, and for human well-being and growth, a major priority for citizens, leaders of all kinds, government, and democracy. While they left intact the traditional sexual division of labor, they established the principle that this social priority should no longer be marginal to mainstream institutions, but should become the obligation of the whole. Organized women, in short, call our attention to what remains to be done today to make women's traditional unpaid social labor also an American public value. This is the agenda with which modern women should begin to change the national public debate.

WOMEN, MOTHERHOOD, AND SOCIAL REFORM

Reconstructing motherhood is the starting point for moving toward a society restructured to value and provide new, more adequate support for family and community welfare. Governing cultural beliefs about public and private have made motherhood central to the moral, social, and political health of the nation by making it central to the way the lives of American women, men, and children are organized. As we saw earlier in discussing the ideal worker, all public institutions—government, for-profit, and nonprofit—are built on the premise that mothers uphold the values of family and community welfare and that society can delegate to them primary, private responsibility for the daily work required to support these values. This premise currently relieves all other social institutions of the obligation to meet society's need for this unpaid labor. As a result, this obligation need not be, and *is* not, an integral part of the missions, priorities, and social responsibility of American institutions.[7]

In a situation, therefore, where the traditional institutional basis for motherhood—a majority of women working primarily in the home—has disappeared, most likely for good, society must resolve anew the problem of how structurally to provide for unpaid social labor. Given the severe erosion of the bonds of mutuality and social obligation the nation is experiencing, the strategy of helping *individual* women to find new ways to combine this unpaid labor with paid labor is simply inadequate. Furthermore, as the demands of paid work are making women's lives more and more like those of men, this already inadequate solution grows increasingly so. The situation requires, instead, a solution that goes to the heart of the problem.

Finding such a solution begins with asking why responsibility for the unpaid social labor that is so crucial to the well-being of American society is *not* shared more broadly by social institutions of all kinds. This question challenges the moral basis of the traditional gendered division of labor that undergirds the distinction between public and private. It asks us not just to think anew about the private sphere, but also to revise the values, priorities, and structures of the public sphere. Getting at the root of the problems that confront our nation requires reorganizing the way the unpaid social labor of family and community welfare is supported and distributed across the entire society.

The need for such reorganization is underscored not only by the need for collective response to the social factors that have caused the disappearance of mothers who work primarily in the home, but also by the multiple other forces in society profoundly reshaping modern motherhood across racial, ethnic, and class lines. These forces include the high poverty rate for women and children, an infant mortality rate that ranks the United States with many "developing" countries, AIDS, the drug epidemic, and growing violence in homes and the world outside them. The obstacles these forces are throwing up to mothers all along the income scale, especially but not only those in poverty, have overwhelmed the traditional ideal of the "good" mother.

On the brink of the twenty-first century, that is, harsh realities from which even "good" mothers are powerless to protect their children are changing the cultural belief that motherhood is a natural capacity that, when properly and dutifully handled, can overcome whatever its social setting presents. Growing recognition of these threatening realities is shifting the social view of mothers. For example, psychologist Bruno Bettelheim popularized experts' move away from the notion of a mother's saving power with publication of his *A Good Enough Parent* (1987). Although the title's gender-neutral language was meant to signal the importance of both parents to a child's development, Bettelheim explicitly assumed he was talking primarily about and to women, reflecting the continuing cultural belief that rearing children is women's work.[8] His contribution was part of new social thinking that being a "good enough" mother is what to hope for, given the large number of obstacles to children's making their way to adulthood today in psychological, physical, and spiritual health. Social analysts too are shifting away from the notion of the perfect mother, a fact illustrated by public health expert Lisbeth Schorr's argument that the capacity to nurture is affected by the degree of family stress stemming from social circumstances and by availability of family supports.[9]

These developments are making American women acutely aware that the social meaning of motherhood has shifted. If they cannot and will not turn their backs on motherhood, it is both because their identities and destinies are inextricably bound up with it, whether they actually experience motherhood or not, and because they have a deep sense of motherhood's importance as a social institution. Yet motherhood no longer plays a central role in the lives of most women in the same way it once did. Today, society increasingly expects motherhood to take place in most women's lives alongside paid work. This has created the need for a new cultural conception of women's lives—one that recognizes their commitments both to family and community and to their paid work, without penalizing either—but this new conception has not yet emerged.

As a result, paradoxically, motherhood and the prospect of motherhood are leading many women to realize that they are individuals with *public* interests (economic, employment, legal, medical, etc.) to establish and defend. And a major public interest of women's that is often overlooked is developing this new cultural conception of women's lives and revising social structures to undergird it. Without this development and revision, women, motherhood, and the wider set of social values associated with the private sphere are all at grave risk.

Yet women receive little encouragement from any quarter, including often the women's movement, to take the initiative in getting society to revalue and reorganize both unpaid and paid work. Instead, most women struggle with the two main *individual* alternatives presented them by the powerful structures of the public world, especially the workplace. The first alternative, conforming to the norms for male adult life and work on which mainstream institutions are predicated, devalues the daily unpaid labor of family and community welfare. The second alternative, accepting an economically marginalized position as second-class employees in order to integrate work with "private" priorities, restricts women's potential as paid workers. In both of these alternatives, the cultural belief that unpaid social labor is primarily women's work not only goes unchallenged, but is institutionalized in new public forms. Even in American organizations that have introduced programs to respond to workers' family needs, the reluctance of men to use such programs demonstrates that combining work, family, and community commitments continues to be seen chiefly as women's problem, and *not* the problem also of male employees, organizations themselves, and society in general.[10] Furthermore,

availing themselves of flexibility "on the margins" of an otherwise unrestructured world of work is not the way to equity for
women, but

> is likely to increase the disadvantages women already face in the work-
> place: being overrepresented among the poor, having lower wages than
> men even when in comparable jobs, and moving more slowly—if at all—
> into the higher ranks of organizations. Flexibility superimposed on exist-
> ing assumptions about the conditions of employment is . . . likely to *in-
> crease* gender inequity.[11]

Women must recognize that the individual search for workplace
flexibility, even were the majority of fathers to participate in it, is
not the way to *change* the public status of the unpaid daily work of
human welfare. Women's situation reveals that the real problem in
American society is that families and their community commitments are of secondary importance to the private sector and most
other institutions. Many organizations expect that women, like
men, will put "private" commitments second to organizations' increasing time demands. These are the corporate social values behind many "family friendly" programs that are actually designed
to increase the amount of time both women and men work by offering services, such as sick-child care, that *relieve* them of their
family responsibilities.[12] While some such relief is, of course, desirable, it is at least as important that mainstream institutions make
time for their employees to *fulfill* family and community commitments. The real problem, in other words, is that the male norm for
adult life and work is inadequate not just for women, but also for
the well-being of society and of men.

Women thus must develop a third alternative, refusing either to
adjust to the existing norms for adult life and work defined by men
and public institutions or to accept second-class status in these institutions. They must offer leadership in changing these norms.
Many women's individual efforts in the workplace to bear privately
the burden of doing justice to motherhood convinces them that this
is an unsatisfactory long-term solution for women, families, and

the country. They recognize in their situation a predicament that is not theirs alone, but society's. Women must act on the *public* significance of this insight, taking responsibility for the larger social predicament they see. Doing so involves exchanging their cultural habit of adapting to men's leadership for recognition that they too are capable of vision about society as a whole.

Concern for the public good need not be the only thing that motivates women to challenge the persisting traditional gendered division of labor. An equally legitimate motive is self-interest, beginning with the need of the majority of women to reduce stress caused by work/family conflict, to have access to equal work and economic opportunity, and to preserve family and community values crucial to the quality and meaning of their personal lives. The road to public-mindedness and public effectiveness, in short, begins with self-interest just as properly as with altruism. In public action, the ability "to understand [one's] own interests and negotiate for them in moments of conflict" may not be sufficient, but it is an ingredient equally as important as commitment to the common good.[13] Indeed, particularly for women, learning to identify, legitimate, and pursue their own interests, rather than depending on men to know or defend those interests for them, is a crucial step toward becoming full public participants. It is a crucial step too in educating institutions to what women's interests are and to strategizing to institutionalize these interests.

Acting on their interests, learning to assess critically the principles that currently guide organizations and, where these principles are deficient, learning to see beyond them, is where women need to start in formulating public vision. Because women's pressing questions cut to the heart of where the country as a whole is headed, they ought to be pursued on this collective level: Why is American society organized so that the unpaid labor of family and community welfare, on which the good order of the economy, society, and state depends, is primarily the responsibility of women? Why is this labor relegated to the private sphere and given minimal public institutional support or priority? What are the social costs

of a gendered division of labor that excludes men and public institutions from active involvement in the unpaid daily work of human
welfare?

Responding to these questions with meaningful structural reform begins with recognizing the inadequacy for *society* of the link
the governing cultural conception of motherhood draws between
women, the domestic sphere, and the work of human welfare.
Women must challenge the exclusiveness of this link if they are to
assert the wider accountability of society to both motherhood and
unpaid social labor, making work they care about work for which
the public world also shares responsibility. They must question the
"natural" gendered hierarchy of work embedded in traditional cultural beliefs about public and private. This hierarchy gives public
respect and precedence to paid labor, especially that of men, but
devalues the unpaid social labor on which society depends. It is not
enough for women to challenge the two-tiered structure of work at
home, striving for equal sharing of social labor with male spouses
or partners. Women also must challenge this two-tiered structure
in public institutions and social policy. At the same time as they
claim the right to equal access to paid employment in public institutions, that is, women must provide leadership in questioning existing norms for paid work and in making unpaid social labor also
a structurally supported, primary public value.

RECONSTRUCTING PUBLIC LIFE

In short, nothing less than a basic restructuring of the values that
shape our public institutions, including the "private" sector, will
address the eroding bonds of family and community that, cutting
across lines of race, ethnicity, and class, have created the nation's
values crisis. The origins of this crisis are broader than those identified by people who see strengthening the *private* responsibility of
families as the moral key to our public problems. New social realities have outstripped the traditional relationship between public
and private values. What is needed is social vision that recognizes
and seeks to address this change, instead of working from a model

of how society should be organized that no longer fits reality. The lack of such vision is a major reason for policymakers' difficulty in formulating, legislating, and implementing effective social policy; in turn, it is a major reason for growing public cynicism about government.

The key to generating effective new public vision lies in systematically revising fundamental aspects of our traditional way of thinking about society, especially the minimal degree of responsibility for families and communities assigned the public world. Redefinition of the standard for adult work that currently shapes public policy and institutions of all kinds, as well as individual lives, is central to this revision. The new standard must combine, for men and women, paid and unpaid labor. In this way, it will recognize that American society is reformulating family life, having grown beyond the sixteenth-century model of families as economic and moral appendages of fathers. Such a standard also will allow fathers to turn to building new family and community roles, now that those based on outmoded notions of authority and "breadwinning" have eroded.

Women especially possess the will to take the initiative in this social reorganization. They are most acutely aware that the unpaid labor of family and community welfare, caught as it is between new realities and old cultural beliefs, is an endangered social value. However, time is short. Women face a window of opportunity narrowed by the threat that mainstream institutional values will overwhelm the unpaid labor of human welfare as a social value. Women themselves will be newcomers to these institutions only for a relatively short time, no matter how long they may need to struggle to become full and equal workers in the public world. In this short time, they can look at these institutions and at the structure and meaning of paid employment with comparatively fresh eyes. Still on the threshold of the public world, pressed to rearrange the meaning and structure of their own lives, they can more easily notice and question the institutional and work norms to which most men have become habituated. As many struggle to maintain family and community commitments in the face of a workplace structured for an ideal worker who delegates both, women can call attention to the personal costs that employed men have been paying for years and to the social implications of these costs. But women too are subject to the socializing power of mainstream values and many soon may be sidetracked in their effort to lead, either by being installed as second-class citizens in the workplace or by having their own values reshaped.

Contrary to what often is assumed, in short, there can be nothing automatic about women's leadership in institutions of the scale and complexity of today's. As women achieve critical mass in public life, reform of basic social patterns will not be accomplished by virtue of qualities they may be thought to possess by nature or nurture. Instead, women today face a challenge similar to that of organized women in advancing human welfare as a public value. Now as then, women's public effectiveness will require self-conscious, hardheaded, and pioneering efforts. Modern women must consciously choose and advance values they see as social priorities, institutionalizing them through persistent education, negotiation, and astute political strategy. Most of all, learning from the successes and shortcomings of the past, they must work with one another and also with men to create new alliances of diverse individuals and groups, beginning in this way to build new bonds of community as they work toward their goals in and outside of institutions.

Their primary goal of changing the gendered hierarchy of labor that still shapes the dominant culture of America will depend on challenging the centuries-old cultural assumption "that the public world of political and economic activity is and should be distinct from the private domain of relationships and care."[14] Only challenging this assumption, as it is institutionalized throughout the public world of paid work, will preserve the unpaid labor of family and community welfare and strengthen it as a social value. Women must take the lead in engaging institutions in the new process of meeting their social obligation to make unpaid social labor a publicly supported *priority*. Public institutions—for-profit, as well as nonprofit and government—possess tremendous power to change the cultural patterns they currently reflect and reinforce. They constitute an arena for women's leadership in shaping American values that is equally as important as the arenas of social policy or formal politics. In part, this is because institutions of all kinds, while they erect barriers to women's public leadership, also provide opportunities, resources, leverage, and sometimes even support for this leadership.

RECONSTRUCTING WORK

What is needed in all institutions is the complete "re-engineering" of work and the workplace, beginning at the top, called for by management expert Lotte Bailyn. The aim of this re-engineering is for American organizations to recognize, not simply in their human resources departments but at the heart of their operations, the legitimacy and social value of employees' need to combine family and community responsibilities with those at work.[15] Reorganizing the operating assumptions of institutions about workers and their private concerns, and recognizing the disappearance of the social structure that formerly provided for these concerns, is a major key to addressing erosion of the nation's social fabric. Giving up counterproductive demands for white-collar employees' constant availability and exclusive commitment is also the way for American organizations to become more productive and competitive.[16]

Re-engineering work and the workplace, challenging the dominant cultural conception of adult work as paid employment that is based on male experience, requires challenging the norm that underpins this conception: that unpaid daily responsibilities for human welfare are incompatible with full public moral status and agency for women or men. It is this norm, as Bailyn argues, that molds individual and organizational life to standards dysfunctional for both. These standards require from technical, professional, and managerial employees overwork and orientation to rigid career pathways and timetables that put advancement ahead of the work itself.. Through these standards, organizations promote the norm that "high-level employees are totally involved in the public, occupational part of their lives and are concerned primarily with moving up a managerial hierarchy."[17] While some adults should be free, if they wish, to organize their lives around this narrow meaning, the well-being of contemporary society depends on the reconception of adult work. In the face of changed social and economic realities, the public good can be fostered and preserved only if the existing norm of the ideal worker's exclusive commitment to paid work and delegation of unpaid social labor is changed.

This means changing the way organizations are designed to delegate to families, specifically to women, responsibility for the unpaid social labor of family and civil welfare on which they too depend. Women, rather than seeking workplace flexibility to help themselves or their partners adjust their worklives to bear this responsibility privately, must challenge organizational policies that "implicitly deny the possibility that the *work situation* could provide a margin for adjustment."[18] Currently, these policies do not acknowledge that organizations have an obligation in return for the unpaid social labor performed mainly by mothers, traditionally as spouses, but increasingly as employees. Yet this labor provides organizations with a workforce and consumer base, allows exclusive work commitment from many male workers whom it continues to relieve of daily personal, family care, and community obligations, and helps build the bonds of communities on which organizations depend in multiple ways.

As economist Juliet Schor argues, at a time when organizations have given up even the degree of social obligation they once felt for helping with the work that guarantees the reproduction of society, they must be challenged to a whole new level of social responsibility. Whereas in the past they paid most men a wage that provided sole or primary support for homemakers' unpaid social labor, the disappearance of the "family wage," forcing the development of dual, full-time earner families, means this unpaid labor is no longer structurally provided for. Worse, institutions now penalize economically and in terms of career success employees who work 30–40-hour weeks in order to make time for unpaid social labor, while rewarding those who work 60–80-hour weeks and are largely unavailable for such labor.[19] They do so, furthermore, despite the fact that time spent is a crude measure of employees' dedication or performance and no guarantee of productivity.[20] The unrecognized costs to individuals, families, and society as a whole of organizations' shift to these practices in recent decades are now evident in the nation's social deterioration. They are especially evident among the working poor, where jobs that are increasingly the kind available—low-wage, often part-time, with minimal or no benefits—prevent many families from being economically self-sufficient. Among disadvantaged women workers with few or no skills, who are at the bottom of the labor force, the situation of single mothers is particularly grave. Organizations' practices are a major reason many disadvantaged women turn to public assistance:

> [P]ersistently high rates of welfare use among single mothers do not primarily indicate that something is wrong with their values, their role models, their work ethic, or their time orientation. Nor do they signal that single mothers have developed an excessive taste for handouts and leisure time. Rather, they attest to the fact that something is very wrong with the presumption that low-wage work is the solution to welfare and poverty.[21]

Along with efforts at the institutional level, citizens' partnership with government in efforts to reshape national policy has a major role to play in re-engineering work and structurally providing the support for families that is now missing. Arguing that public policy must stimulate organizations to systematically rethink the structure of jobs and worktime, Schor notes that worktime has been overlooked as a national policy issue since the 1930s.[22] Her research on the social effects of overwork suggests the kind of mechanisms for restructuring worktime that ought to be considered. For example, Schor proposes that the federal government require all companies to offer employees options that would address their lack of time and flexibility for dealing with family and related responsibilities.[23] Some of these would benefit white-collar workers especially, for instance job sharing or various strategies for trading income for shorter hours *without* incurring penalty regarding job status or career advancement (e.g., a shorter work week, more vacation, reduced daily hours). To help change the traditional sexual division of labor assumed by institutional cultures, Schor suggests policies could provide incentives to encourage men to take time for family responsibilities.[24] In the case of blue- and pink-collar workers, who cannot afford to trade away even a small amount of income, Schor proposes reducing the work week to 35 hours, without reducing pay, and abolishing premium overtime pay, replacing it with a system of compensated time off.[25]

Further, in order to address the nation's values crisis and the erosion of the bonds of mutuality and obligation central to it, government must reorder its *own* priorities as well and its allocation of funding to them. In particular, in addition to helping to restructure jobs and worktime, national policy also must revise the assumptions that have shaped family policy, making it a new priority to help families in need weather the shifting social realities of American life. Family policy too must recognize as a primary social value the combining of paid and unpaid work on which the recovery of social well-being depends. It must provide assistance to adults in both single- and dual-parent families in their struggle not only to be economically self-sufficient, but also to fulfill their moral responsibilities to and within communities. Calling for a policy strategy which "targets within universalism," Theda Skocpol underscores the importance of formulating policies that "speak with a consistent moral voice" to the whole society. These policies should recognize where adults, across races and classes, have legitimate need for help in negotiating the currents of change, while acknowledging that differing social situations mean some adults require more help than others.[26] This was the strategy behind organized women's Sheppard-Towner program for neonatal and maternal health education—a targeting of the special needs of disadvantaged mothers and children by a national policy geared to helping all.[27]

In much the same way, the modern family security program Skocpol proposes would replace our current programs known as welfare, designed to assist only the poor. Addressing the situation of
American children caught in changing family structures, it would
reflect the principle that in order to combine paid and unpaid work
parents need help raising children and finding good jobs. Chief
among its social provisions would be "child support assurance for
all single custodial parents, parental leave and child-care assistance
for all working families, job training and relocation assistance for
displaced workers and new entrants to the labor market, and universal health benefits."[28]

Another priority of new national policy on jobs, worktime,
and family security must be provisions that address the gap between changed social expectations regarding paid work and the social resources and opportunities available to disadvantaged young
women. This gap has ensured that these young women have been
left behind their privileged counterparts in learning to see paid
work, as well as motherhood, as a central source of identity and
meaning in life. As sociologist Luker argues,

> We live in a society that continues to idealize marriage and family as ex-
> pected lifetime roles for women, even as it adds on the expectation that
> women will also work and be self-supporting. Planning for the trade-offs
> entailed in a lifetime of paid employment in the labor market and raising
> a family taxes the skills of our most advantaged young women. We should
> not be surprised that women who face discrimination by race and class in
> addition to that of gender are often even less adept at coping with these
> large and contradictory demands.[29]

Preparing young disadvantaged women to be economically self-
sufficient, while helping young disadvantaged men achieve the
same goal, so that marriage becomes economically feasible for
both, is what we should be striving for. To this end, traditional
cultural incentives must be altered for disadvantaged women
by providing real options for the future, as well as the educational opportunities, professional role models, and other personal-

development resources in their schools, religious institutions, and communities that they have not had.[30] Like other young women, disadvantaged women need the freedom to find meaning and purpose for their lives in a way that does not depend on becoming mothers before they are ready, and that will equip them to enter the future prepared for self-sufficiency.

CONCLUSION

While most liberal leaders seem unable to find the vision required to move the country forward, and the majority of conservative leaders are persuaded that it is possible to go back to the way things used to be, women are well-positioned to look at the new realities of families, work, and communities confronting the nation and to develop public vision to address them. However invested many women may also be in traditional cultural beliefs, the realities of their lives tell them that reweaving the torn social fabric depends to a significant degree on recognizing several things: the new economic expectations society has of women, the cost to society of women's decreased time for civic engagement, the increasing disconnection between many fathers and their families, and the social problems threatening to overwhelm children and adults alike.

Women must begin to look to themselves, therefore, for public vision that reinterprets important traditional values, such as the affective and moral roles of families as part of larger communities, in light of recent structural shifts in American life. In doing so, women must overcome the deep cultural barrier that still keeps many from authoritative public action—from choosing to lead. They are entering uncharted territory with regard to both their own public leadership and the American values crisis they must help to address. At the same time, they can look to earlier traditions of women's public leadership that, in many respects, have brought them to where they are today. To chart their own path, as these traditions warn them to do, women must be as critical of these earlier efforts at reform as of the larger patterns of culture and society from which they sprang. Yet they also may recognize in these efforts some important values that they may choose to critically appropriate for the present and future.

The public traditions of organized women encourage modern women to see that too much is at stake in American life and in their own lives to settle for becoming uncritical followers of the established institutional patterns of the public world. Rather, the challenge of becoming full public participants that women still confront today requires them to assert their own critical view of these patterns. This challenge has a fundamentally moral dimension for women and for the nation. In alliance with men who also recognize the urgency of the task, women must generate progressive, values-based public vision that addresses more adequately than the current public debate the link between women's welfare and the welfare of society as a whole.

Women are poised to shape American values publicly on a scale to which they have never before had access. Much is riding on whether and how they choose to lead.

Notes

CHAPTER ONE

1. The phrase is taken from a Peter Hart and Robert Teeter opinion poll, reported by the *Wall Street Journal* (p. A1) and NBC News on June 17, 1994, in which the American public agreed with the religious right on this basic diagnosis (while registering far more liberal views than the right on such issues as antidiscrimination laws for gays, a woman's right to choose abortion, and the distribution of condoms in schools).

2. Quoted in Arlene Skolnick and Stacey Rosencrantz, "The New Crusade for the Old Family," *American Prospect*, no. 18 (Summer 1994): 61.

3. For an excellent discussion of this view, see Christopher Jencks and Kathryn Edin, "Do Poor Women Have a Right to Bear Children?" *American Prospect*, no. 20 (Winter 1995).

4. See Linda K. Kerber, *Women of the Republic: Intellect and Ideology in Revolutionary America* (Chapel Hill: University of North Carolina Press, 1980), pp. 11 and 283, for her discussion of this historical conception.

5. Skolnick and Rosencrantz, "The New Crusade for the Old Family," p. 59.

6. Michael Wines, "Clinton Speech Stresses Issues of Morality," *New York Times* (September 10, 1994), p. A1.

7. Charles Murray, "The Coming White Underclass," *Wall Street Journal* (October 29, 1993); emphasis added.

8. Ibid.

9. George F. Will, "Mothers Who Don't Know How," *Newsweek* (April 23, 1990), p. 80.

10. Kristin Luker, Women's Policy Agenda Seminar, Harvard Divinity

School (April 8, 1994). See her "Dubious Conceptions: The Controversy over Teen Pregnancy," *American Prospect*, no. 5 (Spring 1991): 73, for analysis of how experts and the American public have become persuaded that a major cause of poverty is not just unwed mothers, but teenage pregnancy, and that decreasing teenage pregnancy will decrease poverty.

11. U.S. Congress, House Committee on Ways and Means, *The Green Book: Background Material and Data on Major Programs within the Jurisdiction of the Committee on Ways and Means* (Washington, D.C.: Government Printing Office, 1994), p. 411, table 10-31. Figures are for 1992 and for AFDC recipients ages eleven through eighteen. Welfare's sharpest critics in Congress have been especially concerned about this age group. Calling for excluding teen-mothers below age eighteen from any benefits, the harshest of proposed "disincentives," they have argued that "illegitimacy" must be attacked here, where it is epidemic and being encouraged by welfare.

12. Luker, "Dubious Conceptions," p. 75.

13. See Jason DeParle, "Clinton Target: Teen-Age Pregnancy," *New York Times* (March 22, 1994), p. A10, for a discussion of Clinton's focus on teenage mothers' lack of character.

14. See Nell Painter, "Hill, Thomas, and the Use of Racial Stereotype," in *Race-ing Justice and En-gendering Power: Essays on Anita Hill, Clarence Thomas, and the Constitution of a Social Reality*, edited by Toni Morrison (New York: Pantheon Books, 1992), and Ann Firor Scott, *Natural Allies: Women's Associations in American History* (Urbana: University of Illinois Press, 1991), pp. 90–92, for discussion of white American stereotypes of the "natural" sexual and parental immorality of black women.

15. Luker, "Dubious Conceptions," p. 81.

16. Quoted in Sara S. McLanahan, "The Consequences of Single Motherhood," *American Prospect*, no. 18 (Summer 1994): 48.

17. Martha L. Fineman also makes this point in relation to poverty discourses in her "Images of Mothers in Poverty," *Duke Law Journal*, no. 2 (April 1991): 285–86. She makes the further point that there is a distinction in these discourses, like the distinction made about the poor, between deserving and undeserving single mothers and the kind (and degree) of public assistance to which each has access. Single mothers who lose their spouses through death—widows—are typically not condemned, remaining deserving (p. 282).

18. The influential article bearing this title and expressing this view was

written by Barbara Dafoe Whitehead and appeared in the *Atlantic Monthly* (April 1993).

19. For a balanced discussion of this evidence, see Sara McLanahan and Gary Sandefur, *Growing Up with a Single Parent: What Hurts, What Helps* (Cambridge: Harvard University Press, 1994), chapter 3.

20. McLanahan, "The Consequences of Single Motherhood," p. 49.

21. Skolnick and Rosencrantz, "The New Crusade for the Old Family," pp. 61–63.

22. Daniel P. Moynihan, *The Negro Family: The Case for National Action* (Washington, D.C.: Office of Planning and Research, U.S. Department of Labor, March 1965).

23. Luker, "Dubious Conceptions," pp. 81–82. Constance Williams and others also argue that these pregnancies often are wanted and meaningful to black teenagers, if unplanned in terms of their exact timing.

24. For a valuable historical discussion of this lack of correspondence, see Mary Ryan, "In Search of the Public," introduction to *Women in Public: Between Banners and Ballots, 1825–1880* (Baltimore: Johns Hopkins University Press, 1990).

25. U.S. Department of Labor statistic, taken from Lotte Bailyn, *Breaking the Mold: Women, Men, and Time in the New Corporate World* (New York: Free Press, 1993), p. 65.

26. Luker, "Dubious Conceptions," pp. 78–79.

27. Ibid., p. 79.

28. McLanahan, "The Consequences of Single Motherhood," pp. 53–54.

29. Ibid., p. 54.

30. Juliet Schor, "Short of Time: American Families and the Structure of Jobs" (paper presented at the Future Directions for American Politics Seminar, Harvard University, March 1994), p. 4.

31. Juliet Schor, *The Overworked American: The Unexpected Decline of Leisure* (New York: Basic Books, 1991), p. 5.

32. This notion of women's citizenship as fundamentally different from (white) men's, based as it is in the private world of the family governed by love, biological ties, and men, is deeply rooted in Western political philosophy and owes much to both the Christian humanists and to Hegel. On the humanists, see Clarissa W. Atkinson, *The Oldest Vocation: Christian Motherhood in the Middle Ages* (Ithaca: Cornell University Press, 1991). On

Hegel, see Carole Pateman, "The Patriarchal Welfare State," in *Democracy and the Welfare State*, edited by Amy Gutmann (Princeton: Princeton University Press, 1988), p. 236.

33. Kerber, *Women of the Republic*, pp. 11 and 283.

34. Kay Lehman Schlozman, Nancy Burns, and Sidney Verba, "Gender and Pathways to Participation: The Role of Resources," *Journal of Politics* 56, no. 4 (November 1994): 968.

35. M. Margaret Conway, *Political Participation in the United States* (Washington, D.C.: Congressional Quarterly Press, 1991), p. 33. Conway cites data on women, politics, and the mass media from Warren E. Miller and Santa A. Traugott, *American National Election Studies Data Sourcebook, 1952–86* (Cambridge: Harvard University Press, 1989), p. 301, table 5.18.

36. See Kay Mills, "Memo: To Good Old Boys and '90's Women," *Columbia Journalism Review* (January/February 1990): 48–49, and Susan Hansen, "Differences?" *News Inc.* (September 1992): 23–38. The latter reports (p. 23) a 1991 study conducted by the Newspaper Advertising Bureau and supported by in-house surveys conducted by major national newspaper chains that shows women's daily readership of newspapers dropped 18 percent between 1970 and 1990, while men's dropped 12.5 percent in the same period.

37. Seyla Benhabib, *Situating the Self: Gender, Community, and Postmodernism in Contemporary Ethics* (New York: Routledge, 1992), p. 13.

38. Katherine Tate, "Double Liabilities or Twin Assets: Gender, Race, and the Senatorial Candidacy of Carol Moseley Braun" (Occasional Paper 93-7, Center for American Political Studies, Harvard University, March 1993), p. 6. Women are not more likely to support the policy objectives and candidates feminist organizations endorse, and even Democratic women identify more often with liberal positions on issues than with female candidates.

39. Ibid., p. 6.

40. Anne Costain, *Inviting Women's Rebellion: A Political Process Interpretation of the Women's Movement* (Baltimore: Johns Hopkins University Press, 1992), pp. 136–42.

41. Joan Scott, "The Sears Case," in *Gender and the Politics of History* (New York: Columbia University Press, 1988), p. 175.

42. See, for example, Jean Bethke Elshtain, *Public Man, Private Woman*

(Princeton: Princeton University Press, 1981), p. 336, and Sara Ruddick, *Maternal Thinking: Toward a Politics of Peace* (Boston: Beacon Press, 1992).

43. Quoted by Ann Firor Scott in *The Southern Lady: From Pedestal to Politics, 1830–1930* (Chicago: University of Chicago Press, 1970), p. 186.

CHAPTER TWO

1. See "Women: The New Providers" (survey conducted by Louis Harris and Associates, Inc., for the Families and Work Institute and the Whirlpool Foundation, May 1995), p. 33.

2. The U.S. Bureau of Labor Statistics projects that by the year 2005 women will make up exactly 48 percent of the U.S. work force, a figure that will represent 63 percent of women aged sixteen or older. Figures taken from "More Women Work, While Fewer Men Do," *Wall Street Journal* (December 31, 1993).

3. Ruth Smith, "Relationality and the Ordering of Differences in Feminist Ethics," *Journal of Feminist Studies in Religion* 9, nos. 1–2 (Spring/Fall 1993): 205.

4. Ibid., p. 200.

5. The prevailing historical interpretation of nineteenth-century American women is that separate-spheres ideology presented morality as an attribute of middle-class women. But this interpretation grows out of a Marxist historical analysis that identifies morality and religion as bourgeois. For a discussion of the dangers of feminist views of morality reiterating the liberal view that minority, lower-class, and poor women are incapable of moral agency, see ibid., p. 202.

6. Ibid., p. 214.

7. Clarissa W. Atkinson, *The Oldest Vocation: Christian Motherhood in the Middle Ages* (Ithaca: Cornell University Press, 1991), pp. 194–201.

8. See ibid., chapter 6.

9. See Rosemary Radford Ruether, *Sexism and God-Talk: Toward a Feminist Theology* (Beacon Press: Boston, 1983), pp. 165–69, for an accessible theological and historical discussion of the problem.

10. Atkinson, *The Oldest Vocation*, p. 6.

11. Ibid., p. 242.

12. Ibid., pp. 199–201.

13. Ibid., p. 195.

14. Ibid., p. 211.

15. Ibid., p. 235.

16. Ibid., p. 234.

17. Ibid., pp. 242–43.

18. Nancy Cott, *The Bonds of Womanhood: "Woman's Sphere" in New England, 1780–1835* (New Haven: Yale University Press, 1977), p. 1.

19. Ibid., p. 200.

20. Ibid., pp. 1–2.

21. For a helpful discussion of such shifts in which social truths that are taken for granted as part of a received natural order become contested, see the focus on culture, hegemony, and ideology in the introduction to Jean and John Comaroff's *Of Revelation and Revolution: Christianity, Colonialism, and Consciousness in South Africa* (Chicago: University of Chicago Press, 1991).

22. Barbara Welter introduced the phrase now standard in historiography. She based her analysis of the phenomenon on a survey of women's magazines, gift annuals, and religious literature published in the mid-1800s. See "The Cult of True Womanhood, 1820–1860," *American Quarterly*, 18, no. 2, part 1 (Summer 1966): 151–74.

23. Cott, *The Bonds of Womanhood*, pp. 5 and ff.

24. Welter, "The Cult of True Womanhood," pp. 152–54.

25. Mrs. Sandford, from *Woman, In Her Social and Domestic Character* (Boston, 1842), p. 15, as quoted in ibid., p. 159.

26. Ibid., p. 156.

27. *The Young Ladies' Class Book*, quoted in ibid., p. 162.

28. Cott, *The Bonds of Womanhood*, pp. 167–68.

29. See Cott's discussion of Catherine Sedgwick, in ibid., p. 193.

30. Welter, "The Cult of True Womanhood," p. 152.

31. Quoted in ibid., p. 173.

32. Ibid., p. 174.

33. Cott, *The Bonds of Womanhood*, p. 199.

34. Ibid., pp. 61–62 and 199.

35. Ibid., p. 17.

36. Ibid., pp. 203–4.

37. For an assessment of the inadequacy of Marx's critique of religion and of how its influence compromises the effectiveness of feminist social theory, see Amy Newman, "Feminist Social Criticism and Marx's Theory of Religion," *Hypatia* 9, no. 4 (Fall 1994).

38. For an example of how this historical interpretation has become a premise of major studies, see Alice Kessler-Harris, *Out to Work: A History of Wage-Earning Women in the United States* (New York: Oxford University Press, 1982), pp. 49–50.

39. Elizabeth Cady Stanton, *The Woman's Bible* (Boston: Northeastern University Press, 1993), p. 7. Originally published by New York European Publishing Company, 1895.

40. Ibid., pp. 11–12.

41. Seyla Benhabib, *Situating the Self: Gender, Community, and Postmodernism in Contemporary Ethics* (New York: Routledge, 1991), p. 108.

42. Gary S. Becker, *A Treatise on the Family* (Cambridge: Harvard University Press, 1981), pp. 21–22. Feminist economists criticize Becker and other economists for their reliance on unexamined anthropological and social assumptions. See, for example, Nancy Folbre and Heidi Hartmann, "The Rhetoric of Self-Interest: Ideology and Gender in Economic Theory," in *The Consequences of Economic Rhetoric*, edited by Arjo Klamer, Donald McCloskey, and Robert Solow (New York: Cambridge University Press, 1988), pp. 184–206. Bringing the history of Christianity to bear on Becker's economic theory tells us more about the cultural moral framework he has appropriated with insufficient criticism.

43. Becker, *A Treatise on the Family*, p. 22.

44. See Sylvia Junko Yanagisako and Jane Fishburn Collier, "Toward a Unified Analysis of Gender and Kinship," in *Gender and Kinship: Essays toward a Unified Analysis*, edited by Collier and Yanagisako (Stanford: Stanford University Press, 1987), pp. 29–35.

45. I am indebted to Clarissa Atkinson for pointing out to me that the parallel between Luther and Becker is especially exact in their making wives of all women. In Western Christianity and culture before the sixteenth century, ideologically, women had an existence as women independent of wifehood.

46. Becker, *A Treatise on the Family*, p. 23.

47. Yanagisako and Collier make this argument in "Toward a Unified

Analysis of Gender and Kinship." See pp. 14ff. for their discussion of the literature on this point.

48. Ibid., pp. 34–35.

49. Carol Gilligan, *In a Different Voice: Psychological Theory and Women's Development* (Cambridge: Harvard University Press, 1982), p. 79. For the classic study of sex-role stereotypes, which recognizes the value-inflectedness of these psychological traits, see Inge K. Broverman et al., "Sex-Role Stereotypes: A Current Appraisal," *Journal of Social Issues* 28, no. 2 (1972): 59–78.

50. Gilligan, *In a Different Voice*, pp. 1–2.

51. For the fullest development of this argument, see Wendy Kaminer, *A Fearful Freedom: Women's Flight from Equality* (Reading: Addison-Wesley, 1990).

CHAPTER THREE

1. See, for example, articles in widely read national news magazines: "White Male Paranoia," *Newsweek* (March 29, 1993), pp. 46–54; "Yet Another Setback for the White Male," *Time* (September 27, 1993) p. 20; "White, Male, and Worried," *Business Week* (January 31, 1994), pp. 50–56.

2. See Elisabeth Schüssler Fiorenza, *In Memory of Her: A Feminist Theological Reconstruction of Christian Origins* (New York: Crossroad Publishing Company, 1983), pp. 251–70.

3. See Clarissa Atkinson, *The Oldest Vocation: Christian Motherhood in the Middle Ages* (Ithaca: Cornell University Press, 1991), p. 204.

4. Martin Luther, *Lectures on Genesis, Chapters 1–5*, p. 202 (WA 42.151), as quoted and discussed in Atkinson, *The Oldest Vocation*, p. 208.

5. Ibid., p. 212.

6. Ibid.

7. See Bernadette Brooten, "Junia . . . Outstanding among the Apostles (Romans 16:7)," in *Women Priests: A Catholic Commentary on the Vatican Declaration*, edited by Leonard Swidler and Arlene Swidler (New York: Paulist Press, 1977), pp. 141–44.

8. Atkinson, *The Oldest Vocation*, p. 198.

9. See Atkinson's discussion of Thomas More and his *Utopia* in ibid., pp. 194ff.

10. In a volume analyzing the hearings, *Race-ing Justice and En-gendering*

Power: Essays on Anita Hill, Clarence Thomas, and the Construction of a Social Reality, edited by Toni Morrison (New York: Pantheon Books, 1992), a number of scholars discuss the inter- and intraracial politics of sex and race at their core. For treatments of the gender hierarchy and conflict within the black community, see especially Nellie Y. McKay, "Remembering Anita Hill and Clarence Thomas: What Really Happened When One Black Woman Spoke Out"; Nell Irvin Painter, "Hill, Thomas, and the Use of Racial Stereotype"; and Christine Stansell, "White Feminists and Black Realities: The Politics of Authenticity." For examination of Thomas's manipulation of the politics of race and gender, see especially Manning Marable, "Clarence Thomas and the Crisis of Black Political Culture," pp. 68–69; and Kimberle Crenshaw, "Whose Story Is It Anyway? Feminist and Antiracist Appropriations of Anita Hill," pp. 416ff.

11. Quoted in "Anita Hill Offers Her Version of Senate Hearings," *New York Times* (October 17, 1992), p. 6.

12. See McKay, "Remembering Anita Hill," p. 285; Painter, "Hill, Thomas and the Use of Racial Stereotype," pp. 200–14.

13. Timothy M. Phelps and Helen Winternitz point out that preserving the accord between members of the exclusive club of the Senate was a priority that initially worked against investigation or hearings of Hill's charges until public furor began to arise. See their *Capitol Games: The Inside Story of Clarence Thomas, Anita Hill, and a Supreme Court Nomination* (New York: HarperPerennial, 1993), pp. 241–42.

14. Opening statement of Judge Clarence Thomas to the Senate Judiciary Committee, October 11, 1991, reprinted in *Court of Appeal: The Black Community Speaks Out on the Record and Sexual Politics of Thomas vs. Hill*, edited by Robert Chisman and Robert L. Allen (New York: Ballantine Books, 1992), p. 13.

15. Phelps and Winternitz point out that if the Committee had been able to ask Thomas about his alleged interest in pornography, dating back to his college years, Hill's case would have been strengthened considerably. See *Capitol Games*, pp. 346–47. Thomas took advantage of the Committee's ruling that questions to him or Hill about their personal lives would be out of order.

16. Phelps and Winternitz make the point that before the hearings on Hill's charges even began, the fact that political negotiations among the Senators had reduced postponement of the vote on Thomas's nomination

to only a week meant the allotted time for them was too short for serious investigation of the charges. See ibid., pp. 274–75.

17. Phelps and Winternitz discuss these and other reasons for Hill's decision to follow Thomas, including the fact that it was President Reagan's objective at the time to abolish the Department of Education, in ibid., p. 325.

18. See polls cited in "For Oklahoma, Anita Hill's Story Is Open Wound," *New York Times* (April 19, 1993), pp. A1 and B12.

19. Tom R. Tyler, "Justice, Self-Interest, and the Legitimacy of Legal and Political Authority," in *Beyond Self-Interest*, edited by Jane J. Mansbridge (Chicago: University of Chicago Press, 1990), pp. 175–76. Tyler's essay provides an important discussion of the role played by considerations of justice, in addition to self-interest, in public choice.

20. Quoted in "Law Firms Begin Reining In Sex-Harassing Partners," *New York Times* (February 25, 1994), p. A19.

21. See "Some Workers Lose Right to File Suit for Bias at Work," *New York Times* (March 18, 1994), pp. A1 and B6.

22. Quoted in "Final Tailhook Report Portrays a Navy Troubled by Social Changes at Home," *Wall Street Journal* (April 26, 1993), p. A14.

23. Editorial, "The Tailhook Fiasco," *New York Times* (February 17, 1994), p. A22.

24. Quoted in "Senate Approves a Four-Star Rank for Admiral in Tailhook Affair," *New York Times* (April 20, 1994), pp. A1 and B10.

25. "Military Women Say Complaints of Sex Harassment Go Unheeded," *New York Times* (March 10, 1993), pp. A1 and A19.

26. The account in the *New York Times* drew attention to the use of the media by the Democratic and Republican women Representatives and Senators, suggesting their concern for giving their act maximum public exposure. See "Senate Approves a Four-Star Rank for Admiral in Tailhook Affair."

27. See, for example, another editorial on the Navy and sexual harassment in the *New York Times* (March 12, 1994), p. 20: "the idea that women might be committed to their careers and determined to be given equal opportunity is even newer to the military than it is to corporate America."

28. Study reported in "The Evolving Concept of Sexual Harassment," *New York Times* (October 13, 1991), p. 28.

29. Study cited in Marable, "Clarence Thomas and the Crisis of Black Political Culture," p. 66.

30. Susan P. Phillips and Margaret Schneider, "Sexual Harassment of Female Doctors by Patients, *New England Journal of Medicine* 329, no. 26 (1993): 1936–39.

31. Nationwide survey conducted by the American Jewish Congress in 1993 and a survey conducted by the United Methodist Church in 1990 reported in the *New York Times* (August 28, 1993), p. L5.

32. See, for example, Gertrude Himmelfarb, *The De-Moralization of Society: From Victorian Virtues to Modern Values* (New York: Alfred A. Knopf, 1995), pp. 259–63.

33. Joe Klein, "The Politics of Promiscuity," *Newsweek* (May 9, 1994), pp. 16–20.

34. Kathleen Gerson, *No-Man's Land: Men's Changing Commitments to Family and Work* (New York: Basic Books, 1993), p. 5. According to Gerson, the number of American households in 1990 depending solely or primarily on a male earner rises to a total of only about one-third when those in which the woman works part-time and those headed by a single father are included.

35. Ibid., pp. 3–4.

36. Iris Marion Young, "Mothers, Citizenship, and Independence: A Critique of Pure Family Values," *Ethics* 105, no. 3 (April 1995): 542.

37. Robert L. Griswold, *Fatherhood in America: A History* (New York: Basic Books, 1993), pp. 218 and 223.

38. Barbara Ehrenreich, *The Hearts of Men: American Dreams and the Flight from Commitment* (Garden City: Anchor Press/Doubleday, 1984), p. 12.

39. Ibid., p. 169.

40. Sara S. McLanahan, "The Consequences of Single Motherhood," *American Prospect*, no. 18 (Summer 1994): 48.

41. See Sheila Ards, "Understanding Patterns of Child Maltreatment," *Contemporary Policy Issues* 10, no. 4 (October 1992): 48–49.

42. National Research Council, "Etiology of Child Maltreatment," in *Understanding Child Abuse and Neglect* (Washington, D.C.: National Academy Press, 1993), p. 141.

43. Ibid., pp. 113 and 127.

44. Angela Browne, "Violence against Women" (Report B of the Council on Scientific Affairs to the American Medical Association, 1991), p. 13.

45. William Safire, "What Fathers Want," *New York Times* (June 16, 1994), p. A27.

46. Susan Chira, "War over Role of American Fathers," *New York Times* (June 19, 1994), p. 22.

47. The number 400 was reported in "Parish Priest Is Sentenced in Sexual Assault of Boys," *New York Times* (April 15, 1994), p. B5.

48. Peter Steinfels, "The Church Faces the Trespasses of Priests," *New York Times* (June 27, 1993), pp. 1 and 5. Steinfels reported that national estimates of the pattern varied at the time. Sociologist Andrew M. Greeley estimated that 2,500 priests had abused 100,000 minors over the last twenty-five years. Philip J. Murnion, also a priest-sociologist, estimated 15,000 victims over forty years.

49. Peter Steinfels, "Beliefs," *New York Times* (June 12, 1993), p. 6.

50. In the first class-action complaint in a sexual abuse case involving the church, racketeering charges were lodged in New Jersey against four Roman Catholic bishops charged with covering up a pattern of abuse of 50 to 100 potential claimants by two priests. Reported in the *Wall Street Journal* (June 11, 1993), p. B10.

51. Steinfels, "Beliefs."

52. Angela Browne, "Violence against Women by Male Partners: Prevalence, Outcomes, and Policy Implications," *American Psychologist* 48 (October 1993): 1077.

53. Ibid., p. 1078.

54. Ibid., pp. 1077–79.

55. Browne, "Violence against Women" (Report B), p. 10.

56. "Violence against Women: Relevance for Medical Practitioners," *Journal of the American Medical Association* 267, no. 23 (June 17, 1992): 3187.

57. Browne, "Violence against Women" (Report B), p. 12.

58. Ibid., pp. 14–16.

59. Melinda Henneberger and Michel Marriott, "For Some, Youthful Courting Has Become a Game of Abuse," *New York Times* (July 11, 1993), pp. A1 and 33; and Michel Marriott, "A Malevolent Ritual Is Called Common in New York Pools," *New York Times* (July 7, 1993), pp. A1 and B2.

60. Quoted in N. R. Kleinfield, "Admitting Guilt, Wachtler Offers Account of Plot," *New York Times* (April 1, 1993), p. A1.

61. Letter to the editor, *New York Times Magazine* (March 28, 1993), responding to "The Campus Crime Wave," *New York Times Magazine* (March 7, 1993).

62. See, for example, David Blankenhorn's *Fatherless America: Confronting Our Most Urgent Social Problem* (New York: Basic Books, 1995). Proposing that a more nurturing daddy, the "Good Family Man," replace the traditional father, Blankenhorn claims not to be calling for a return to a traditional model. However, the description he gives of this father's distinctive male role as provider, protector, nurturer, and sponsor is based on the traditional ideology of gender complementarity. The "Good Family Man" differs from traditional fatherhood chiefly in the way his claim to traditional authority as head of family is presented in more egalitarian language. See chapter 11, "The Good Man," pp. 201–21.

63. The idea that there are master cultural narratives that "block" others comes from Edward W. Said's discussion of narratives and power in the context of imperialism, in *Culture and Imperialism* (New York: Alfred A. Knopf, 1993), p. xiii.

64. Barbara Ehrenreich makes the point in *The Hearts of Men*, p. 169, that the "male revolt" she describes is part of the erosion of the American moral climate that has been the subject of study from David Riesman to Christopher Lasch.

65. For illuminating discussion of this problem, see Nellie Y. McKay, "Acknowledging Differences: Can Women Find Unity through Diversity?" in *Theorizing Black Feminisms: The Visionary Pragmatism of Black Women*, edited by Stanlie M. James and Abena P. A. Busia (New York: Routledge, 1993). See also Crenshaw, "Whose Story Is It Anyway?"

CHAPTER FOUR

1. This is especially true for men, given their greater access to jobs requiring education and training. See Kay Lehman Schlozman, Nancy Burns, and Sidney Verba, "Gender and Pathways to Participation: The Role of Resources," *Journal of Politics* 56, no. 4 (November 1994): 974–78.

2. For a discussion of these barriers, see Lynn C. Burbridge, "The Glass Ceiling in Different Sectors of the Economy: Differences between Government, Non-Profit, and For-Profit Organizations" (report submitted to

the U.S. Department of Labor Glass Ceiling Commission, June 23, 1994).

3. For an analysis that links class with gender and race in examining barriers to women, see Sharon L. Harlan and Catherine White Berheide, "Barriers to Workplace Advancement Experienced by Women in Low-Paying Occupations" (report submitted to the U.S. Department of Labor Glass Ceiling Commission, January 1994).

4. Judith Shklar, *American Citizenship: The Quest for Inclusion* (Cambridge: Harvard University Press, 1991).

5. Ibid., p. 64.

6. Ibid., pp. 63–64.

7. See Derek Bok, *The Cost of Talent: How Executives and Professionals Are Paid and How It Affects America* (New York: Free Press, 1993).

8. Many discussions of the work/family conflict highlight the gendered structure of paid work. Legal scholar Joan C. Williams has formulated a theoretical model, on which I draw here, of what she calls the "dominant family ecology" and its relationship to the market. See her "Gender Wars: Selfless Women in the Republic of Choice," *New York University Law Review* 66, no. 6 (December 1991), and "Is Coverture Dead? Beyond a New Theory of Alimony," *Georgetown Law Journal* 82, no. 7 (September 1994).

9. Juliet Schor, *The Overworked American: The Unexpected Decline of Leisure* (New York: Basic Books, 1992), p. 37.

10. Harriet B. Presser, "Employment Schedules among Dual-Earner Spouses and the Division of Household Labor by Gender," *American Sociological Review* 59, no. 3 (June 1994): 358.

11. See Lynne M. Casper, Mary Hawkins, and Martin O'Connell, "Who's Minding the Kids: Child Care Arrangements, Fall 1991" (report to the U.S. Department of Commerce, May 1994), pp. 6 and 15.

12. Presser, "Employment Schedules among Dual-Earner Spouses," pp. 358–60.

13. Ibid., p. 362.

14. Williams, "Is Coverture Dead?" p. 2242.

15. Schor, *The Overworked American*, p. 38.

16. Joan C. Williams, "Deconstructing Gender," *Michigan Law Review* 87 (February 1989): 801.

17. The most recent figures available are for 1993. *Employment in Perspective: Women in the Labor Force* (Bureau of Labor Statistics, U.S. Department of Labor, Fourth Quarter 1993), table A.

18. Heidi Hartmann and Roberta Spalter-Roth, "A Feminist Approach to Policymaking for Women and Families" (paper delivered at the Future Directions for American Politics and Public Policy Seminar, Harvard University, March 1994), p. 3.

19. Juliet Schor developed her concept of the on-demand system of employment in "Short of Time: American Families and the Structure of Jobs" (paper delivered at the Future Directions for American Politics and Public Policy Seminar, Harvard University, March 1994).

20. Williams, "Is Coverture Dead?" pp. 2236ff.

21. Williams, "Gender Wars," pp. 1596–97.

22. Schor, "Short of Time," pp. 8–10.

23. Williams, "Gender Wars," p. 1603.

24. Schor, *The Overworked American*, p. 29.

25. Schor, "Short of Time," p. 11.

26. Williams, "Is Coverture Dead?" pp. 2237ff.

27. Williams, "Gender Wars," pp. 1608–12.

28. Ibid., p. 1612.

29. Williams, "Is Coverture Dead?" pp. 2241ff.

30. Schor, *The Overworked American*, pp. 8 and 20.

31. Ibid., pp. 20–21 and 83.

32. Ibid., pp. 36–37.

33. Ella L. J. Edmondson Bell and Stella M. Nkomo discuss the African-American case in "Barriers to Work Place Advancement Experienced by African-Americans" (report submitted to the U.S. Department of Labor Glass Ceiling Commission, March 1994), pp. 31–34.

34. Burbridge, "The Glass Ceiling in Different Sectors of the Economy," p. 4.

35. Bureau of Labor statistics taken from Catalyst, "Successful Initiatives for Breaking the Glass Ceiling to Upward Mobility for Minorities and Women" (report submitted to the U.S. Department of Labor Glass Ceiling Commission, December 1993), pp. 4–6.

36. "Good for Business: Making Full Use of the Nation's Human Capi-

tal" (report of the U.S. Department of Labor Glass Ceiling Commission, March 1995), p. 10.

37. Catalyst, "Successful Initiatives," p. 9.

38. For a review of research on structural barriers to women's advancement see Bette Woody and Carol Weiss, "Barriers to Work Place Advancement: The Experience of the White Female Workforce" (report submitted to the U.S. Department of Labor Glass Ceiling Commission, (April 19, 1994), pp. 59–62; and Catalyst, "Successful Initiatives."

39. Harlan and Berheide, "Barriers to Workplace Advancement Experienced by Women in Low-Paying Occupations," p. 9.

40. Ibid., p. 19.

41. Mona Harrington, *Women Lawyers: Rewriting the Rules* (New York: Alfred A. Knopf, 1994), p. 37. For her discussion of the "mommy track," see p. 34.

42. Kathryn Edin, "The Myths of Dependency and Self-Sufficiency: Women, Welfare, and Low-Wage Work" (manuscript, April 1994), pp. 15 and 23.

43. See in particular chapter 5 in Constance Williard Williams, *Black Teenage Mothers: Pregnancy and Child Rearing from Their Perspective* (Lexington: Lexington Books, 1991).

44. Williams, "Deconstructing Gender," p. 823.

45. Bok, *The Cost of Talent*, p. 297.

46. For Schor's discussion of this consumer culture, see *The Overworked American*, in particular chapter 5, pp. 107–38.

47. Peter T. Kilborn, "More Women Take Low-Wage Jobs Just So Their Families Can Get By," *New York Times* (March 13, 1994), p. 24.

48. See, for example, the study reported in Barbara Presley Noble, "Women Pay More for Success," *New York Times* (July 4, 1993), Business Section, p. 25.

49. Harrington, *Women Lawyers*, chapter 7, and Catalyst, "Successful Initiatives," p. 8.

50. Primary examples include Carol Gilligan, *In a Different Voice: Psychological Theory and Women's Development* (Cambridge: Harvard University Press, 1982); Mary Belenky et al., *Women's Ways of Knowing: The Development of Self, Voice, and Mind* (New York: Basic Books, 1986); Judy B. Rosener, "Ways Women Lead," *Harvard Business Review* 68 (November/

December 1990); Sara Ruddick, *Maternal Thinking: Toward a Politics of Peace* (Boston: Beacon Press, 1989); and Deborah Tannen, *You Just Don't Understand: Women and Men in Conversation* (New York: William E. Morrow and Company, 1990).

51. Madeleine Kunin, *Living a Political Life* (New York: Alfred A. Knopf, 1994), p. 10.

52. "Dole: Women Can Offer Hope in a Cynical World," *Harvard Gazette* (June 1993), pp. 1 and 15.

53. "Pastoral Letter: The General Association of Massachusetts to the Churches under Their Care," *New England Spectator* (July 12, 1837), reprinted in *The Public Years of Sarah and Angelina Grimké: Selected Writings, 1835–1839*, edited by Larry Ceplair (New York: Columbia University Press, 1989), p. 211.

54. Rosener, "Ways Women Lead," pp. 120–24.

55. *Washington Post* (March 15, 1994), p. A6; emphasis added.

56. For a useful discussion of this point, see Ruth Hubbard and Elijah Wald, *Exploding the Gene Myth* (Boston: Beacon Press, 1993), chapters 1 and 7 especially.

57. Kathleen Gerson, *Hard Choices: How Women Decide about Work, Career, and Motherhood* (Berkeley: University of California Press, 1985), p. 33.

58. For discussion of domesticity's embedded criticism of self-interest, see Williams's "Gender Wars," especially p. 1634, and "Deconstructing Gender," pp. 810–13.

CHAPTER FIVE

1. The phrase is taken from Kathryn Kish Sklar, who identifies this capacity as one of the main features of Progressive women's political culture. See her "Religious and Moral Authority as Factors Shaping the Balance of Power for Women's Political Culture in the Twentieth Century" (paper presented at the 100th Anniversary of the Founding of Hull House, Rockford, Illinois, October 1989), p. 18.

2. Nancy F. Cott introduces her discussion of modern feminism by making a similar point. See *The Grounding of Modern Feminism* (New Haven: Yale University Press, 1987), p. 3.

3. Foremost among these important new studies are those by Paula Baker, "The Domestication of Politics: Women and American Political

Society, 1780–1920," in *Women, the State, and Welfare*, edited by Linda Gordon (Madison: University of Wisconsin Press, 1990); Paula Baker, *The Moral Frameworks of Public Life: Gender, Politics, and the State in Rural New York, 1870–1920* (New York: Oxford University Press, 1991); Ellen Fitzpatrick, *Endless Crusade: Women, Social Scientists, and Progressive Reform* (New York: Oxford University Press, 1990); Janet Zollinger Giele, *Two Paths to Women's Equality: Temperance, Suffrage, and the Origins of Modern Feminism* (New York: Twayne Publishers, 1995); Evelyn Brooks Higginbotham, *Righteous Discontent: The Women's Movement in the Black Baptist Church, 1880–1920* (Cambridge: Harvard University Press, 1993); Molly Ladd-Taylor, *Mother-Work: Women, Child-Welfare, and the State* (Urbana: University of Illinois Press, 1994); Ann Firor Scott, *Natural Allies: Women's Associations in American History* (Urbana: University of Illinois Press, 1991); Kathryn Kish Sklar, *Florence Kelley and the Nation's Work* (New Haven: Yale University Press, 1995); and Theda Skocpol, *Protecting Soldiers and Mothers: The Political Origins of Social Policy in the United States* (Cambridge: Harvard University Press, 1992).

4. Scott, *Natural Allies*, p. 3.

5. Ibid., p. 178.

6. See, for example, Robert D. Putnam, "The Prosperous Community: Social Capital and Public Life," *American Prospect*, no. 13 (Spring 1993): 38. Putnam recognizes the central importance of civic ties for a healthy democracy and economy, and focuses on the problem of creating and sustaining social capital. But these processes, their history, and the very notion of social capital itself are deeply gendered. Therefore, systematic analysis of gender (in the context of race, ethnicity, and class) as a variable in both the theory and practice of civil society is crucial to addressing our current national situation.

7. See the works cited in note 3.

8. Ellen C. DuBois established the framework of interpretation that has dominated historiography of nineteenth- and early-twentieth-century women in her classic work, *Feminism and Suffrage: The Emergence of an Independent Women's Movement in America, 1848–1869* (Ithaca: Cornell University Press, 1978). See especially her introduction to that volume (pp. 15–20).

9. From the resolution passed at the 1856 National Women's Rights Convention, quoted in ibid., p. 41.

10. See, for example, Hazel V. Carby, "'On the Threshold of Woman's Era': Lynching, Empire, and Sexuality in Black Feminist Theory," in *"Race," Writing, and Difference*, edited by Henry Louis Gates, Jr. (Chicago: University of Chicago Press, 1986), and *Unequal Sisters: A Multi-Cultural Reader in U.S. Women's History*, edited by Vicki L. Ruiz and Ellen DuBois (New York: Routledge, 1994).

11. DuBois, *Feminism and Suffrage*, pp. 37–38.

12. Elizabeth Battelle Clark, "The Politics of God and The Woman's Vote: Religion in the American Suffrage Movement, 1848–1895" (Ph.D. dissertation, Princeton University, 1989), p. 33.

13. See Ellen DuBois, "Women's Rights and Abolition," *Antislavery Reconsidered: New Perspectives on the Abolitionists*, edited by Lewis Perry and Michael Fellman (Baton Rouge: Louisiana State University Press, 1979), pp. 240–42.

14. See Clark, "The Politics of God," pp. 12–18, for discussion of this point in relationship to the ideological split between the National Woman Suffrage Association and Elizabeth Cady Stanton and the WCTU and Frances Willard.

15. For example, see Nancy F. Cott, "What's in a Name? The Limits of 'Social Feminism'; or, Expanding the Vocabulary of Women's History," *Journal of American History* 76, no. 3 (December 1989): 826.

16. Lori Ginzberg, *Women and the Work of Benevolence: Morality, Politics, and Class in the Nineteenth-Century United States* (New Haven: Yale University Press, 1990), pp. 206–7.

17. Sklar, "Religious and Moral Authority," p. 1.

18. Maureen Fitzgerald makes this point as well in asserting, against the dominant historical interpretation, that Stanton's was a claim to moral equality. See her foreword to the 1993 edition of Elizabeth Cady Stanton's *The Woman's Bible* (Boston: Northeastern University Press, 1993), pp. ix–x.

19. Quoted in Mary D. Pellauer, *Toward a Tradition of Feminist Theology: The Religious Social Thought of Elizabeth Cady Stanton, Susan B. Anthony, and Anna Howard Shaw* (Brooklyn: Carlson Publishing, 1991), p. 136, from "Prisons and Punishments," *The Revolution* (January 7, 1869), p. 9. Stanton made this remark in an 1869 speech on prison reform.

20. Indeed, even radicals differed among themselves on this point. For a

discussion of how, see Fitzgerald's foreword to *The Woman's Bible*, pp. xxii–xxvii.

21. Elizabeth Battelle Clark, "Religion, Rights, and Difference in the Early Woman's Rights Movement," *Wisconsin Women's Law Journal* 3 (1987): 30.

22. For a discussion of the impact of the Second Great Awakening, see Dorothy C. Bass, "'Their Prodigious Influence': Women, Religion, and Reform in Antebellum America," in *Women of Spirit: Female Leadership in the Jewish and Christian Traditions*, edited by Rosemary Radford Ruether and Eleanor McLaughlin (New York: Simon and Schuster, 1979), pp. 279–300.

23. See especially in Ann Douglas, *The Feminization of American Culture* (New York: Alfred A. Knopf, 1977), the chapter entitled "The Loss of Theology: From Dogma to Fiction." Her argument not only overlooks the nontextual arena in which women were active theologically, but also privileges male theological ideas as "serious" theology. Furthermore, Douglas takes this position in the context of analysis of a historical period when women were still formally denied access to both theological education and religious leadership in most Christian traditions and in Judaism.

24. For a full-length study of the Spiritualists, see Ann Braude, *Radical Spirits: Spiritualism and Women's Rights in Nineteenth-Century America* (Boston: Beacon Press, 1989). For a discussion of Stanton and the religious roots of her thought, see Fitzgerald's foreword to *The Woman's Bible*, pp. ix–x.

25. Braude, ibid., p. 62.

26. Pellauer, *Toward a Tradition of Feminist Theology*, p. 297, and general discussion of Stanton's religious thought.

27. Stanton, introduction to *The Woman's Bible*, pp. 7–13; Pellauer, *Toward a Tradition of Feminist Theology*, p. 135. Pellauer's study provides a rare and especially good analysis of Stanton's "religious social" thinking.

28. Carolyn De Swarte Gifford also makes this point and quotes Stanton's resolution passed at the women's rights convention of 1878, marking the thirtieth anniversary of Seneca Falls, in "Politicizing the Sacred Texts: Elizabeth Cady Stanton and *The Woman's Bible*," in *Searching the Scriptures*, vol. 1, *A Feminist Introduction*, edited by Elisabeth Schüssler Fiorenza (New York: Crossroad Publishing Company, 1993), pp. 55–56.

29. Ruth Bordin, *Frances Willard: A Biography* (Chapel Hill: University of North Carolina Press, 1986), p. 4.

30. Ruth Bordin, *Woman and Temperance: The Quest for Power and Liberty, 1873–1900* (Philadelphia: Temple University Press, 1981), p. 202 n. 111.

31. Frances Willard, *"Writing Out My Heart": Selections from the Journal of Frances E. Willard, 1855–1896*, edited by Carolyn De Swarte Gifford (Urbana: University of Illinois Press, 1995), p. 17.

32. Ibid., p. 17.

33. Clark, "The Politics of God," p. 267, quoting from Nancy Hardesty, *Women Called to Witness: Evangelical Feminism in the Nineteenth Century* (Nashville: Abingdon Press, 1984), p. 154.

34. I am grateful to biblical scholar Bernadette Brooten for conversations in which she has pointed out that biblical teachings about the family diverge and that the Gospel texts by no means promote the idea of a traditional family. The illustrative citations referred to here are Matthew 12:46–50, Mark 10:28–31, and Luke 14:25–33.

35. Sklar, "Religious and Moral Authority," p. 6.

36. Ibid., pp. 25–26 n. 27.

37. For a recent study that confirms the special role voluntary associations, especially religious ones, still play today in teaching women civic skills and bringing women into political life, see Kay Lehman Schlozman, Nancy Burns, and Sidney Verba, "Gender and Pathways to Participation: The Role of Resources," *Journal of Politics* 56, no. 4 (November 1994): 963–90.

38. Higginbotham, *Righteous Discontent*, pp. 9 and 17.

39. Ginzberg, *Women and the Work of Benevolence*, p. 34.

40. For an extended argument to this effect, see analysis of the "ideology of benevolence" in ibid., pp. 5–6.

41. See also, for example, Alice Kessler-Harris, *Out to Work: A History of Wage-Earning Women in the United States* (New York: Oxford University Press, 1982), pp. 49–50.

42. Ibid., p. xi.

43. For a discussion of "Good and Evil as Male and Female" in Western Christianity and culture, see Rosemary Radford Ruether, *Sexism and God-Talk: Toward a Feminist Theology* (Boston: Beacon Press, 1983), pp. 165–73. See also Mary Daly, *Beyond God the Father: Toward a Philosophy of*

Women's Liberation (Boston: Beacon Press, 1973), chapter 2, for a more extended theological analysis.

44. For an example of the emerging scholarship on American Jewish women in this period, see Karla Goldman, "Ambivalent Benevolence: Female Jewish Philanthropy and the Immigrant Jew" (paper given at the Berkshire Conference on the History of Women, June 1993).

45. Quoted in Kessler-Harris, *Out to Work*, p. 96.

46. Clark, "The Politics of God," p. 31.

47. The Garrisonian split was a schism in the abolitionist movement between radicals, who followed William Lloyd Garrison, and moderates over the rights and role of women in the movement and society, and whether or not to continue working within inherited structures, especially religious institutions. For an example of other historians who follow DuBois's analysis, see Ginzberg, *Women and the Work of Benevolence*, pp. 98ff. Ginzberg argues there was a midcentury shift from women's morally and locally based reform initiatives to a more politically effective discourse and nationally oriented effort.

48. See DuBois's discussion of "Abolitionist Politics," in *Feminism and Suffrage*, pp. 31–40.

49. See, for example, the distinction Kathryn Kish Sklar draws between black women's "voluntary activity" and white women's "reform activity" on the basis of the latter's access (due to their race privilege) to state resources. Sklar, "Historical Foundations of Women's Power," in *Mothers of a New World: Maternalist Politics and the Origins of Welfare States*, edited by Seth Koven and Sonya Michel (New York: Routledge, 1993), pp. 43–44.

50. Ginzberg, *Women and the Work of Benevolence*, p. 173.

51. Bordin, *Woman and Temperance*, p. 13.

52. Ginzberg, *Women and the Work of Benevolence*, p. 206.

53. I am indebted in pursuing this line of argument to the work of Theda Skocpol in *Protecting Soldiers and Mothers*, and also that of Linda Kerber in *Women of the Republic: Intellect and Ideology in Revolutionary America* (Chapel Hill: University of North Carolina Press, 1980). Both Skocpol and Kerber demonstrate unusual sensitivity to and respect for the normative dimension of historical women's political thought—in particular, women's attempts to develop their own political values, identities, and styles. In

doing so, Skocpol and Kerber set aside old verities in the interpretation of American politics and reach for new and more complex readings. Neither scholar addresses to a significant degree the role of religion in women's political development. Their intellectual openness, however, allows religion to be brought back to the center of the debate, where his-torical women thought it belonged.

54. Skocpol, *Protecting Soldiers and Mothers*, p. 371.

55. Clark, "The Politics of God," p. 224.

56. Linda Gordon, *Pitied but Not Entitled: Single Mothers and the History of Welfare, 1890–1935* (New York: Free Press, 1994).

57. Linda Gordon, "Putting Children First: Women, Maternalism, and Welfare in the Twentieth Century," Discussion Papers, no. 991-93 (Madison: Institute for Research on Poverty, University of Wisconsin, 1993), p. 13.

58. Linda Gordon, "Gender, State, and Society: A Debate with Theda Skocpol," *Contention* 2, no. 3 (Spring 1993): 146–47.

59. Theda Skocpol, "Soldiers, Workers, and Mothers: Gendered Iden-tities in Early U.S. Social Policy," *Contention* 2, no. 3 (Spring 1993): 173.

60. Molly Ladd-Taylor, "Mother-Work: Ideology, Public Policy, and the Mothers' Movement, 1890–1930" (Ph.D. dissertation, Yale University, 1986), p. 1.

61. Eileen Boris, "The Power of Motherhood: Black and White Activist Women Redefine the 'Political,'" in Koven and Michel's *Mothers of a New World*, pp. 232 and 235.

62. Ladd-Taylor, "Mother-Work," p. 10.

63. Sklar, "Historical Foundations of Women's Power," p. 45.

64. See especially Stephanie J. Shaw, "Black Club Women and the Cre-ation of the National Association of Colored Women," *Journal of Women's History* 3, no. 2 (Fall 1991).

65. See on this distinction Boris, "The Power of Motherhood," p. 214.

66. Gordon, "Putting Children First," p. 2.

67. Gwendolyn Mink, "The Lady and the Tramp: Gender, Race, and the Origins of the American Welfare State," in Gordon, *Women, the State, and Welfare*, p. 111.

CHAPTER SIX

1. Elizabeth Battelle Clark, "Religion, Rights, and Difference in the Early Women's Rights Movement," *Wisconsin Women's Law Journal* 3 (1987): 39.

2. Ann Braude, *Radical Spirits: Spiritualism and Women's Rights in Nineteenth-Century America* (Boston: Beacon Press, 1989), p. 9.

3. Higginbotham makes this point with regard to black women in *Righteous Discontent: The Women's Movement in the Black Baptist Church, 1880–1920* (Cambridge: Harvard University Press, 1993), p. 122. It is true also for white women reformers.

4. For Stanton, see Mary D. Pellauer, *Toward a Tradition of Feminist Theology: The Religious Social Thought of Elizabeth Cady Stanton, Susan B. Anthony, and Anna Howard Shaw* (Brooklyn: Carlson Publishing, 1991), p. 34; for Broughton, see Higginbotham, *Righteous Discontent*, pp. 128–29; for Angelina Grimké, see *The Public Years of Sarah and Angelina Grimké: Selected Writings, 1835–1839*, edited by Larry Ceplair (New York: Columbia University Press, 1989), pp. 195–96 and 204–10.

5. See Higginbotham's discussion of the biblical exegesis of black leaders Mary Cook and Virginia Broughton, *Righteous Discontent*, pp. 128–29, as well as Pellauer on Stanton and Anthony.

6. I am indebted to Carolyn De Swarte Gifford, editor of Willard's journal, for this information. Private conversation, May 11, 1995.

7. Pellauer, *Toward a Tradition of Feminist Theology*, pp. 34–35 and 125–26.

8. Angelina Grimké, Letter 12, "Human Rights Not Founded on Sex" (1837), in Ceplair, *The Public Years of Sarah and Angelina Grimké*, p. 195. Both Grimkés argued that when moral being was the issue or "standard" there was no difference between men and women. Although they believed in gender difference, they saw it as a distinction having no influence on men's and women's moral status and duties.

9. Dorothy C. Bass elaborates this point in her discussion of Garrisonian perfectionism's critique of moral inequality in " 'In Christian Firmness and Christian Meekness': Feminism and Pacificism in Antebellum America," in *Immaculate and Powerful: The Female and Sacred Image and Social Reality*, edited by Clarissa Atkinson, Constance H. Buchanan, and Margaret Miles (Boston: Beacon Press, 1985).

10. Angelina Grimké, Letter 11, "The Sphere of Woman and Man as

Moral Beings the Same" (1837), pp. 188–89, and Sarah Grimké, Letter 4, "Social Intercourse of the Sexes" (1837), p. 219, Letter 8, "On the Condition of Women in the United States" (1837), p. 221, and Letter 14, "What Are the Duties of Woman at the Present Time?" (1837), p. 261, in Ceplair, *The Public Years of Sarah and Angelina Grimké.*

11. See, for example, Ellen C. DuBois, *Feminism and Suffrage: The Emergence of an Independent Women's Movement in America, 1848–1869* (Ithaca: Cornell University Press, 1978), pp. 37–38.

12. Sarah Grimké, Letter 8, "On the Condition of Women in the United States" (1837), in Ceplair, *The Public Years of Sarah and Angelina Grimké*, p. 220.

13. Sarah Grimké, Letter 4, "Social Intercourse of the Sexes" (1837), in ibid., p. 218.

14. In DuBois's judgment, women's independence and the end of their subordination lay with the vote. See *Feminism and Suffrage*, p. 17. But nineteenth-century women never separated moral equality from other forms, whether they came early or late to support suffrage.

15. Sarah Grimké, Letter 3, "The Pastoral Letter of the General Association of Congregational Ministers of Massachusetts" (1837), in Ceplair, *The Public Years of Sarah and Angelina Grimké*, p. 216.

16. Ellen DuBois, "Women's Rights and Abolition," in *Antislavery Reconsidered: New Perspectives on the Abolitionists*, edited by Lewis Perry and Michael Fellman (Baton Rouge: Louisiana State University Press, 1979), p. 241–42.

17. I have borrowed this distinction from philosopher of religion Cornel West, who drew it in general remarks on a panel on religion as a resource for criticism of public reason, "Political Liberalism: Religion and Public Reason" (Harvard Divinity School, May 3, 1995). Maureen Fitzgerald makes a similar distinction in her discussion of Stanton's awareness of the need for systematic social change. See her foreword to *The Woman's Bible* (Boston: Northeastern University Press, 1993), pp. ix–x.

18. Carroll Smith-Rosenberg, *Religion and the Rise of the American City* (Ithaca: Cornell University Press, 1971), pp. 66–67.

19. Harry C. Boyte, "The Pragmatic Ends of Popular Politics," in *Habermas and the Public Sphere*, edited by Craig Calhoun (Cambridge: Massachusetts Institute of Technology Press, 1992), p. 347.

20. Frances Willard, *"Writing Out My Heart": Selections from the Journal of*

Frances E. Willard, 1855–1896, edited by Carolyn De Swarte Gifford (Urbana: University of Illinois Press, 1995), introduction, part 1, 14 February 1859–28 March 1861, p. 33.

21. Ibid., p. 9.

22. See references to Brooks in Higginbotham, *Righteous Discontent*.

23. See also Elizabeth Battelle Clark's discussion of this point in "The Politics of God and the Woman's Vote: Religion in the American Suffrage Movement, 1848–1895" (Ph.D. dissertation, Princeton University, 1989), p. 34 and n. 19. Even DuBois makes this point in "Women's Rights," p. 246.

24. Speech quoted in Pellauer, *Toward a Tradition of Feminist Theology*, p. 112.

25. Quoted in ibid., pp. 118–19.

26. Quoted in ibid., p. 122; Pellauer points out that Hagar was the biblical figure whom Stanton used as a model of this female strength.

27. Quoted in Higginbotham, *Righteous Discontent*, p. 150.

28. Quoted in Ruth Bordin, *Frances Willard: A Biography* (Chapel Hill: University of North Carolina Press, 1986), p. 173.

29. Quoted in Pellauer, *Toward a Tradition of Feminist Theology*, p. 36.

30. Quoted in Bordin, *Frances Willard*, p. 131.

31. Quoted in Pellauer, *Toward a Tradition of Feminist Theology*, p. 80.

32. Ibid., pp. 131–32 and 36.

33. Pellauer, quoting Stanton, makes this point in ibid., p. 84.

34. Ibid., pp. 77–81.

35. Quoted in ibid., pp. 79–80.

36. Anna Julia Cooper, *A Voice from the South*, Schomburg Library Edition (New York: Oxford University Press, 1988), pp. 23–24.

37. Ibid., pp. 29 and 28; emphasis in original.

38. Ibid., p. 29.

39. Mary Helen Washington's introduction to ibid., p. xxxi.

40. Clark, "The Politics of God," p. 67. See, for the larger discussion, the section "Law, Nature, and Rights," pp. 47–80.

41. Stanton made this clear in her criticism of institutional religion. See

her 1852 speech, quoted in Pellauer, *Toward a Tradition of Feminist Theology*, p. 29.

42. Jane Addams, *Twenty Years at Hull House, with Autobiographical Notes* (Urbana: University of Illinois Press, 1990), p. 70.

43. Ibid., pp. 43–44.

44. Pellauer, *Toward a Tradition of Feminist Theology*, pp. 100–101.

45. Cooper, *A Voice from the South*, p. 117.

46. *The Journal of Frances E. Willard*, 4 January 1870, deposited at the Frances E. Willard Memorial Library, WCTU National Headquarters, Evanston, Illinois (emphasis in original).

47. Willard, "*Writing Out My Heart*," entry for December 6, 1860, p. 101.

48. Quoted in Pellauer, *Toward a Tradition of Feminist Theology*, pp. 196–97.

49. Cooper, "Woman versus the Indian," *A Voice from the South*, pp. 124–25.

50. Ann Firor Scott, *Natural Allies: Women's Associations in American History* (Urbana: University of Illinois Press, 1991), p. 183.

51. Ibid., p. 180.

52. The phrase "unlikely sisterhood" is from Higginbotham, *Righteous Discontent*.

53. Ibid., p. 91; see also pp. 88–119.

54. Quoted in Karla Goldman, "Ambivalent Benevolence: Female Jewish Philanthropy and the Immigrant Jew" (paper presented at the Berkshire Conference on the History of Women, June 1993), p. 6.

55. Quoted in ibid., p. 7.

56. The notion of moral universe is used by Theda Skocpol in describing the action of middle-class, married Progressive women on behalf of pensions for needy widows. Skocpol, *Protecting Soldiers and Mothers: The Political Origins of Social Policy in the United States* (Cambridge: Harvard University Press), p. 479.

57. For a comparison, see especially Eileen Boris, "The Power of Motherhood: Black and White Activist Women Redefine the 'Political,'" in *Mothers of a New World: Maternalist Politics and the Origins of Welfare States*, edited by Seth Koven and Sonya Michel (New York: Routledge, 1993). See also p. 236.

58. Scott, *Natural Allies*, p. 39.

59. For a detailed discussion, see Ruth Bordin, *Woman and Temperance: The Quest for Power and Liberty, 1873–1900* (Philadelphia: Temple University Press, 1981), pp. 110–11.

60. Ibid., pp. 58 and 119.

61. Quoted in Skocpol, *Protecting Soldiers and Mothers*, pp. 334–35.

62. Ibid., p. 353.

63. Sonya Michel, "The Limits of Maternalism," in *Mothers of a New World*, p. 297.

64. Ibid., p. 297.

65. Skocpol, *Protecting Soldiers and Mothers*, p. 479.

66. See Skocpol's discussion of pensions, distinguishing the policy intent to honor rather than give poor relief to mothers, in ibid., pp. 424–79.

67. Ibid., p. 466.

68. Ibid., pp. 33 and 479. See Skocpol's discussion of patriarchal domination theorists on this point, pp. 30–35.

69. See Michel's discussion of the failure of maternalists to recognize childcare as a public service in "The Limits of Maternalism," p. 308.

70. Quoted in Allen F. Davis, *American Heroine: The Life and Legend of Jane Addams* (New York: Oxford University Press, 1973), p. 65.

71. Higginbotham, *Righteous Discontent*, pp. 16–17.

72. Scott, *Natural Allies*, p. 178. Women's clubs initiated 75 percent of the public libraries existing in 1933, see Karen J. Blair, *The Clubwoman as Feminist: True Womanhood Redefined, 1868–1914* (New York: Holmes and Meier Publishers, 1980), pp. 100–101.

73. Bordin, *Woman and Temperance*, p. 98.

74. Ruth Bordin, *Frances Willard: A Biography* (Chapel Hill: University of North Carolina Press, 1986), pp. 173–74.

75. Ibid., p. 189.

76. Skocpol, *Protecting Soldiers and Mothers*, p. 428.

77. Quoted in ibid., pp. 427–28.

78. Quoted in Scott, *Natural Allies*, p. 141.

79. Blair, in *The Clubwoman as Feminist*, pp. 3–5, notes how use of traditional male definitions of activity has led many historians of women to

focus on suffrage and to overlook clubwomen's search for autonomy and their politicization. Paula Baker, in "The Domestication of Politics: Women and American Political Society, 1780–1920," in *Women, the State, and Welfare,* edited by Linda Gordon (Madison: University of Wisconsin Press, 1990), points out that not one, but two political cultures were in operation in the nineteenth century.

80. Skocpol, *Protecting Soldiers and Mothers,* pp. 319 and 416.

81. This example is taken from Paula Baker's *The Moral Frameworks of Public Life: Gender, Politics, and the State in Rural New York, 1870–1930* (New York: Oxford University Press, 1991), pp. 56–57.

82. Ibid., pp. 56–57 and 80.

83. Quoted in Molly Ladd-Taylor, *Raising a Baby the Government Way: Mothers' Letters to the Children's Bureau, 1915–1932* (New Brunswick: Rutgers University Press, 1986), p. 25.

84. Baker, "The Domestication of Politics," p. 70.

85. Ibid., p. 72.

86. Scott, *Natural Allies,* p. 177.

87. Bordin, *Woman and Temperance,* p. 159.

88. Skocpol, *Protecting Soldiers and Mothers,* p. 319. However, a collective female consciousness did not disappear altogether from American politics. Women like Molly Dewson developed influential public roles in government which connected this collective consciousness of the Progressive period with the revival of the women's movement in the 1960s. See Susan Ware, *Partner and I: Molly Dewson, Feminism, and New Deal Politics* (New Haven: Yale University Press, 1987).

89. Baker, "The Domestication of Politics," p. 75.

90. Molly Ladd-Taylor, "Mother-Work: Ideology, Public Policy, and the Mothers' Movement, 1890–1930" (Ph.D. dissertation, Yale University, 1986), p. 378.

91. Jane Addams, *The Second Twenty Years at Hull House* (New York: Macmillan Company, 1973), pp. 109–10.

92. Skocpol, *Protecting Soldiers and Mothers,* p. 319.

93. See ibid., p. 477, and the analysis of the relationship between original supporters' intent in setting up the pensions and how the pensions were implemented, pp. 471–79.

94. Ibid., p. 479.

95. Ladd-Taylor, *Raising a Baby the Government Way*, pp. 22–23. See also Ladd-Taylor's "Mother-Work," p. 378.

96. Ladd-Taylor, *Raising a Baby the Government Way*, p. 32.

97. Ladd-Taylor, "Mother-Work," p. 383.

98. Ibid., p. 13.

99. Ibid., p. 7.

CHAPTER SEVEN

1. Several scholars have made proposals that are related to the proposal for reconstructing motherhood I set forth here, but at the same time quite different. Legal scholar Mary Berry argues for making childcare equally a responsibility of men; see her *The Politics of Parenthood: Child Care, Women's Rights, and the Myth of the Good Mother* (New York: Viking, 1993). Historian Molly Ladd-Taylor calls for developing feminist family and welfare policies focused chiefly on empowering mothers, which would involve a redefinition of work; see her *Mother-Work: Women, Child-Welfare, and the State, 1890–1930* (Urbana: University of Illinois Press, 1994), pp. 204–5. And economist Nancy Folbre offers a comprehensive set of policy proposals which recasts social responsibilities for caregiving based on an egalitarian family, and includes public and private compensation for family labor; see her *Who Pays for the Kids? Gender and the Structure of Constraint* (New York: Routledge, 1994).

2. Ruth Smith, "Relationality and the Ordering of Differences in Feminist Ethics," *Journal of Feminist Studies in Religion* 9, nos. 1–2 (Spring/Fall 1993): 214.

3. Kathleen Hall Jamieson, dean of the Annenberg School for Communication at the University of Pennsylvania, quoted in "Hype in Health Debate Hides Its Seriousness," *New York Times* (February 5, 1994). The article also reports a survey conducted by the Harvard School of Public Health showing a large number of Americans poorly informed about the details of various health policy proposals.

4. See Kay Lehman Schlozman, Nancy Burns, and Sidney Verba, "Gender and Pathways to Participation: The Role of Resources," *Journal of Politics* 56, no. 4 (November 1994), and Robert D. Putnam, "Bowling Alone: America's Declining Social Capital," *Journal of Democracy* 6, no. 1 (January 1995).

5. See Robert Putnam, "The Prosperous Community: Social Capital and Public Life," *American Prospect*, no. 13 (Spring 1993): 42.

6. Political scientist Carole Pateman discusses the notion of the welfare society as the logical product of women's full integration into modern public life, representing the dawn of "genuine democracy," in her essay "The Patriarchal Welfare State," in *Democracy and the Welfare State*, edited by Amy Gutmann (Princeton: Princeton University Press, 1988), pp. 231–60. While organized women's vision was less radical in several respects than what Pateman proposes, it had more in common with this notion of the welfare society than with that of the welfare state, in which responsibility for welfare is vested in government.

7. Juliet Schor also makes this point in "Short of Time: American Families and the Structure of Jobs" (paper given at the Future Directions for American Politics and Public Policy Seminar, Harvard University, March 1994), p. 15, as does Lotte Bailyn in *Breaking the Mold: Women, Men, and Time in the New Corporate World* (New York: Free Press, 1993).

8. Bruno Bettelheim, *A Good Enough Parent* (New York: Vintage, 1987), pp. xi and xiii.

9. Lisbeth B. Schorr, with Daniel Schorr, *Within Our Reach: Breaking the Cycle of Disadvantage* (New York: Doubleday, 1988), p. 151.

10. Bailyn, *Breaking the Mold*, p. 8.

11. Ibid., pp. 69–70.

12. Schor, "Short of Time," pp. 13–14.

13. Jane J. Mansbridge, "The Rise and Fall of Self-Interest in the Explanation of Political Life," in *Beyond Self-Interest*, edited by Jane J. Mansbridge (Chicago: University of Chicago Press, 1990), p. 22.

14. Bailyn, *Breaking the Mold*, p. 4.

15. Ibid., pp. 3–4.

16. Ibid., pp. xi–xii and 95–96. Bailyn argues that revising workplace standards is in the self-interest of organizations, as well as socially responsible.

17. Ibid., p. 39.

18. Ibid., p. 104; emphasis added.

19. Schor, "Short of Time," p. 15.

20. Bailyn, *Breaking the Mold*, pp. 86–87.

21. Kathryn Edin, "The Myths of Dependency and Self-Sufficiency: Women, Welfare, and Low-Wage Work" (manuscript, April 1994), p. 2.

22. Schor, "Short of Time," p. 19.

23. Ibid, pp. 16–19.

24. Ibid., pp. 14–15.

25. Ibid., pp. 18–19.

26. Skocpol emphasizes the importance for policy of recognizing that Americans inhabit the same moral universe. See her discussion of the political importance of policy that sets forth consistent values and opportunities for all: "Targeting within Universalism: Politically Viable Policies to Combat Poverty in the United States," in *The Urban Underclass*, edited by Christopher Jencks and Paul E. Petersen (Washington, D.C.: Brookings Institution, 1991), pp. 428–29.

27. Ibid., p. 424.

28. Ibid., p. 429.

29. Kristin Luker, "Dubious Conceptions: The Controversy over Teen Pregnancy," *American Prospect*, no. 5 (Spring 1991): 83.

30. Constance Willard Williams, *Black Teenage Mothers: Pregnancy and Childrearing from Their Perspective* (Lexington: Lexington Books, 1991), p. 131.

Bibliography

Addams, Jane. *The Second Twenty Years at Hull House.* New York: Macmillan Company, 1973.

————. *Twenty Years at Hull House, with Autobiographical Notes.* Urbana: University of Illinois Press, 1990.

Ards, Sheila. "Understanding Patterns of Child Maltreatment." *Contemporary Policy Issues* 10, no. 4 (October 1992): 39–51.

Atkinson, Clarissa W. *The Oldest Vocation: Christian Motherhood in the Middle Ages.* Ithaca: Cornell University Press, 1991.

Atkinson, Clarissa W., Constance H. Buchanan, and Margaret Miles. *Immaculate and Powerful: The Female and Sacred Image and Social Reality.* Boston: Beacon Press, 1985.

Bailyn, Lotte. *Breaking the Mold: Women, Men, and Time in the New Corporate World.* New York: Free Press, 1993.

Baker, Paula. "The Domestication of Politics: Women and American Political Society, 1780–1920." In *Women, the State, and Welfare,* edited by Linda Gordon. Madison: University of Wisconsin Press, 1990.

————. *The Moral Frameworks of Public Life: Gender, Politics, and the State in Rural New York, 1870–1930.* New York: Oxford University Press, 1991.

Bass, Dorothy C. "'Their Prodigious Influence': Women, Religion, and Reform in Antebellum America." In *Women of Spirit: Female Leadership in the Jewish and Christian Traditions,* edited by Rosemary Radford Ruether and Eleanor McLaughlin. New York: Simon and Schuster, 1979.

Becker, Gary S. *A Treatise on the Family.* Cambridge: Harvard University Press, 1981.

Belenky, Mary. *Women's Ways of Knowing: The Development of Self, Voice, and Mind*. New York: Basic Books, 1986.

Benhabib, Seyla. *Situating the Self: Gender, Community, and Postmodernism in Contemporary Ethics*. New York: Routledge, 1992.

Berry, Mary. *The Politics of Parenthood: Child Care, Women's Rights, and the Myth of the Good Mother*. New York: Viking, 1993.

Bettelheim, Bruno. *A Good Enough Parent*. New York: Vintage, 1987.

Blair, Karen J. *The Clubwoman as Feminist: True Womanhood Redefined, 1868–1914*. New York: Holmes and Meier Publishers, 1980.

Bok, Derek. *The Cost of Talent: How Executives and Professionals Are Paid and How It Affects America*. New York: Free Press, 1993.

Bordin, Ruth. *Frances Willard: A Biography*. Chapel Hill: University of North Carolina Press, 1986.

———. *Woman and Temperance: The Quest for Power and Liberty, 1873–1900*. Philadelphia: Temple University Press, 1981.

Boris, Eileen. "The Power of Motherhood: Black and White Activist Women Redefine the 'Political.'" In *Mothers of a New World: Maternalist Politics and the Origins of Welfare States*, edited by Seth Koven and Sonya Michel. New York: Routledge, 1993.

Boyte, Harry C. "The Pragmatic Ends of Popular Politics." In *Habermas and the Public Sphere*, edited by Craig Calhoun. Cambridge: Massachusetts Institute of Technology Press, 1992.

Braude, Ann. *Radical Spirits: Spiritualism and Women's Rights in Nineteenth-Century America*. Boston: Beacon Press, 1989.

Brooten, Bernadette. "Junia . . . Outstanding among the Apostles (Romans 16:7)." In *Women Priests: A Catholic Commentary on the Vatican Declaration*, edited by Leonard Swidler and Arlene Swidler. New York: Paulist Press, 1977.

Broverman, Inge K., et al. "Sex-Role Stereotypes: A Current Appraisal." *Journal of Social Issues* 28, no. 2 (1972).

Browne, Angela. "Violence against Women." Report B of the Council on Scientific Affairs to the American Medical Association, 1991.

———. "Violence against Women by Male Partners: Prevalence, Outcomes, and Policy Implications." *American Psychologist* 48 (October 1993): 1077–88.

Carby, Hazel V. "'On the Threshold of Woman's Era': Lynching, Empire, and Sexuality in Black Feminist Theory." In *"Race," Writing, and Difference*, edited by Henry Louis Gates, Jr. Chicago: University of Chicago Press, 1986.

Ceplair, Larry, ed. *The Public Years of Sarah and Angelina Grimké: Selected Writings, 1835–1839*. New York: Columbia University Press, 1989.

Chisman, Robert, and Robert L. Allen, eds. *Court of Appeal: The Black Community Speaks Out on the Record and Sexual Politics of Thomas vs. Hill*. New York: Ballantine Books, 1992.

Clark, Elizabeth Battelle. "The Politics of God and the Woman's Vote: Religion in the American Suffrage Movement, 1848–1895." Ph.D. dissertation, Princeton University, 1989.

———. "Religion, Rights, and Difference in the Early Women's Rights Movement." *Wisconsin Women's Law Journal* 3 (1987): 29–57.

Comaroff, Jean, and John Comaroff. *Of Revelation and Revolution: Christianity, Colonialism, and Consciousness in South Africa*. Chicago: University of Chicago Press, 1991.

Conway, M. Margaret. *Political Participation in the United States*. Washington, D.C.: Congressional Quarterly Press, 1991.

Cooper, Anna Julia. *A Voice from the South*. Schomburg Library Edition. New York: Oxford University Press, 1988.

Costain, Anne. *Inviting Women's Rebellion: A Political Process Interpretation of the Women's Movement*. Baltimore: Johns Hopkins University Press, 1992.

Cott, Nancy. *The Bonds of Womanhood: "Woman's Sphere" in New England, 1780–1835*. New Haven: Yale University Press, 1977.

———. *The Grounding of Modern Feminism*. New Haven: Yale University Press, 1987.

———. "What's in a Name? The Limits of 'Social Feminism'; or, Expanding the Vocabulary of Women's History." *Journal of American History* 76, no. 3 (December 1989): 809–30.

Crenshaw, Kimberle. "Whose Story Is It Anyway? Feminist and Anti-racist Appropriations of Anita Hill." In *Race-ing Justice and En-gendering Power: Essays on Anita Hill, Clarence Thomas, and the Construction of a Social Reality*, edited by Toni Morrison. New York: Pantheon Books, 1992.

Daly, Mary. *Beyond God the Father: Toward a Philosophy of Women's Liberation.* Boston: Beacon Press, 1973.

Davis, Allen F. *American Heroine: The Life and Legend of Jane Addams.* New York: Oxford University Press, 1973.

Douglas, Ann. *The Feminization of American Culture.* New York: Alfred A. Knopf, 1977.

DuBois, Ellen C. *Feminism and Suffrage: The Emergence of an Independent Women's Movement in America, 1848–1869.* Ithaca: Cornell University Press, 1978.

———. "Women's Rights and Abolition." In *Antislavery Reconsidered: New Perspectives on the Abolitionists*, edited by Lewis Perry and Michael Fellman. Baton Rouge: Louisiana State University Press, 1979.

Edin, Kathryn. "The Myths of Dependency and Self-Sufficiency: Women, Welfare, and Low-Wage Work." Manuscript, April 1994.

Ehrenreich, Barbara. *The Hearts of Men: American Dreams and the Flight from Commitment.* Garden City: Anchor Press/Doubleday, 1984.

Elshtain, Jean Bethke. *Public Man, Private Woman.* Princeton: Princeton University Press, 1981.

Fineman, Martha L. "Images of Mothers in Poverty." *Duke Law Journal*, no. 2 (April 1991): 274–95.

Fitzpatrick, Ellen. *Endless Crusade: Women, Social Scientists, and Progressive Reform.* New York: Oxford University Press, 1990.

Folbre, Nancy. *Who Pays for the Kids? Gender and the Structure of Constraint.* New York: Routledge, 1994.

Folbre, Nancy, and Heidi Hartmann. "The Rhetoric of Self-Interest: Ideology and Gender in Economic Theory." In *The Consequences of Economic Rhetoric*, edited by Arjo Klamer, Donald McCloskey, and Robert Solow. New York: Cambridge University Press, 1988.

Gerson, Kathleen. *Hard Choices: How Women Decide about Work, Career, and Motherhood.* Berkeley: University of California Press, 1985.

———. *No-Man's Land: Men's Changing Commitments to Family and Work.* New York: Basic Books, 1993.

Giele, Janet Zollinger. *Two Paths to Women's Equality: Temperance, Suffrage, and the Origins of Modern Feminism.* New York: Twayne Publishers, 1995.

Gifford, Carolyn De Swarte. "Politicizing the Sacred Texts: Elizabeth Cady Stanton and *The Woman's Bible.*" In *Searching the Scriptures*. Vol. 1, *A Feminist Introduction*, edited by Elisabeth Schüssler Fiorenza. New York: Crossroad Publishing Company, 1993.

————, ed. *"Writing Out My Heart": Selections from the Journal of Frances E. Willard, 1855–1896*. Urbana: University of Illinois Press, 1995.

Gilligan, Carol. *In a Different Voice: Psychological Theory and Women's Development*. Cambridge: Harvard University Press, 1982.

Ginzberg, Lori. *Women and the Work of Benevolence: Morality, Politics, and Class in the Nineteenth-Century United States*. New Haven: Yale University Press, 1990.

Goldman, Karla. "Ambivalent Benevolence: Female Jewish Philanthropy and the Immigrant Jew." Paper presented at the Berkshire Conference on the History of Women, June 1993.

Gordon, Linda. "Gender, State, and Society: A Debate with Theda Skocpol." *Contention* 2, no. 3 (Spring 1993).

————. *Pitied but Not Entitled: Single Mothers and the History of Welfare, 1890–1935*. New York: Free Press, 1994.

————. "Putting Children First: Women, Maternalism, and Welfare in the Twentieth Century." Discussion Papers, no. 991-93. Madison: Institute for Research on Poverty, University of Wisconsin, 1993.

Griswold, Robert L. *Fatherhood in America: A History*. New York: Basic Books, 1993.

Hansen, Susan. "Differences?" *News Inc.*, September 1992.

Harrington, Mona. *Women Lawyers: Rewriting the Rules*. New York: Alfred A. Knopf, 1994.

Hartmann, Heidi, and Roberta Spalter-Roth. "A Feminist Approach to Policymaking for Women and Families." Paper delivered at the Future Directions for American Politics and Public Policy Seminar, Harvard University, March 1994.

Higginbotham, Evelyn Brooks. *Righteous Discontent: The Women's Movement in the Black Baptist Church, 1880–1920*. Cambridge: Harvard University Press, 1993.

Hubbard, Ruth, and Elijah Wald. *Exploding the Gene Myth*. Boston: Beacon Press, 1993.

Jencks, Christopher, and Kathryn Edin. "Do Poor Women Have a Right to Bear Children?" *American Prospect*, no. 20 (Winter 1995): 43–53.

Kaminer, Wendy. *A Fearful Freedom: Women's Flight from Equality*. Reading: Addison-Wesley, 1990.

Kerber, Linda K. *Women of the Republic: Intellect and Ideology in Revolutionary America*. Chapel Hill: University of North Carolina Press, 1980.

Kessler-Harris, Alice. *Out to Work: A History of Wage-Earning Women in the United States*. New York: Oxford University Press, 1982.

Klein, Joe. "The Politics of Promiscuity." *Newsweek*, 9 May 1994, pp. 16–20.

Koven, Seth, and Sonya Michel, eds. *Mothers of a New World: Maternalist Politics and the Origins of Welfare States*. New York: Routledge, 1993.

Kunin, Madeleine. *Living a Political Life*. New York: Alfred A. Knopf, 1994.

Ladd-Taylor, Molly. "Mother-Work: Ideology, Public Policy, and the Mothers' Movement, 1890–1930." Ph.D. dissertation, Yale University, 1986.

———. *Mother-Work: Women, Child-Welfare, and the State*. Urbana: University of Illinois Press, 1994.

———. *Raising a Baby the Government Way: Mothers' Letters to the Children's Bureau, 1915–1932*. New Brunswick: Rutgers University Press, 1986.

Luker, Kristin. "Dubious Conceptions: The Controversy over Teen Pregnancy." *American Prospect*, no. 5 (Spring 1991).

Mansbridge, Jane J. "The Rise and Fall of Self-Interest in the Explanation of Political Life." In *Beyond Self-Interest*, edited by Jane J. Mansbridge. Chicago: University of Chicago Press, 1990.

Marable, Manning. "Clarence Thomas and the Crisis of Black Political Culture." In *Race-ing Justice and En-gendering Power: Essays on Anita Hill, Clarence Thomas, and the Construction of a Social Reality*, edited by Toni Morrison. New York: Pantheon Books, 1992.

McKay, Nellie Y. "Acknowledging Differences: Can Women Find Unity through Diversity?" In *Theorizing Black Feminisms: The Visionary Pragmatism of Black Women*, edited by Stanlie M. James and Abena P. A. Busia. New York: Routledge, 1993.

———. "Remembering Anita Hill and Clarence Thomas: What Really Happened When One Black Woman Spoke Out." In *Race-ing Justice and En-gendering Power: Essays on Anita Hill, Clarence Thomas, and the Construction of a Social Reality*, edited by Toni Morrison. New York: Pantheon Books, 1992.

McLanahan, Sara S. "The Consequences of Single Motherhood." *American Prospect*, no. 18 (Summer 1994): 48–59.

McLanahan, Sara S., and Gary Sandefur. *Growing Up with a Single Parent: What Hurts, What Helps*. Cambridge: Harvard University Press, 1994.

Michel, Sonya. "The Limits of Maternalism." In *Mothers of a New World: Maternalist Politics and the Origins of Welfare States*, edited by Seth Koven and Sonya Michel. New York: Routledge, 1993.

Miller, Warren E., and Santa A. Traugott. *American National Election Studies Data Sourcebook, 1952–86*. Cambridge: Harvard University Press, 1989.

Mills, Kay. "Memo: To Good Old Boys and '90's Women." *Columbia Journalism Review* (January/February 1990): 48–50.

Mink, Gwendolyn. "The Lady and the Tramp: Gender, Race, and the Origins of the American Welfare State." In *Women, the State, and Welfare*, edited by Linda Gordon. Madison: University of Wisconsin Press, 1990.

Moynihan, Daniel P. *The Negro Family: The Case for National Action*. Washington, D.C.: Office of Planning and Research, U.S. Department of Labor, March 1965.

National Research Council. "Etiology of Child Maltreatment." In *Understanding Child Abuse and Neglect*. Washington, D.C.: National Academy Press, 1993.

Newman, Amy. "Feminist Social Criticism and Marx's Theory of Religion." *Hypatia* 9, no. 4 (Fall 1994): 15–38.

Painter, Nell Irvin. "Hill, Thomas, and the Use of Racial Stereotype." In *Race-ing Justice and En-gendering Power: Essays on Anita Hill, Clarence Thomas, and the Construction of a Social Reality*, edited by Toni Morrison. New York: Pantheon Books, 1992.

Pateman, Carole. "The Patriarchal Welfare State." In *Democracy and the Welfare State*, edited by Amy Gutmann. Princeton: Princeton University Press, 1988.

Pellauer, Mary D. *Toward a Tradition of Feminist Theology: The Religious Social Thought of Elizabeth Cady Stanton, Susan B. Anthony, and Anna Howard Shaw*. Brooklyn: Carlson Publishing, 1991.

Phelps, Timothy M., and Helen Winternitz. *Capitol Games: The Inside Story of Clarence Thomas, Anita Hill, and a Supreme Court Nomination.* New York: HarperPerennial, 1993.

Phillips, Susan P., and Margaret Schneider. "Sexual Harassment of Female Doctors by Patients." *New England Journal of Medicine* 329, no. 26 (1993): 1936–39.

Presser, Harriet B. "Employment Schedules among Dual-Earner Spouses and the Division of Household Labor by Gender." *American Sociological Review* 59, no. 3 (June 1994): 348–65.

Putnam, Robert D. "Bowling Alone: America's Declining Social Capital." *Journal of Democracy* 6, no. 1 (January 1995): 65–79.

———. "The Prosperous Community: Social Capital and Public Life." *American Prospect*, no. 13 (Spring 1993): 4–10.

Rosener, Judy B. "Ways Women Lead." *Harvard Business Review* 68 (November/December 1990): 119–26.

Ruddick, Sara. *Maternal Thinking: Toward a Politics of Peace.* Boston: Beacon Press, 1989.

Ruether, Rosemary Radford. *Sexism and God-Talk: Toward a Feminist Theology.* Beacon Press: Boston, 1983.

Ruether, Rosemary Radford, and Eleanor McLaughlin, eds. *Women of Spirit: Female Leadership in the Jewish and Christian Traditions.* New York: Simon and Schuster, 1979.

Ruiz, Vicki L., and Ellen DuBois. *Unequal Sisters: A Multi-Cultural Reader in U.S. Women's History.* New York: Routledge, 1994.

Ryan, Mary. *Women in Public: Between Banners and Ballots, 1825–1880.* Baltimore: Johns Hopkins University Press, 1990.

Said, Edward. *Culture and Imperialism.* New York: Alfred A. Knopf, 1993.

Schlozman, Kay Lehman, Nancy Burns, and Sidney Verba. "Gender and Pathways to Participation: The Role of Resources." *Journal of Politics* 56, no. 4 (November 1994): 963–90.

Schor, Juliet. *The Overworked American: The Unexpected Decline of Leisure.* New York: Basic Books, 1991.

———. "Short of Time: American Families and the Structure of Jobs." Paper presented at the Future Directions for American Politics and Public Policy Seminar, Harvard University, March 1994.

Schorr, Lisbeth B., with Daniel Schorr. *Within Our Reach: Breaking the Cycle of Disadvantage*. New York: Doubleday, 1988.

Schüssler Fiorenza, Elisabeth. *In Memory of Her: A Feminist Theological Reconstruction of Christian Origins*. New York: Crossroad Publishing Company, 1983.

Scott, Ann Firor. *Natural Allies: Women's Associations in American History*. Urbana: University of Illinois Press, 1991.

———. *The Southern Lady: From Pedestal to Politics, 1830–1930*. Chicago: University of Chicago Press, 1970.

Scott, Joan. "The Sears Case." In *Gender and the Politics of History*. New York: Columbia University Press, 1988.

Shaw, Stephanie J. "Black Club Women and the Creation of the National Association of Colored Women." *Journal of Women's History* 3, no. 2 (Fall 1991).

Shklar, Judith. *American Citizenship: The Quest for Inclusion*. Cambridge: Harvard University Press, 1991.

Sklar, Kathryn Kish. *Florence Kelley and the Nation's Work*. New Haven: Yale University Press, 1995.

———. "Historical Foundations of Women's Power." In *Mothers of a New World: Maternalist Politics and the Origins of Welfare States*, edited by Seth Koven and Sonya Michel. New York: Routledge, 1993.

———. "Religious and Moral Authority as Factors Shaping the Balance of Power for Women's Political Culture in the Twentieth Century." Paper presented at the 100th Anniversary of the Founding of Hull House, Rockford, Illinois, October 1989.

Skocpol, Theda. *Protecting Soldiers and Mothers: The Political Origins of Social Policy in the United States*. Cambridge: Harvard University Press, 1992.

———. "Soldiers, Workers, and Mothers: Gendered Identities in Early U.S. Social Policy." *Contention* 2, no. 3 (Spring 1993).

———. "Targeting within Universalism: Politically Viable Policies to Combat Poverty in the United States." In *The Urban Underclass*, edited by Christopher Jencks and Paul E. Petersen. Washington, D.C.: Brookings Institution, 1991.

Skolnick, Arlene, and Stacey Rosencrantz. "The New Crusade for the Old Family." *American Prospect*, no. 18 (Summer 1994): 59–66.

Smith, Ruth. "Relationality and the Ordering of Differences in Feminist Ethics." *Journal of Feminist Studies in Religion* 9, nos. 1–2 (Spring/Fall 1993): 199–215.

Smith-Rosenberg, Carroll. *Religion and the Rise of the American City*. Ithaca: Cornell University Press, 1971.

Stansell, Christine. "White Feminists and Black Realities: The Politics of Authenticity." In *Race-ing Justice and En-gendering Power: Essays on Anita Hill, Clarence Thomas, and the Construction of a Social Reality*, edited by Toni Morrison. New York: Pantheon Books, 1992.

Stanton, Elizabeth Cady. *The Woman's Bible*. Foreword by Maureen Fitzgerald. Boston: Northeastern University Press, 1993.

Tannen, Deborah. *You Just Don't Understand: Women and Men in Conversation*. New York: William E. Morrow and Company, 1990.

Tate, Katherine. "Double Liabilities or Twin Assets: Gender, Race, and the Senatorial Candidacy of Carol Moseley Braun." Occasional Paper 93-7, Center for American Political Studies, Harvard University, March 1993.

Tyler, Tom R. "Justice, Self-Interest, and the Legitimacy of Legal and Political Authority." In *Beyond Self-Interest*, edited by Jane J. Mansbridge. Chicago: University of Chicago Press, 1990.

U.S. Congress, House Committee on Ways and Means. *The Green Book: Background Material and Data on Major Programs within the Jurisdiction of the Committee on Ways and Means*. Washington, D.C.: Government Printing Office, 1994.

U.S. Department of Commerce. "Who's Minding the Kids: Child Care Arrangements, Fall 1991." Prepared by Lynne M. Casper, Mary Hawkins, and Martin O'Connell. May 1994.

U.S. Department of Labor. Bureau of Labor Statistics. "Employment in Perspective: Women in the Labor Force." Fourth Quarter, 1993.

U.S. Department of Labor Glass Ceiling Commission. "Barriers to Workplace Advancement Experienced by African-Americans." Prepared by Ella L. J. Edmondson Bell and Stella M. Nkomo. March 1994.

———. "Barriers to Workplace Advancement Experienced by Women in Low-Paying Occupations." Prepared by Sharon L. Harlan and Catherine White Berheide. January 1994.

———. "Barriers to Workplace Advancement: The Experience of the White Female Workforce." Prepared by Bette Woody and Carol Weiss. April 1994.

———. "The Glass Ceiling in Different Sectors of the Economy: Differences between Government, Non-Profit, and For-Profit Organizations." Prepared by Lynn C. Burbridge. June 1994.

———. "Good for Business: Making Full Use of the Nation's Human Capital." March 1995.

———. "Successful Initiatives for Breaking the Glass Ceiling to Upward Mobility for Minorities and Women." Prepared by Catalyst. December 1993.

Ware, Susan. *Partner and I: Molly Dewson, Feminism, and New Deal Politics.* New Haven: Yale University Press, 1987.

Welter, Barbara. "The Cult of True Womanhood, 1820–1860." *American Quarterly* 18, no. 2, part 1 (Summer 1966).

Whitehead, Barbara Dafoe. "Dan Quayle Was Right." *Atlantic Monthly* (April 1993): 47–68.

Will, George F. "Mothers Who Don't Know How." *Newsweek*, 23 April 1990, pp. 80–81.

Willard, Frances E. "The Journal of Frances E. Willard." Frances E. Willard Memorial Library, Women's Christian Temperance Union National Headquarters, Evanston, Ill.

Williams, Constance Willard. *Black Teenage Mothers: Pregnancy and Childrearing from Their Perspective.* Lexington: Lexington Books, 1991.

Williams, Joan C. "Deconstructing Gender." *Michigan Law Review* 87 (February 1989): 797–845.

———. "Gender Wars: Selfless Women in the Republic of Choice." *New York University Law Review* 66, no. 6 (December 1991): 1559–1634.

———. "Is Coverture Dead? Beyond a New Theory of Alimony." *Georgetown Law Journal* 82, no. 7 (September 1994): 2227–90.

Yanagisako, Sylvia Junko, and Jane Fishburn Collier. "Toward a Unified Analysis of Gender and Kinship." In *Gender and Kinship: Essays toward a Unified Analysis*, edited by Collier and Yanagisako. Stanford: Stanford University Press, 1987.

Young, Iris Marion. "Mothers, Citizenship and Independence: A Critique of Pure Family Values." *Ethics* 105, no. 3 (April 1995): 535–56.

Index

LIBRARY OF CONGRESS CATALOGING-IN-PUBLICATION DATA

Buchanan, Constance H.
    Choosing to lead : women and the crisis of American values /
Constance H. Buchanan.
        p.   cm.
    Includes bibliographical references and index.
    ISBN 0-8070-2002-8
    1. Women—United States.   2. Women and religion—United States.
I. Title.
HQ1410.B77 1996
305.4'0973—dc20   95-43515